Teach Yourself
VISUALLY™
Flash® CS3 Professional

Visual

by Sherry Kinkoph Gunter

BICENTENNIAL
1807
WILEY
2007
BICENTENNIAL

Wiley Publishing, Inc.

Teach Yourself VISUALLY™ Flash® CS3 Professional

Published by
Wiley Publishing, Inc.
111 River Street
Hoboken, NJ 07030-5774

Published simultaneously in Canada

Library of Congress Control Number: 2007934452

ISBN: 978-0-470-17123-3

Manufactured in the United States of America

10 9 8 7 6 5 4 3 2 1

Trademark Acknowledgments

Contact Us

For general information on our other products and services please contact our Customer Care Department within the U.S. at 800-762-2974, outside the U.S. at 317-572-3993 or fax 317-572-4002.

For technical support please visit www.wiley.com/techsupport.

Wiley Publishing, Inc.

Sales

Contact Wiley
at (800) 762-2974 or
fax (317) 572-4002.

Praise for Visual Books

"Like a lot of other people, I understand things best when I see them visually. Your books really make learning easy and life more fun."

John T. Frey (Cadillac, MI)

"I have quite a few of your Visual books and have been very pleased with all of them. I love the way the lessons are presented!"

Mary Jane Newman (Yorba Linda, CA)

"I just purchased my third Visual book (my first two are dog-eared now!), and, once again, your product has surpassed my expectations.

Tracey Moore (Memphis, TN)

"I am an avid fan of your Visual books. If I need to learn anything, I just buy one of your books and learn the topic in no time. Wonders! I have even trained my friends to give me Visual books as gifts."

Illona Bergstrom (Aventura, FL)

"Thank you for making it so clear. I appreciate it. I will buy many more Visual books."

J.P. Sangdong (North York, Ontario, Canada)

"I have several books from the Visual series and have always found them to be valuable resources."

Stephen P. Miller (Ballston Spa, NY)

"Thank you for the wonderful books you produce. It wasn't until I was an adult that I discovered how I learn – visually. Nothing compares to Visual books. I love the simple layout. I can just grab a book and use it at my computer, lesson by lesson. And I understand the material! You really know the way I think and learn. Thanks so much!"

Stacey Han (Avondale, AZ)

"I absolutely admire your company's work. Your books are terrific. The format is perfect, especially for visual learners like me. Keep them coming!"

Frederick A. Taylor, Jr. (New Port Richey, FL)

"I have several of your Visual books and they are the best I have ever used."

Stanley Clark (Crawfordville, FL)

"I bought my first Teach Yourself VISUALLY book last month. Wow. Now I want to learn everything in this easy format!"

Tom Vial (New York, NY)

"Thank you, thank you, thank you...for making it so easy for me to break into this high-tech world. I now own four of your books. I recommend them to anyone who is a beginner like myself."

Gay O'Donnell (Calgary, Alberta, Canada)

"I write to extend my thanks and appreciation for your books. They are clear, easy to follow, and straight to the point. Keep up the good work! I bought several of your books and they are just right! No regrets! I will always buy your books because they are the best."

Seward Kollie (Dakar, Senegal)

"Compliments to the chef!! Your books are extraordinary! Or, simply put, extra-ordinary, meaning way above the rest! THANK YOU THANK YOU THANK YOU! I buy them for friends, family, and colleagues."

Christine J. Manfrin (Castle Rock, CO)

"What fantastic teaching books you have produced! Congratulations to you and your staff. You deserve the Nobel Prize in Education in the Software category. Thanks for helping me understand computers."

Bruno Tonon (Melbourne, Australia)

"Over time, I have bought a number of your 'Read Less - Learn More' books. For me, they are THE way to learn anything easily. I learn easiest using your method of teaching."

José A. Mazón (Cuba, NY)

"I am an avid purchaser and reader of the Visual series, and they are the greatest computer books I've seen. The Visual books are perfect for people like myself who enjoy the computer, but want to know how to use it more efficiently. Your books have definitely given me a greater understanding of my computer, and have taught me to use it more effectively. Thank you very much for the hard work, effort, and dedication that you put into this series."

Alex Diaz (Las Vegas, NV)

Credits

Project Editor
Timothy J. Borek

Acquisitions Editor
Jody LeFevere

Copy Editor
Kim Heusel

Technical Editor
Jon McFarland

Editorial Manager
Robyn Siesky

Business Manager
Amy Knies

Sr. Marketing Manager
Sandy Smith

Manufacturing
Allan Conley
Linda Cook
Paul Gilchrist
Jennifer Guynn

Book Design
Kathie Rickard

Production Coordinator
Adrienne Martinez

Layout
Carrie A. Foster
Jennifer Mayberry

Screen Artist
Jill Proll

Illustrators
Ronda David-Burroughs
Cheryl Grubbs
Shane Johnson
Jake Mansfield

Proofreader
Nancy L. Reinhardt

Quality Control
Dwight Ramsey

Indexer
Broccoli Information
Managament

Special Help
Jody LeFevere
Alissa Birkel

Vice President and Executive Group Publisher
Richard Swadley

Vice President and Publisher
Barry Pruett

Composition Director
Debbie Stailey

Wiley Bicentennial Logo
Richard J. Pacifico

About the Author

Sherry Kinkoph Gunter has written and edited oodles of books over the past 11 years covering a variety of computer topics, including Internet subjects, Microsoft Office programs, digital photography, and more. Her recent titles include *Teach Yourself VISUALLY Microsoft Office 2007, Master VISUALLY Dreamweaver CS3 and Flash CS3, Teach Yourself VISUALLY HTML,* and *Office 2007 Simplified.* Sherry's ongoing quest is to help users of all levels master ever-changing computer technologies. No matter how many times software manufacturers and hardware conglomerates throw out a new version or upgrade, Sherry vows to be there to make sense of it all and help computer users get the most out of their machines.

Author's Acknowledgments

Special thanks go out to publisher Barry Pruett and to acquisitions editor Jody LeFevere for allowing me the opportunity to tackle this project; to project editor Tim Borek for his impeccable dedication and patience in guiding this project from start to finish; to copy editor Kim Heusel for ensuring that all the *i*'s were dotted and *t*'s were crossed; to technical editor Jon McFarland for skillfully checking each step and offering valuable input along the way; and finally to the production team at Wiley for their able efforts in creating yet another visual masterpiece. Extra special thanks go to my favorite fireman, Matty Gunter, my hero in every way.

Table of Contents

Table of Contents

chapter **5** **Working with Text**

chapter **6** Working with Layers

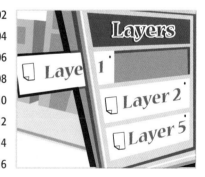

chapter **7** **Working with Flash Symbols and Instances**

Table of Contents

chapter 10 Adding Special Effects

chapter 11 Creating Buttons

chapter 12 Adding Interactivity

chapter 13 Adding Sound

chapter 14 Working with Video

chapter 15 Distributing Flash Movies

How to use this book

How to Use this Teach Yourself VISUALLY Book

Do you look at the pictures in a book or newspaper before anything else on a page? Would you rather see an image instead of read about how to do something? Search no further. This book is for you. Opening *Teach Yourself VISUALLY Flash CS3 Professional* allows you to read less and learn more about the Flash CS3 program.

Who Needs This Book

This book is for a reader who has never used this particular technology or software application. It is also for more computer-literate individuals who want to expand their knowledge of the different features that Flash CS3 Professional has to offer. We assume that you already know the basics of your computer's operating system as well as how to use your mouse and other input devices.

Book Organization

Teach Yourself VISUALLY Flash CS3 Professional has 15 chapters.

Chapter 1, "Flash Fundamentals," covers the basic elements of using the program, including opening and saving files, setting the Stage size, working with the Flash panels, and other fundamental tasks.

Chapters 2 and 3, "Creating Objects" and "Enhancing and Editing Objects," explain how to use the Flash drawing tools to create original artwork for your Flash projects and how to manipulate the artwork to change its appearance.

Chapter 4, "Working with Imported Graphics," shows you how to bring in artwork from other sources to use in your Flash movies.

Chapter 5, "Working with Text," teaches you how to add and edit text for use in your Flash projects.

Chapter 6, "Working with Layers," explains how to use layers in your movies to organize elements, create dimension, and create masks.

Chapter 7, "Working with Flash Symbols and Instances," instructs you in how to reuse artwork in your movies and keep movie elements organized in the Flash Library.

Chapters 8 and 9, "Creating Basic Animation in Flash," and "Creating Animation by Tweening," show you how to build animations in Flash and work with frames.

Chapter 10, "Adding Special Effects," explain how to add filters, transitions, and blends to add special effects to your projects.

Chapter 11, "Creating Buttons," demonstrates how to add buttons to your project and assign button behaviors.

Chapter 12, "Adding Interactivity," introduces you to basic Flash actions and behaviors you can assign to add interactivity, such as stop and play actions.

Chapter 13, "Adding Sound," shows you how to add sound to enhance your Flash movies.

Chapter 14, "Working with Video," explains how to utilize Flash video features to control embedded video clips.

Chapter 15, "Distributing Flash Movies," instructs you on the various ways you can publish your Flash projects so others can see them.

Chapter Organization

This book consists of sections, all listed in the book's table of contents. A *section* is a set of steps that show you how to complete a specific computer task.

Each section, usually contained on two facing pages, has an introduction to the task at hand, a set of full-color Windows screen shots and steps that walk you through the task, and a set of tips. This format allows you to quickly look at a topic of interest and learn it instantly.

Chapters group together three or more sections with a common theme. A chapter may also contain pages that give you the background information needed to understand the sections in a chapter.

What You Need to Use This Book

To perform the steps in this book, you need a personal computer with Adobe Flash CS3 installed.

Windows requirements:

- Intel Pentium 4, Intel Centrino, Intel Xeon, or Intel Core Duo (or compatible) processor
- Windows XP with Service Pack 2 or Windows Vista
- 512MB of RAM
- 2.5GB of available hard-disk space
- 16-bit video card
- DVD-ROM drive
- Internet connection (for product activation and online help access)

Mac requirements:

- 1GHz PowerPC G4 or G5 or multicore Intel processor

- Mac OS X v. 10.4.8
- 512MB of RAM
- 2.5GB of available hard disk space
- 16-bit video card
- DVD-ROM drive
- Internet connection (for product activation and online help access)

Using the Mouse

This book uses the following conventions to describe the actions you perform when using the mouse:

Click

Press your left mouse button once. You generally click your mouse on something to select something on the screen.

Double-click

Press your left mouse button twice. Double-clicking something on the computer screen generally opens whatever item you have double-clicked.

Right-click

Press your right mouse button. When you right-click anything on the computer screen, the program displays a shortcut menu containing commands specific to the selected item.

Click and Drag, and Release the Mouse

Move your mouse pointer and hover it over an item on the screen. Press and hold down the left mouse button. Now, move the mouse to where you want to place the item and then release the button. You use this method to move an item from one area of the computer screen to another.

The Conventions in This Book

A number of typographic and layout styles have been used throughout *Teach Yourself VISUALLY Flash CS3 Professional* to distinguish different types of information.

Bold

Bold type represents the names of commands and options that you interact with. Bold type also indicates text and numbers that you must type into a dialog box or window.

Italics

Italic words introduce a new term and are followed by a definition.

Numbered Steps

You must perform the instructions in numbered steps in order to successfully complete a section and achieve the final results.

Bulleted Steps

These steps point out various optional features. You do not have to perform these steps; they simply give additional information about a feature.

Indented Text

Indented text tells you what the program does in response to your following a numbered step. For example, if you click a certain menu command, a dialog box may appear, or a window may open. Indented text may also tell you what the final result is when you follow a set of numbered steps.

Notes

Notes give additional information. They may describe special conditions that may occur during an operation. They may warn you of a situation that you want to avoid, for example the loss of data. A note may also cross-reference a related area of the book. A cross-reference may guide you to another chapter, or another section within the current chapter.

Icons and Buttons

Icons and buttons are graphical representations within the text. They show you exactly what you need to click to perform a step.

 You can easily identify the tips in any section by looking for the TIPS icon. Tips offer additional information, including tips, hints, and tricks. You can use the TIPS information to go beyond what you have learned in the steps.

Operating System Difference

You can follow along with the steps in this book regardless of whether your computer is running the Mac OS or Windows operating system. Where steps are provided for both operating systems, the Windows instructions precede the Mac OS instructions. For example, "Press Enter (Return)."

CHAPTER 1

Flash Fundamentals

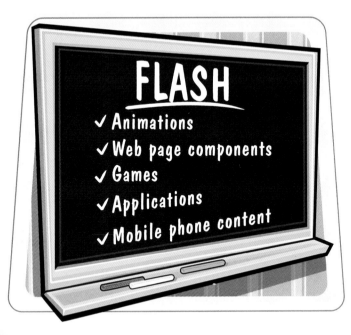

FLASH
- ✓ Animations
- ✓ Web page components
- ✓ Games
- ✓ Applications
- ✓ Mobile phone content

The Flash authoring program is the perfect tool for both new and experienced Web page designers who want to create expressive, dynamic Web page elements. In this chapter, you learn all the basics for starting Flash files and finding your way around the program window.

Adobe Flash is the program of choice for multimedia authoring projects. You can use Flash to create animations, Web page components, games, applications, and mobile phone content. Using the Flash Player plug-in, just about every Web browser available today supports Flash-based content. In the strictest sense, Flash is an integrated development environment, while the Flash Player is a virtual machine for running Flash files.

Create Animation Content

Flash includes a variety of tools you can use to draw your own graphic objects to use in your projects. Flash-created vector graphics are much smaller in file size than raster graphics, such as JPEGs and GIFs. Vector graphics display much faster on a downloading Web page and are a more efficient method of delivering images over the Internet. To learn more about creating objects, see Chapters 2 and 3. To learn how to import artwork, see Chapter 4. See Chapter 5 to learn about adding text.

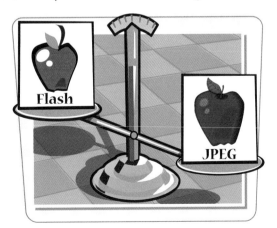

Work with Symbols

After creating new objects or importing artwork from other sources, you can turn objects into symbols to reuse in your Flash movie. Every time you use a symbol, you use an instance of the original object. If you make changes to the original, the instance changes as well. Flash keeps track of your symbols in the file's Library. To learn more about using symbols and instances, see Chapter 7.

Build Animation Sequences

You can use the Flash animation tools to create all kinds of animation effects, from making an object move across the screen to complex animations that follow paths and action commands. You can create animations using frames. A frame stores content, and the total number of frames determines the length of your movie. For more on creating animations, see Chapters 8 and 9. To learn how to add sound to your animations, see Chapter 13.

Organize with Layers

You can use layers in your Flash movies to organize content and add depth to your animations. Each layer acts like a transparent sheet, allowing you to view underlying layers. You can manage layers in the Flash Timeline window. To learn more about working with layers and the Flash Timeline, see Chapter 6

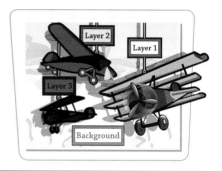

Add Interactive Elements

You can also use the Flash tools to create interactive elements in your movie and assign actions. For example, you can add a button that, when clicked, activates another movie. A programming language called *ActionScript* controls interactivity in Flash. You do not need to know how to write ActionScript to add interactivity; Flash includes numerous prewritten scripts that you can apply. To learn more about adding buttons, see Chapter 11. To learn about adding actions, see Chapter 12.

Publish Your Movies

There are a variety of ways you can share your animations with others. Flash includes options for publishing movies to Web pages, as Flash movie files, or as self-extracting animations. The program also includes features to help you preview a movie before publishing, test download performance, and more. To learn more about publishing your Flash projects, see Chapter 15.

The Flash program window has several components for working with graphics and movies. Take time to familiarize yourself with the on-screen elements. If you use Flash on a Macintosh computer, the program elements may look a bit different than those displayed in the following Windows example.

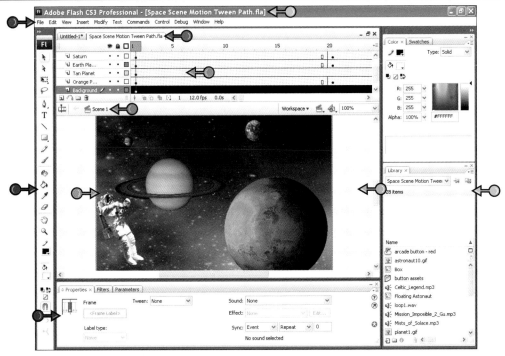

TITLE BAR

Displays the name of the open file.

MENU BAR

Displays Flash menus which, when clicked, reveal commands.

FILE TAB

The tab at the top of the work area represents the current file. If two or more files are open, you can switch from file to file by clicking a tab.

TIMELINE

Contains all the frames, layers, and scenes that make up a movie.

TOOLS PANEL

Contains the basic tools needed to create and work with vector graphics.

CURRENT SCENE

Displays the name of the scene on which you are currently working.

STAGE OR MOVIE AREA

The area where a movie or graphic displays, where you can view a frame's contents and draw graphic objects. This area is also called the Flash Editor.

WORK AREA

The area surrounding the Stage. Anything placed on the work area does not appear in the movie.

PROPERTY INSPECTOR

Use this panel to view and edit properties of the current object.

PANELS

Allow quick access to options for controlling and editing Flash movies.

The Flash Timeline contains the frames, layers, and scenes that make up a movie. You can use the Timeline to organize and control your movies. By default, the Timeline appears docked near the top of the program window. If you are new to Flash, take a moment and familiarize yourself with the Timeline elements.

See Chapters 8, 9, and 10 for more on working with the Flash Timeline.

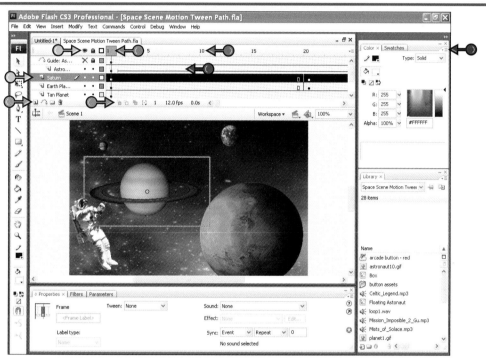

LAYERS

Use layers to organize artwork, animation, sound, and interactive elements. Layers enable you to keep pieces of artwork separate and combine them to form a cohesive image, such as a company logo that includes a layer of text and another layer with a graphic shape.

FRAMES

Lengths of time in a Flash movie are divided into frames. They enable you to control what appears in animation sequences and which sounds play.

FRAME NUMBERS

Frames appear in chronological order in the Timeline, and each frame has a number.

PLAYHEAD

Also called the Current Frame Indicator, the playhead marks the current frame displayed on the Stage.

PANEL MENU

Displays a drop-down menu of customizing options for controlling how frames are displayed in the Timeline.

TIMELINE BUTTONS

Scattered around the Timeline are buttons for controlling frames, layers, and movies.

LAYER BUTTONS

Click to add and delete layers.

LAYER CONTROLS

Display the status of a layer, such as hidden, locked, or outlined.

Open a Flash File

Flash files are called *documents* or *movies*. When you save a file, you can open it and work on it again. You can make Flash files as simple as a drawing you create using the Flash drawing tools, or as complex as an animation sequence consisting of scenes and interactive elements.

You can also start a new Flash file at any time, even if you are currently working on another file. Every new file you start uses a default Stage size. If the file windows are maximized, each open file appears as a tab at the top of the Timeline.

Open a Flash File

OPEN A FLASH FILE

① Click **File**.

② Click **Open**.

If the Main toolbar is displayed, you can click the **Open** button (🗁) to display the Open dialog box.

You can also press Ctrl + O (⌘ + O) to open the Open dialog box.

● You can open a recent file by clicking here and clicking the file name.

Note: When you first open Flash, you can use the Welcome screen to open existing files or create new files. Click **Open** to display the Open dialog box.

The Open dialog box appears.

③ Click 🔽 to navigate to the folder or drive containing the file you want to open.

④ Click the file name.

● You can change the file types listed by clicking here and choosing a file type.

⑤ Click **Open**.

The file opens in the Flash window.

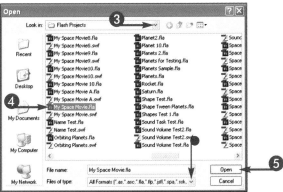

OPEN A NEW FLASH FILE

1 Click **File**.

2 Click **New**.

If the Main toolbar is displayed, you can click the **New** button (□) to display the New Document dialog box.

You can also press `Ctrl`+`N` (`⌘`+`N`) to open the New Document dialog box.

Note: *When you first open Flash, you can use the Welcome screen to open existing files or create new files. From the Create New column, click the type of file you want to create.*

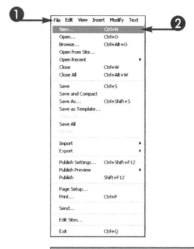

The New Document dialog box appears.

3 Click the type of document you want to create.

● A description of each type appears here.

4 Click **OK**.

A blank document appears in the Flash window.

You can have several Flash files open and switch between them using the tabs at the top of the Timeline.

Note: *You can also use the Window menu to switch between open files.*

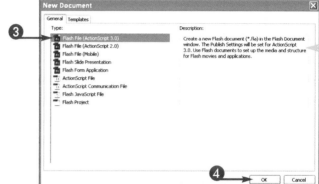

Why does Flash not show a Main toolbar by default?

The Main toolbar includes access to common commands, such as Open and Save. For example, to open a file, click the **Open** button (📂). By default, Flash does not display the Main toolbar, but you can turn it on if you want. Click **Windows**, **Toolbars**, and then **Main**.

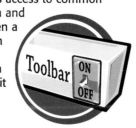

Is there a limit to how many Flash files I can have open?

No. However, the more files you open, the slower your computer runs. Graphics files, such as those that you author in Flash, can take up more processing power than other programs. Unless you are sharing data between the files, it is a good idea to close Flash files you are no longer using.

Save and Close a Flash File

As you create movies in Flash, you need to save them to work on them again. By default, Flash saves all files in the FLA format. Because Flash does not offer an automatic save feature, it is a good practice to save your work frequently.

You can close Flash files no longer in use to free up computer memory. Be sure to save your changes before closing a file.

Saving graphics to the Flash Library works a bit differently than saving a file. See Chapter 7 for more information about saving symbols.

Save and Close a Flash File

SAVE A FILE

1 Click **File**.

2 Click **Save**.

If the Main toolbar is displayed, you can click the **Save** button (🖫) to display the Save As dialog box.

You can also press `Ctrl`+`S` (`⌘`+`S`) to open the Save As dialog box.

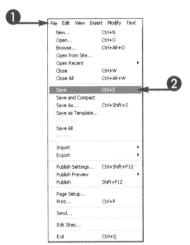

The Save As dialog box appears.

Note: If you have previously saved a file, Flash saves the changes without displaying the Save As dialog box.

3 Type a unique name for the file.

● To save to another folder or drive, click ⌄ and select another location.

● To save the file as another file type, click ⌄ and click a file type.

4 Click **Save**.

Flash saves your file.

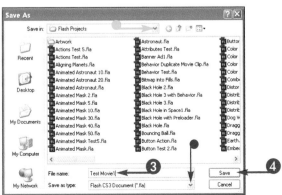

CLOSE A FLASH FILE

1 Save your file.

Note: See the previous steps to learn how to save a Flash file.

2 Click **File**.

3 Click **Close**.

Flash closes the file you are working on, but the program window remains open.

Note: If you have not saved your changes, Flash prompts you to do so before closing a file.

USE THE CLOSE BUTTON

1 Save your file.

2 Click the **Close** button (⌧).

Note: Clicking the program window's ⌧ button closes the Flash application entirely and might result in lost data.

Note: If you have not saved your changes, Flash prompts you to do so before closing a file.

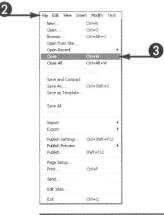

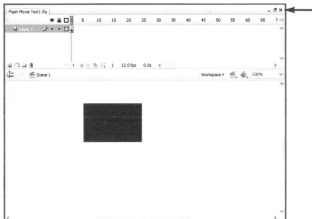

TIPS

How do I save a previously saved file under a new name?

You can copy a previously saved file and save it under a new file name. You can then make changes to the file copy without worrying about changing the original file. To do so, click **File**, then click **Save As**. In the Save As dialog box that appears, type a new name for the file and click Save.

Can I save a Flash file in another format?

Yes; however, you cannot use the Save command unless you want to save the file in an older Flash program version. Instead, you must export the movie to another file format. See Chapter 13 to learn how.

Change the Document Size

The document you create in Flash appears on the Stage, which is the on-screen area where you can view the contents of a frame and draw graphic objects. You can control the size and appearance of the document you create on the Stage. The size of the document determines the size of your Flash movie screen.

It is a good idea to set your movie size before adding any content to your frames. If you set a size after creating your movie, you may end up needing to reposition objects to fit the new size.

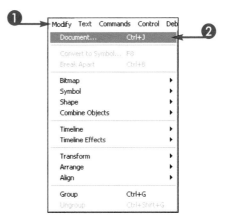

Change the Document Size

1 Click **Modify**.

2 Click **Document**.

You can also click on the **Size** button in the Property inspector to display the Document Properties dialog box.

The Document Properties dialog box appears.

3 To change the stage's dimensions in pixels, type new dimensions in the width and height boxes.

Note: *You can also use the Document Properties dialog box to set a frame rate for your movie. See Chapter 8 to learn more about frame rates.*

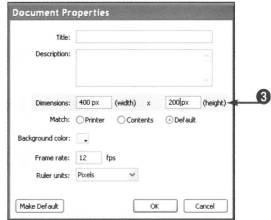

- You can select **Printer** (○ changes to ◉) if you want to match the Stage dimensions to the maximum available print area size for your printer.

- You can select **Contents** (○ changes to ◉) to change the Stage dimensions to match the contents of your movie, with equal spacing all around.

- You can select **Default** (○ changes to ◉) to return the Stage size to the default size.

④ Click **OK**.

- Flash resizes the Stage area according to your new settings.

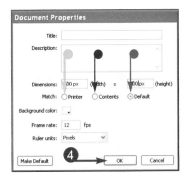

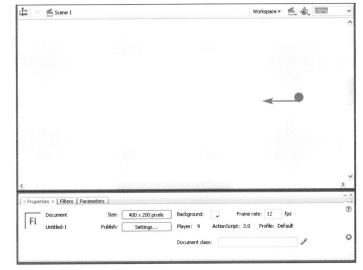

TIPS

How do I specify different units of measurement for the Stage?

From the Document Properties dialog box, click the **Ruler units** ☑ and then click the unit of measurement you want to apply. The unit of measurement immediately changes in the width and height text boxes and you can now set the appropriate measurements.

Ruler Units
- Pixels
- Inches
- Points
- Centimeters
- Millimeters

How do I set a new background color?

By default, Flash sets the Stage background color to white. To set another background color, click the **Background Color** button (▢) in the Document Properties dialog box. A palette of color choices appears. Click the color you want to apply and the color becomes the new background color throughout your movie.

Using the Property Inspector

You can use the Property inspector to see and edit the properties of the object with which you are currently working. The Property inspector changes to reflect the properties associated with the object you select on the Stage. By default, the Property inspector appears open when you first open a Flash file.

The Property inspector acts as a panel that you can collapse, hide from view, or move. By default, Flash docks the Property inspector at the bottom of the program window. You can collapse or close the Property inspector when you do not need it to free up workspace.

Using the Property Inspector

COLLAPSE AND EXPAND THE PROPERTY INSPECTOR

① Click the panel's title bar or name to collapse or minimize the panel.

● You can also click the **Minimize** button (⊟) to collapse the panel (⊟ becomes ⊡).

Note: *This example shows the text properties listed in the Property inspector panel.*

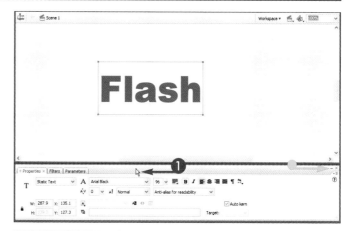

● The Property inspector panel collapses.

② To expand the panel again, click the panel's title bar.

● You can also click the **Maximize** button (⊡).

CLOSE THE PANEL

① To close the panel, click the **Close** button (☒).

Flash closes the Property inspector.

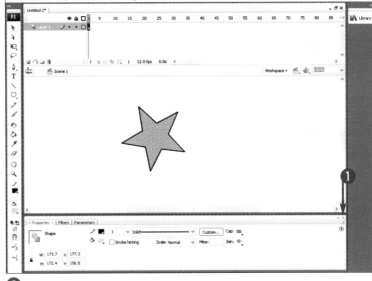

OPEN THE PANEL

② To display the panel, click **Window**.

③ Click **Properties**.

④ Click **Properties**.

You can also press **Ctrl** + **F3** (**⌘** + **F3**) to quickly open the panel.

Flash opens the Property inspector.

TIPS

What do the other tabs in the Property inspector do?

In addition to the Properties tab and depending on what version of Flash CS3 you are using, the Property inspector panel displays two other tabs: Parameters and Filters. The Parameters tab displays information about components. See Chapter 12 to learn how to use components in Flash. If you are using Flash CS3 Professional, the Filters tab appears. You can use the Filters tab to apply filters to your movie objects. To learn more about filters, see Chapter 10.

Can I move the Property inspector panel?

Yes. Like all panels in Flash, you can move the Property inspector to create a floating panel or you can dock the panel on another side of the screen. To move the panel, click and drag the drag area, the upper-left corner of the panel. To collapse a floating panel, simply click the panel's title bar. To expand it again, click the bar again.

Work with Panels

You can use the Flash panels to access additional controls. Flash offers over a dozen different panels, each displaying options related to a specific task. Panels can appear docked to the side of the program window or they can appear as floating panels. When you no longer need them, you can close panels to free up on-screen workspace.

You can open a default set of commonly used panels in Flash that include the Color, Swatches, and Library panels. Flash considers the Property inspector, Library, Actions, and Movie Explorer panels as main authoring panels. You can find all the Flash panels listed on the Window menu.

Work With Panels

OPEN PANELS

① Click **Window**.

② Click the panel you want to open.

Note: A check mark next to the panel name indicates the panel is open; no check mark means the panel is closed.

● The panel appears on-screen.

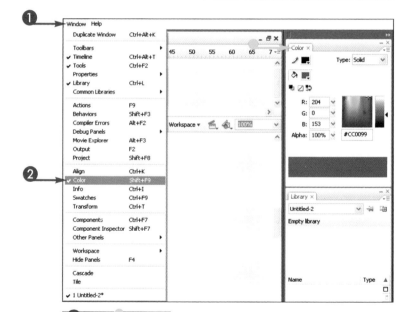

COLLAPSE AND EXPAND PANELS

① Click the panel's title bar or name to collapse or minimize the panel.

● You can also click the **Minimize** button (☐) to collapse the panel (☐ becomes ☐) and click the **Maximize** button (☐) to expand the panel again.

MOVE A PANEL

1 Click and drag the panel's title bar to undock and move a panel.

When you undock a docked panel, it becomes a floating panel that you can move freely about the program window.

To resize a panel, move the ↳ over the border of a panel (↳ changes to ↕), then click and drag to resize the panel.

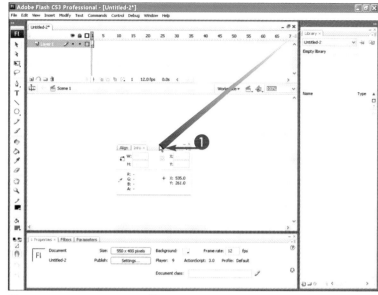

CLOSE PANELS

1 Click the panel's **Close** button (⊠).

The panel closes.

To hide a panel instead of close it, click the panel's title bar.

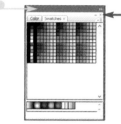

 TIPS

Can I hide all the panels at once?

Yes. Click the **Window** menu and click **Hide Panels** or simply press **F4**. Flash closes all the panels, including the Tools panel of drawing tools. Only the Timeline and the Stage area are left on-screen. This frees up workspace to see the Stage and any animations you want to view. You can use the Window menu to reopen any individual panels you want to view and use again, or you can press **F4** again to toggle the panel display back again.

Can I create a custom workspace with only the panels I want to use?

Yes. To create a custom workspace, open all the panels you want to save as your custom workspace and arrange them how you want them to appear in the program window. Next, click the **Window** menu and click **Workspace**, **Save Current**. The Save Workspace Layout dialog box appears. Type a name for the layout and click **OK**. Flash saves the layout. To restore it at any time, click **Window**, **Workspace**, and the name of the layout, or click the **Workspace** button at the top of the Stage and click a layout.

Zoom Out or In

When working with various elements on the Stage, you can zoom in or out for a better view. For example, you may need to zoom in to see the details of an object you are editing, or you might need to zoom out to see the entire Stage area.

Zooming your view merely changes the magnification of the Stage area and does not change the size of the objects you are viewing.

Zoom Out or In

ZOOM OUT

① Click **View**.

② Click **Zoom Out**.

● Flash zooms your view of the Stage.

  You can select the command again to zoom out another magnification level.

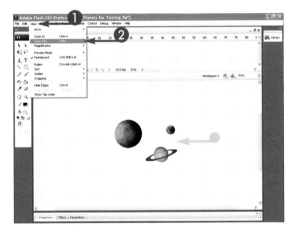

ZOOM IN

① Click **View**.

② Click **Zoom In**.

● Flash zooms your view of the Stage.

  You can select the command again to zoom in another magnification level.

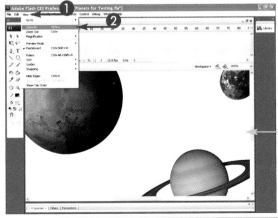

SELECT A ZOOM PERCENTAGE

1 Click ⌄.

2 Click a magnification percentage.

Flash immediately adjusts the view.

● In this example, the window zooms to 50%.

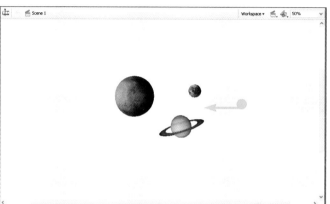

TIPS

How do I use the Zoom tool button?

You can also use the Zoom button on the Tools panel to change the Stage magnification. Click the **Zoom** button (🔍) and click either the **Enlarge** modifier (🔍) or the **Reduce** modifier (🔍) at the bottom of the Tools panel. Next, click the area of the Stage you want to view. Flash immediately enlarges or reduces the view.

Is there a quicker way to zoom in Flash?

You can temporarily zoom from Enlarge to Reduce and vice versa by pressing and holding the Alt key (Option) as long as the Zoom tool is active on the Tools panel. You can also temporarily zoom your view while using another tool on the Tools panel simply by pressing Ctrl + Shift + Spacebar (Spacebar). You can also press Ctrl+1 (⌘+1) to zoom to 100%, or press Ctrl+- and Ctrl++ to zoom out and in.

Using Rulers and Grids

To help you draw with more precision, turn on the Flash Rulers and grid lines. Both tools can help you position objects on the Stage. The rulers and grids do not appear in the final movie.

You can use rulers to measure the various elements on the Stage. You can use gridlines to help you quickly position elements on the Stage.

Using Rulers and Grids

ACTIVATE THE FLASH RULERS

1 Click **View**.

2 Click **Rulers**.

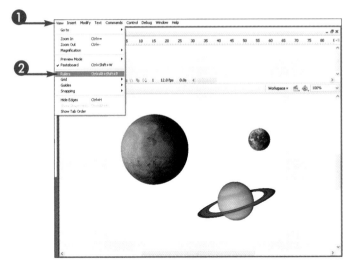

● Flash opens horizontal and vertical rulers in the Stage area.

You can repeat steps **1** and **2** to turn off the rulers.

TURN ON GRID LINES

1 Click **View**.

2 Click **Grid**.

3 Click **Show Grid**.

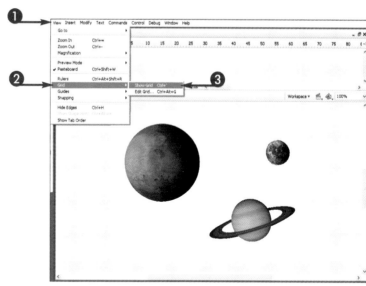

● Grid lines appear on the Stage.

You can repeat steps **1** to **3** to turn off the grid lines.

 TIPS

How can I precisely align objects with the grid?

Use the Snap tool to help you quickly align objects to the grid lines. To activate the tool, click **View**, click **Snapping**, and click a snapping command. You can also click **View**, **Snapping**, and then click **Snap To Grid**.

What are guides?

Guides are lines you can drag onto the Stage to help you as you move items and control positioning. You can turn on the Flash guides as another tool to help you position objects on the Stage. To display the guides, click the **View** menu and then click **Guides**, **Show Guides**. You must also turn on the Flash rulers in order to use guides. To add a guide to the Stage, drag a guideline off of the ruler and onto the Stage. To remove a guide, drag it back to the ruler.

Find Help with Flash

When you run across a program feature or technique that you do not understand, consult the Flash Help system. The Flash Help files offer a wide variety of topics ranging from basic Flash features, such as how to use on-screen buttons and drawing tools, to advanced features, such as how to write scripts using ActionScript.

You display the Flash Help information in the Help panel. Like the other panels available in Flash, you can move, resize, collapse, and expand the Help panel. See the section "Work with Panels" to learn more.

Find Help with Flash

OPEN THE HELP PANEL

① Click **Help**.

② Click **Flash Help**.

● The Help panel opens.

③ Double-click a topic category you want to know more about.

● You can click a subtopic to reveal a list of Help topics to choose from.

④ Click a topic.

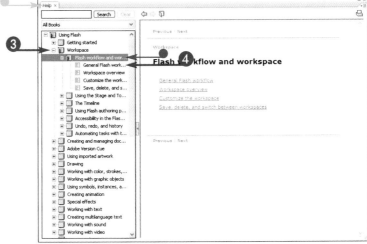

● The Help information appears and you can read more about the topic.

● You can click the navigation buttons, **History Back** (⬅) and **History Forward** (➡) to move back and forth between topics.

Some topics include additional links in the help text you can click to view more information or related topics.

● You can look up a topic by typing a keyword or phrase here and pressing Enter (Return) or clicking the **Search** button.

● Click here to return to the main list of Help topics.

CLOSE THE HELP PANEL

⑤ Click the **Close** button (✕).

Flash closes the Help panel.

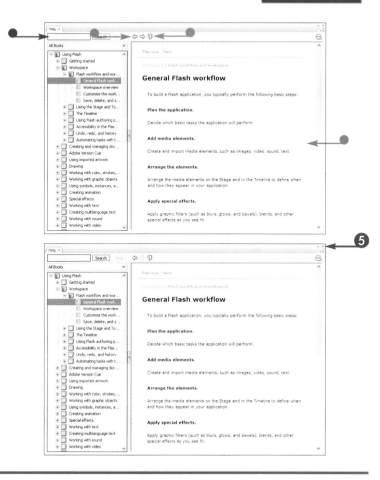

 TIPS

Where else can I find Flash help?

Adobe's Web site (www.adobe.com/support/flash/) is a good place to start if you are looking for additional information about the Flash program. To access the site from Flash, click the **Help** menu and select **Help Resources Online** or **Flash Support Center**. This opens your default Web browser. You may need to log on to your Internet connection first. You can also find numerous sites on the Internet dedicated to Flash users by performing a simple search for the keyword *Flash* using your favorite search engine.

Is there an easy way to find out what new features appear in Flash CS3?

You can open the Help panel directly to a link to learn about new program features. To do so, click **Help, What's New in Flash CS3**. The Help panel opens to the information and you can read all about the new program features and improvements.

Flash includes a variety of templates you can use to create new Flash files. Templates are a great way to build a document and create specialized content. After you open a template, you can add content to the file and save it to reuse again.

Flash installs with a variety of templates you can use to create content for mobile devices, slide shows, advertising presentations, quizzes, and more.

Open a Flash Template

① Click **File**.

② Click **New**.

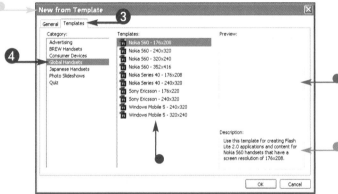

The New Document dialog box appears.

③ Click the Templates tab.

● New from Template appears as the dialog box title.

④ Click a category.

● A list of related templates appears.

● Click a template and view a preview here.

Note: *Not all templates include a preview.*

● A description of the template appears here.

5 Click the template for the type of document that you want to create.

6 Click **OK**.

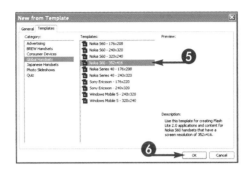

● A blank template appears in the Flash window.

You can add content to create the new file.

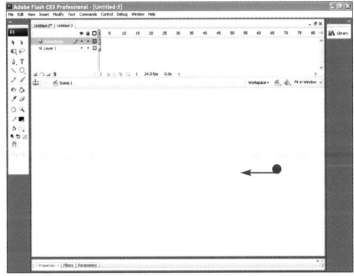

Can I make my own templates in Flash?

Yes. To turn any Flash file into a template file, click **File**, **Save As Template** to open the Save As Template dialog box. Type a unique name for the template, select a category to save the template to, and type a brief description. Click **Save** and Flash saves the file and adds it to the templates list.

How do I save a file I create with a template?

After you finish working on the template, you can save it as a regular Flash file. Click **File**, **Save**, and assign a unique name for the file in the Save As dialog box. To learn more about saving files, see the section "Save and Close a Flash File" earlier in this chapter.

Creating Objects

Do you want to draw your own illustrations to animate? Whether you call them graphics, illustrations, or images, Flash offers many tool you can use to make all sort of artwork for Flash movies and other projects.

Introducing Flash Objects

You can create all kinds of original drawings in Flash. The program includes a variety of tools for creating simple shapes or complex images to use in your Flash movies. Drawings you create in Flash are composed of lines, called *strokes*, and the solid colors, called *fills*, that fill the interior of connected lines. An item you draw, such as a single square or a detailed image, is called an *object*.

Drawing Models

When you draw in Flash, you can use either the Merge Drawing model or the Object Drawing model. The Merge Drawing model is the default drawing mode for anything you draw on the Flash Stage. To draw by using the Object Drawing Model, you must turn on the Object Drawing modifier before you begin drawing. The Object Drawing modifier is available for each drawing tool.

Merge Drawing Model

With the Merge Drawing model, Flash automatically merges shapes and lines that overlap on the Stage. For example, if you have two shapes that overlap, the shapes merge and you cannot separate them into their original forms again. Any part of a shape that appeared beneath the overlapping area is now gone. The Merge Drawing model allows you to combine shapes and lines to create new shapes.

Object Drawing Model

When you draw by using the Object Drawing model, Flash groups your objects as a stand-alone unit and does not merge shapes. With Object Drawing, each shape you draw is a separate object you can manipulate without affecting any other object on the Stage. As you create your shapes, Flash surrounds them with a rectangular bounding box. You can use the Selection tool to reposition objects around the Stage.

Drawing Preferences

It is not always easy to draw with a computer mouse, but Flash makes it simpler with shape and line recognition settings. For example, when shape recognition is turned on, you can draw a rough idea of a shape on the Stage and Flash automatically cleans it up for you. You can find Drawing controls in the Preferences dialog box.

Import Graphics

You do not have to rely on your drawing skills to create objects for your Flash projects. You can import graphics from other programs and manipulate them with the Flash drawing and editing tools. For example, you might import a company logo to use as an interactive button, or import a sequence of photographic images to use in a Flash movie.

Reuse Objects

You can store graphics you create in Flash as symbols to reuse again throughout your Flash project. Symbols are stored in the Flash Library. Any graphics you import are also added to the Library. You use the library to keep track of the various elements you use in your projects, such as artwork, audio, video clips, and buttons.

Using the Flash Tools

Packed with tools, the Tools panel helps you create and work with graphic and text objects. By default, it appears docked on the far-left side of the program window. To hide the Tools panel at any time, click Window, then Tools. You can also expand or collapse the tools by clicking the arrows at the top of the panel.

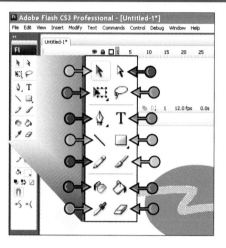

Selection
Also called the Pointer or Arrow tool, you can use this tool to grab, select, and move items on the Stage.

Subselection
Displays edit points you can adjust to change a line's shape.

Free Transform
Use this tool to scale, rotate, or skew a selected item. This tool shares space with the Gradient Transform tool on the panel.

Lasso
Use this tool to select irregularly shaped objects on the Stage.

Pen
Use this tool to draw precise curves. When you click the button's ⌄, you can control anchor points.

Text
Use this tool to draw text boxes or edit text.

Line
Use this tool to draw straight lines.

Rectangle
Use this tool to draw square and rectangle shapes. This tool shares space on the Tools panel with the Oval, Rectangle Primitive, Oval Primitive, and PolyStar tools..

Pencil
Use this tool to draw free-form lines.

Brush
Use this tool to draw with a fill color, much like a paintbrush.

Ink Bottle
Use this tool to change the style, thickness, and color of lines.

Paint Bucket
This tool fills shapes or lines with color.

Eyedropper
Use this tool to copy the attributes of one object to another.

Eraser
This tool erases parts of a graphic object.

View Tools

HAND

Use to move your view of the objects on the Stage or in the work area.

ZOOM

Magnifies your view or zooms out for a better look at the Stage.

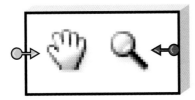

Option Tools

Some of the drawing tools you select might offer modifiers that enable you to set additional controls for the tool.

See Chapter 1 to learn how to display or hide the Tools panel.

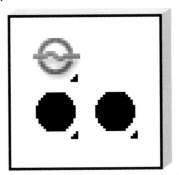

Color Tools and Controls

STROKE COLOR

Click to display a palette of colors for strokes, or lines.

FILL COLOR

Click to display a palette of colors for fills.

BLACK AND WHITE

Changes the line color to black and the fill color to white.

SWAP COLORS

Switches the line color to the fill color and vice versa.

NO COLOR

Use to draw shapes without fill colors.

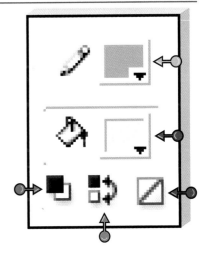

Draw Line Segments

You can draw all sorts of objects with lines. The easiest way to draw straight lines in Flash is to use the Line tool. To draw a free-form line, use the Pencil tool. Lines, also called *strokes* in Flash, can connect with other lines and shapes to create a drawing.

Draw Line Segments

DRAW A STRAIGHT LINE

① Click the **Line** tool (⟍).

② Move the mouse pointer over the Stage area. (⟍ changes to ＋).

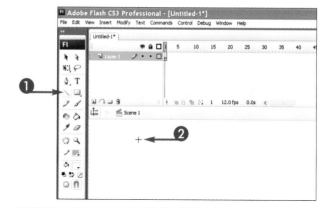

③ Click and drag to draw a line to your desired length.

④ Release the mouse button.

The line appears to your specifications.

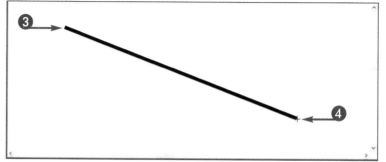

DRAW A FREE-FORM LINE

1 Click the **Pencil** tool (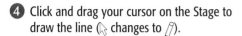).

2 Click the Pencil Mode button.

3 Click a pencil mode.

○ draws straight lines.

● draws curvy lines

● draws free-form lines.

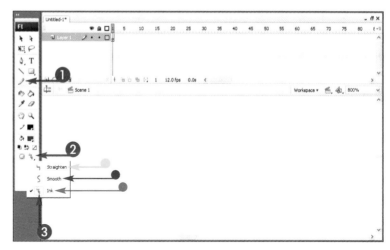

4 Click and drag your cursor on the Stage to draw the line (cursor changes to pencil).

5 Release the mouse button.

The line appears to your specifications.

TIPS

How do I control the line thickness?

You can set a line thickness before you start drawing the actual line segment using the Property inspector panel. If the panel is not open, press Ctrl + F3. When the Line or Pencil tool is selected, the Property inspector displays options for controlling line thickness, style, and color of any strokes you draw on the Stage. For example, to change the line thickness, drag the Stroke height slider up or down. You can apply a new line thickness to an existing line by first clicking the line to select it and then dragging the slider. See Chapter 1 to learn more about the Property inspector panel.

How do I keep a straight line vertical or horizontal?

Using the Line tool, press and hold down the Shift key and draw a line that is pretty much vertical or horizontal. Flash makes the line perfectly vertical or horizontal. This trick also works when drawing a 45-degree line.

Draw Lines with the Pen Tool

You can draw precise lines and curves with the Pen tool. Using this tool takes some getting used to, but with a little practice, you can draw lines easily. Lines that you create with the Pen tool are composed of points, which appear as dots on the line segment and represent changes in the line's curvature.

The quickest way to draw curves is to drag the Pen tool along with its handles on the Flash Stage. The handle is a straight line with two solid points at either end. You can rotate the bar to create different degrees of curvature.

Draw Lines with the Pen Tool

① Click the Pen tool (image).

② Move the pointer over the Stage area (image changes to image).

A line appears.

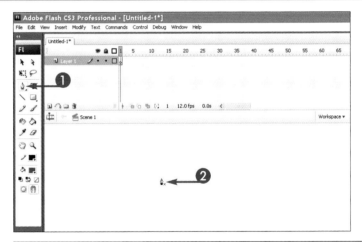

③ Click and begin dragging to start drawing the line.

● Control handles appear.

You can rotate a control handles by dragging the pointer to achieve the bend and line length you want for the curve.

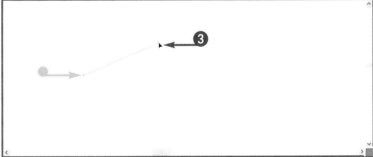

④ Stop dragging and release the mouse button.

⑤ Click and drag where you want the line to end.

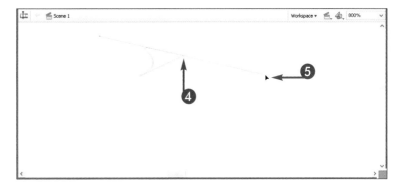

⑥ Release the mouse button.

● The curved line appears on the Stage.

You can add more curves to an existing curved line as long as the Pen tool is still active by simply dragging another line segment.

Flash automatically attaches the second line segment to the first curved line.

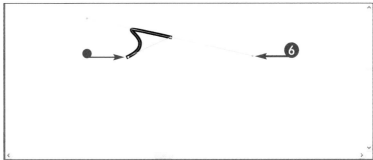

TIPS

How can I edit points on a curved line?
Use the Subselection tool to make changes to a curved line you created using the Pen tool. Click and move the cursor over a handle on the line or at the end of the line. Drag to reposition and reshape the line or curve.

Is there a way to constrain the degree of curvature?
Yes. You can press and hold down the Shift key (⌘ for Mac users) while dragging the Pen tool to keep the curves at 45-degree angles.

Draw Shapes

You can create simple shapes in Flash and then fill them with a color or pattern or use them as part of a drawing. You can create shapes using many of the tools on the Tools panel, but for more uniform shapes, such as circles, ovals, squares, and rectangles, you can use the Rectangle, Oval, or PolyStar tools.

DRAW AN EMPTY SHAPE

1 Click the **Rectangle** (□) tool to draw a rectangle shape.

To draw an oval shape, click the Rectangle tool's ∨ and then click **Oval Tool**.

To draw a polygon, click the Rectangle tool's ∨ and then click **PolyStar Tool**.

2 Click the **Fill Color** palette (▣).

3 Click the **No Color** icon (☑).

Note: You can also click the Fill Color button in the Properties inspector and click the No Color option.

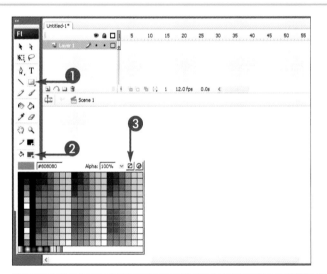

3 Move the cursor over the Stage area (☒ changes to +).

4 Click and drag to draw the shape you want.

Flash completes the shape.

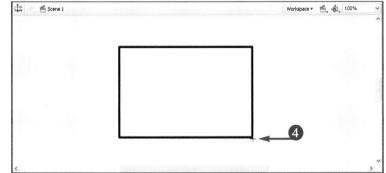

36

DRAW A SHAPE WITH A FILL COLOR

1 Click the shape you want to draw.

Note: See the previous steps to learn how to choose a shape.

2 Click the Fill Color palette.

3 Click a fill color (⛏ changes to 🖌).

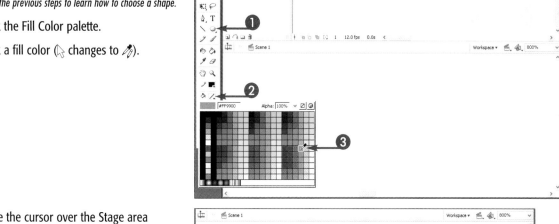

4 Move the cursor over the Stage area (⛏ changes to +).

5 Click and drag to draw the shape.

Flash completes the filled shape.

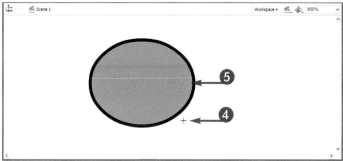

TIPS

How do I draw a rectangle with rounded corners?

You can use the Property inspector to modify the corners of a rectangle shape. If the Property inspector is not open, press Ctrl + F3. Change the Rectangle Corner Radius setting to create the type of rounded corners you want for the shape. Drag the slider control up to designate how much curvature you want for the corners, or drag the slider down to create inverted corners.

How can I change the number of sides for a polygon shape?

If you use the PolyStar tool to draw a shape, you can change the number of sides for the shape through the Property inspector panel. Simply click the PolyStar tool, then click the **Options** button in the Property inspector panel. This opens the Tool Settings dialog box, and you can change the number of sides for the shape.

Tool Settings
Style: polygon
# of Sides: 8

Draw Objects with the Brush Tool

You can use the Brush tool to draw with brush strokes, much like a paintbrush. You can control the size and shape of the brush as well as how the brush strokes appear on the Stage.

Draw Objects with the Brush Tool

① Click the **Brush** tool (✐).

● The ⌖ changes to ●.

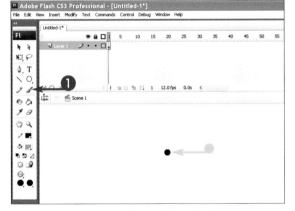

② Click the **Brush Size** modifier.

③ Click a Brush size.

④ Click the **Brush Shape** modifier.

⑤ Click a shape.

⑥ Click and drag to begin drawing.

A brush stroke appears to your specifications.

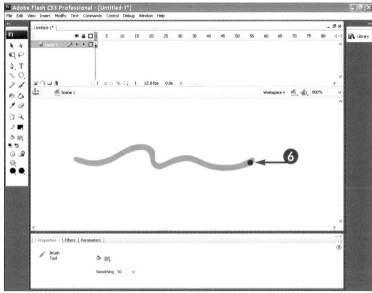

TIP

What do the brush modes do?

You can find five brush modes by clicking the Brush Mode modifier at the bottom of the Tools panel.

 Paint Normal

Lets you paint over anything on the Stage

 Paint Fills

Paints inside fill areas but not on lines

 Paint Behind

Paints beneath any existing objects on the Stage

 Paint Selection

Paints only inside the selected area

 Paint Inside

Begins a brush stroke inside a fill area without affecting any lines

Fill Objects with the Paint Bucket Tool

You can use the Paint Bucket tool to quickly fill in objects, such as shapes. You can fill objects with a color, a gradient effect, or even a picture. The Flash color palette comes with numerous colors and shades, as well as several premade gradient effects from which to choose.

A gradient is two or more colors that blend together. See Chapter 3 to learn more about creating new gradient effects.

Fill Objects with the Paint Bucket Tool

ADD A FILL

① Click the **Paint Bucket** tool (🪣).

　⌖ changes to ◇.

② Click the **Fill Color** palette.

③ Click a fill color (◇ changes to 🖉).

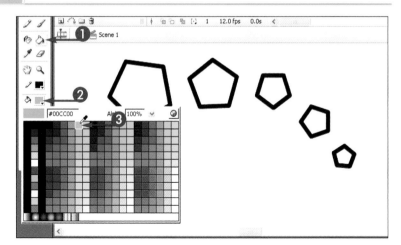

④ Click the shape you want to fill.

　The color fills the shape.

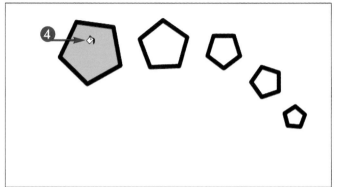

ADD A GRADIENT FILL

5. Click the **Paint Bucket** tool ( ).

   changes to .

6. Click the **Fill Color** palette.

7. Click a gradient color effect (changes to).

Note: *See Chapter 3 to learn more about creating new gradient effects.*

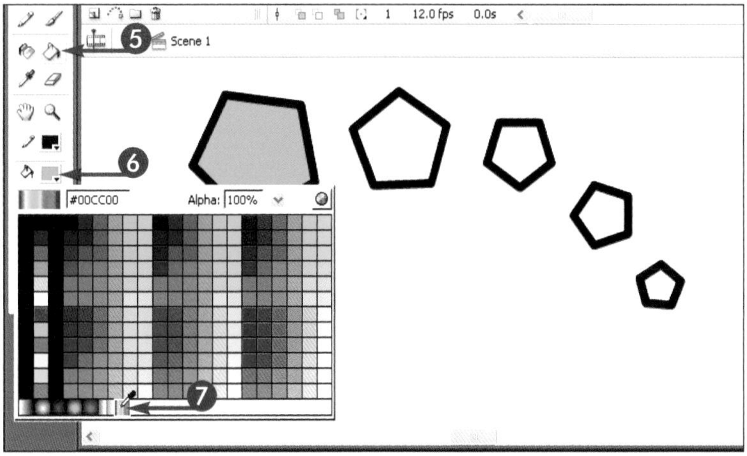

8. Click the shape you want to fill.

   The color fills the shape.

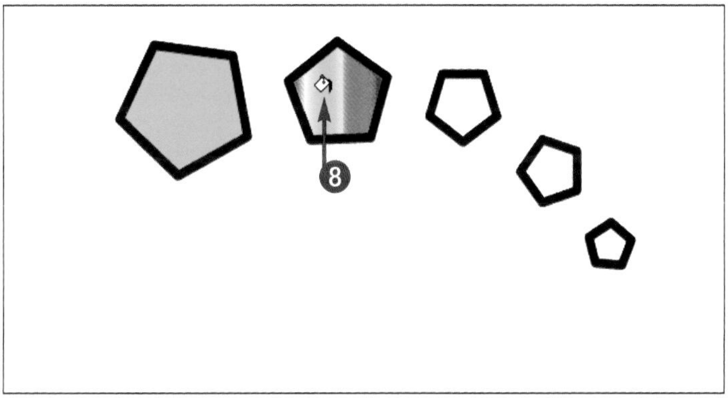

TIPS

What is a gradient effect?

A *gradient effect* shows two or several colors of different intensities. With Flash, you can create a linear gradient effect that intensifies color shading from left to right or top to bottom, or create a radial gradient effect that intensifies color shading from the middle to the outer edges or vice versa.

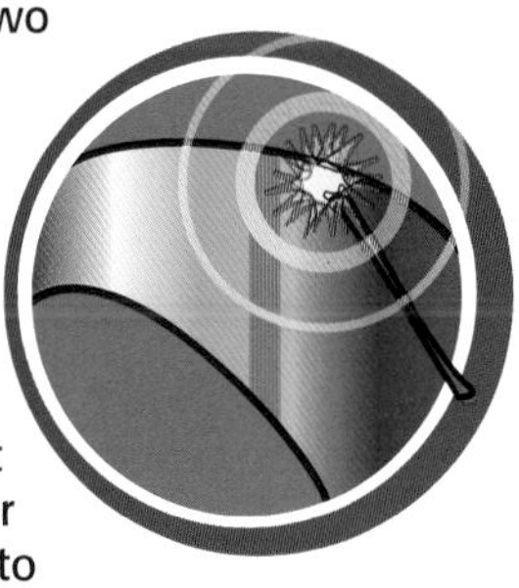

What does the Gap Size modifier do?

When you select the Paint Bucket tool, the Gap Size modifier appears at the bottom of the Tools panel. Click the Gap Size modifier to display a menu list of four settings. These settings determine how the Paint Bucket tool treats any gaps that appear in the shape you are trying to fill. For very large gaps, you may need to close the gaps yourself before applying the fill color.

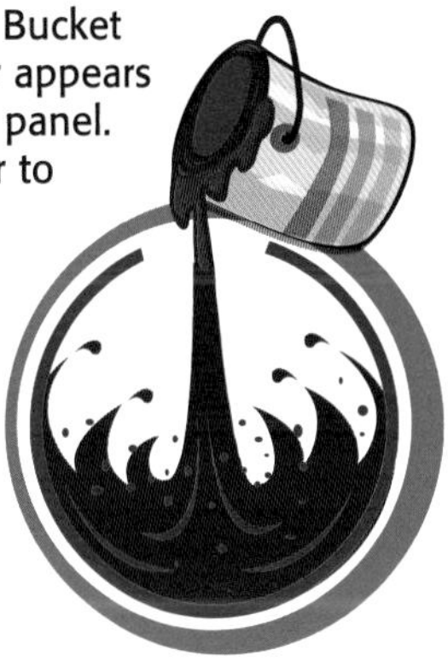

Enhancing and Editing Objects

Need to enhance your drawn object or give it some depth? This chapter shows you how to use a variety of editing tools to enhance shapes and lines, as well as adjust stacking order, change fill colors, and format strokes. You can also use these same tools to edit graphics you import into Flash.

Select Objects

You can use several techniques to select objects in Flash. To work with objects you draw or place on the Flash Stage, whether you want to edit or reposition the objects, you must first select them. The more lines and shapes you place on the Stage, the trickier it is to select only the ones you want.

You can use the Selection tool, also called the Pointer or Arrow tool, to quickly select any single object, such as a line segment or fill. To select several objects, you can click and drag a marquee around the items.

CLICK TO SELECT OBJECTS

1 Click the **Selection** tool (⬆).

2 Move ⬆ over the object you want to select, and then click.

You can select a fill and its surrounding line border by double-clicking the fill.

Note: When working with multiple layers, click the layer containing the object you want to select, and then click the object. See Chapter 6 to learn about layers.

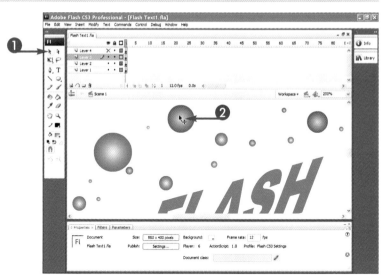

● Selected objects appear highlighted with a pattern.

After selecting an object, you can edit the object.

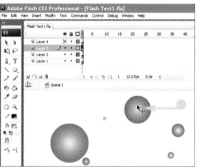

SELECT BY DRAGGING

① Click ▶.

② Click and drag a square selection box around the object you want to select.

Note: When working with multiple layers, click the layer containing the object you want to select, and then click the object. See Chapter 6 to learn more about layers.

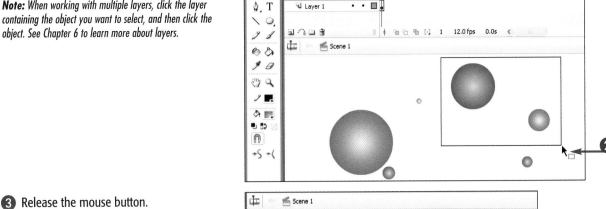

③ Release the mouse button.

● Flash selects everything inside the selection box.

 TIPS

How do I select multiple objects?

Hold down the Shift key while clicking objects when you want to select more than one at a time. For example, if a line is composed of several segments, you can select all of them for editing. Click ▶, and then and hold the Shift key and click each line segment you want to select.

How do I select everything on the Stage?

You can use the Select All command to apply global edits to all the objects on the Stage. You can also use the Select All command to select and delete everything on the stage at one time. To activate the command, click **Edit** and then **Select All**. You can also press Ctrl+A (⌘+A).

continued

You can use the Lasso tool to select irregular objects or multiple objects scattered on the Stage. The Lasso tool draws a freehand "rope" around the item you want to select. This allows you to select an oddly shaped object or just a small portion of an object.

If you make a mistake and lasso a part of the drawing you do not want to select, click anywhere on-screen and try again.

Select Objects (continued)

LASSO AN OBJECT

① To select an irregularly shaped object, click the **Lasso** tool (🔘)

When you move 🔖 over the Stage area, it changes to 🔘.

② Click and drag the lasso around the object until you reach the point where you started.

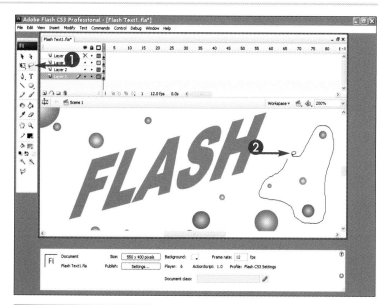

Note: *When working with multiple layers, click the layer containing the object you want to select, and then click the object. See Chapter 6 to learn more about layers.*

③ Release the mouse button.

● Flash highlights anything inside the lasso shape.

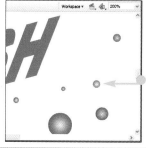

SELECT PART OF AN OBJECT

① Click ▶ or ⌷.

You can click ▶ for simple shapes or lines.

You can click ⌷ for irregularly shaped objects.

② Click and drag the pointer to surround the object part you want to select.

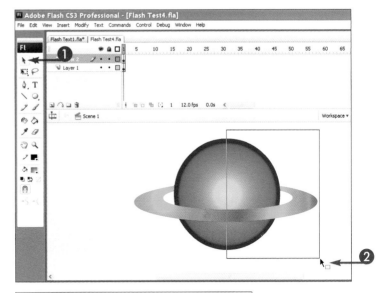

③ Release the mouse button.

● Everything inside the area you dragged over is selected.

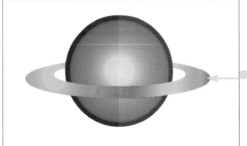

TIPS

How can I select complex shapes?

Drawing around irregular items with the Lasso tool can be difficult. For additional help, use the Lasso tool's Polygon Mode modifier. Click ⌷ and then click the **Polygon Mode** modifier button (⬦) in the Modifier Tray at the bottom of the Tools panel. Now click your way around the object you want to select. Every click creates a connected line to the last click. To turn off the Polygon Mode, double-click.

How do I select just a fill and not its border?

Using the Selection tool (▶), simply click the fill to select it. To select both the fill and the fill's border, double-click the fill. To deselect a fill or border at any time, just click anywhere outside the selected object.

Format Line Segments

You can change a line, also called a stroke in Flash, by adjusting its length or reshaping its curve. For example, you might want to change the angle of a line, extend a curved line to make it appear longer, or just simply make the curve more curvy. You can edit any line segment by altering its endpoints.

Unlike other editing techniques, you do not need to first select the line in order to modify its endpoints.

Format Line Segments

RESIZE A LINE SEGMENT

1. Click ▶.

2. Move ▷ over an end of the line.

Note: Do not click the line to select it.

A ◥ appears next to the ▷.

3. Click and drag the end of the line to shorten or lengthen the segment.

● As you drag the corner pointer in any direction, you can change the line's angle.

4. Release the mouse button.

The line is resized.

RESIZE A LINE SEGMENT

1 Click 🔲.

2 Move ▷ over the area of the line you want to curve.

Note: *Do not click the line to select it.*

A ▶ appears next to the ▷.

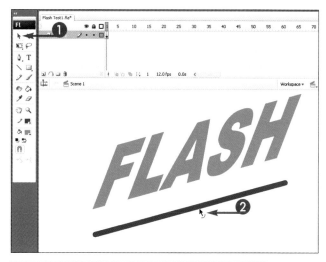

3 Click and drag the line to add or reshape the curve.

4 Release the mouse button.

Flash reshapes the line.

 TIPS

How do I draw perfect vertical and horizontal lines?

You may find it difficult keep a steady hand while drawing a line on the Stage. You can draw perfectly straight horizontal and vertical lines if you press and hold the **Shift** key while dragging the **Line** tool (◿) across the Stage. This technique also works for drawing perfect squares with the Rectangle tool or perfect circles with the Oval tool.

Can I see precise edit points on a line?

Yes. Click the **Subselection** tool (▷) and then click the line. Edit points appear at either end of the line, and if the line consists of more than one segment, edit points also appear at each change of segment. You can drag any edit point to reshape the line.

Smooth or Straighten Line Segments

You can create subtle or dramatic changes in your drawing by smoothing or straightening line segments or *strokes*. For example, perhaps you have painstakingly drawn a tree with several curving branches. You now decide a few of your branches need some modifications. You can use the Arrow tool's Smooth or Straighten options to adjust your lines.

Smooth or Straighten Line Segments

SMOOTH A LINE

① Click ▸.

② Click the line segment you want to smooth.

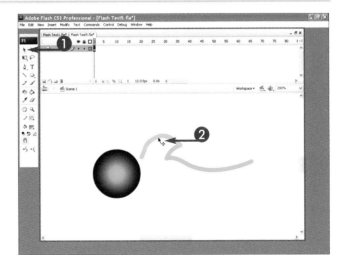

③ Click the **Smooth** modifier (⇥S).

● The line is altered slightly.

You can keep clicking ⇥S until you achieve the desired effect.

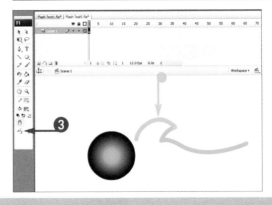

STRAIGHTEN A LINE

1 Click ⬉.

2 Click the line segment you want to straighten.

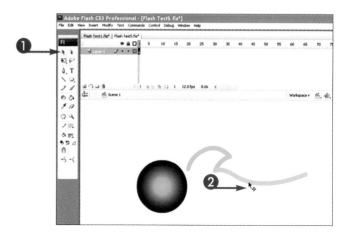

3 Click the **Straighten** tool (⊢⟨).

● The line is altered slightly.

You can keep clicking ⊢⟨ until you achieve the desired effect.

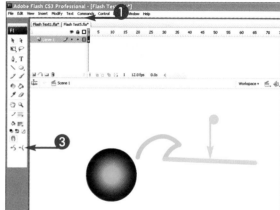

 TIPS

Can I draw in Smooth or Straighten mode?

Yes. Flash can help you with your line-drawing skills using the Pencil mode modifiers. You can activate a mode before you begin drawing. When you click the **Pencil** tool (⟋), the Pencil mode modifier button appears at the bottom of the Tools panel. Click the button and choose a drawing mode. Click **Straighten** (⊢⟨) or **Smooth** (⊢S). When you finish drawing a line, Flash smoothes or straightens it for you. To draw free-form lines, click the **Ink** (⟨) modifier.

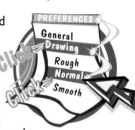

Why do my curved lines appear so rough?

A previous user may have made some adjustments to the program's preferences. You can adjust settings for drawing lines and shapes through the Preferences dialog box. Click **Edit** and then **Preferences** to display the Preferences dialog box. Click the **Drawing** category; then click the **Smooth Curves** ⌄ and select **Normal**. Click **OK** to exit the dialog box and apply the new setting.

Edit Fills

With Flash, you can change a fill shape by adjusting the sides of the fill. A *fill* is a color or pattern that fills a closed outline or shape. You can also change the fill color at any time to create additional changes to the shape or object.

You must select the fill first in order to apply a new color. As long as the fill is highlighted on the Stage, you can continue trying different colors from the Fill Color palette.

RESHAPE A FILL

1 Click ▶.

2 Move ↳ over the edge of the fill.

Note: Do not select the fill.

When you move the pointer near an edge of a fill, ↳ appears next to the pointer.

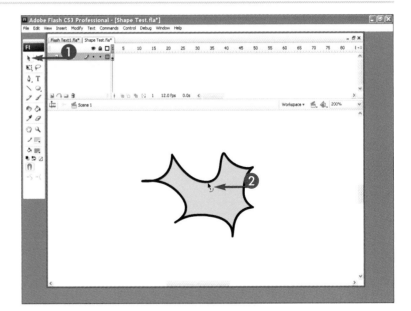

3 Drag the fill's edge in or out to reshape the fill.

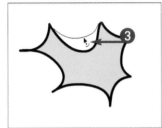

④ Release the mouse button.

● Flash reshapes the fill.

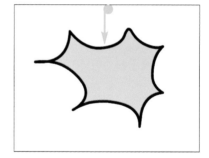

EDIT THE FILL COLOR

① Click [▶].

② Click the fill.

③ Click the **Fill Color** button (■) to open the color palette.

④ Click a color.

The fill immediately shows the new color selection.

Note: See the section "Create a Gradient Effect" to learn how to work with gradient fills.

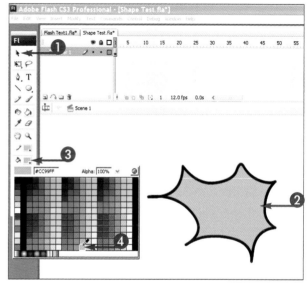

(TIPS)

My fill object does not include an outside stroke. Can I add an outline around the fill?

Yes. Click the **Ink Bottle** tool (●), and then click the edge of the object. To set stroke properties, such as line thickness, before applying the outline, open the Property inspector panel and set stroke properties first. To learn more about the Property inspector panel, see Chapter 1.

Are there other ways to edit fill shapes?

Yes. You can find additional commands for altering shapes on the Modify menu that can help you edit fills. For example, to soften a fill's edges, select the fill, and then click **Modify**, **Shape**, and then **Soften Fill Edges**. From the Soften Fill Edges dialog box, adjust the settings and click **OK**. Experiment with the settings to see what sort of effects you can create.

Modify Objects with the Free Transform Tool

You can use the Free Transform tool in Flash to rotate, skew, scale, distort, and envelope objects, thus creating new shapes to use in your animations and Flash movies. The Free Transform tool includes four modifier tools: Rotate and Skew, Scale, Distort, and Envelope.

You can apply the Rotate and Skew and the Scale modifiers to objects you create or import. You can apply the Distort and Envelope modifiers to objects you draw in Flash.

Modify Objects with the Free Transform Tool

SCALE AN OBJECT

1 Select the object you want to resize.

2 Click the **Free Transform** tool ( ).

Note: You can also click Modify, Transform, Free Transform.

● Flash surrounds the object with edit points, called *handles*.

● Four transform modifiers appear on the Tools palette.

Note: You can use the Scale modifier to resize objects you draw and objects you import.

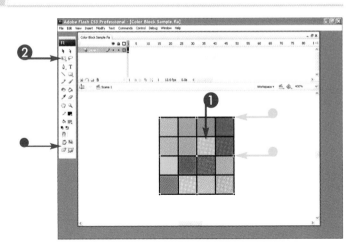

3 Click the **Scale** modifier ( ).

4 Click and drag a handle to scale the object.

● Click and drag corner handles to resize the object but maintain its proportions.

● Click and drag middle handles to stretch or compress an object, distorting its shape.

5 Release the mouse button.

Flash resizes the object.

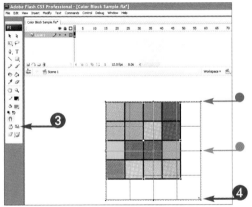

DISTORT AN OBJECT

① Select the object you want to distort.

② Click ▓.

Flash surrounds the object with handles.

③ Click the **Distort** modifier (◹).

④ Click and drag a handle to distort the object (◈ changes to ▷).

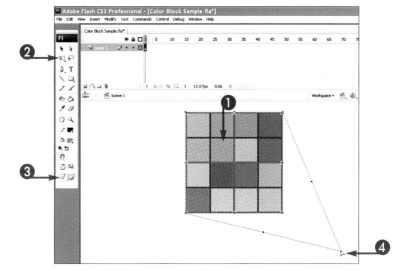

⑤ Release the mouse button.

Flash distorts the object.

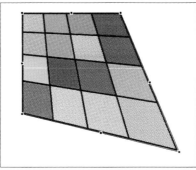

TIPS

How do I set a precise size?

If you need to size an object to a precise measurement, click **Window**, **Info** to open the Info panel. Here you can set a precise size for the object using the width (W) and height (H) text boxes. Simply type the measurement you want, and press Enter (Return) to see the changes take effect.

Info x

W: 67.0

H: 67.0

What happens if I resize an item beyond the Stage?

In some cases, the object you resize may reach beyond the Stage area. Not to worry, because the object is still there. You may need to zoom out to see the object. You can move the item back onto the Stage or resize the Stage to fit the larger object. Any part of the object that hangs off the Stage is still considered in the work area; however, the part may not be visible when you play your Flash movie. See Chapter 1 to learn more about resizing the Stage area.

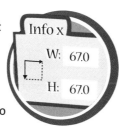

continued

Modify Objects with the Free Transform Tool *(continued)*

You can use the Free Transform tool's skew and envelope features to warp and distort an object or shape, which is useful for creating morphed elements for animations. The skew feature allows you to distort an object by slanting it on one or both axes. The Envelope modifier allows you to enclose the object with edit points, then use the points to control the shape.

Modify Objects with the Free Transform Tool *(continued)*

SKEW AN OBJECT

① Select the object you want to distort.

② Click 🔲.

● Flash surrounds the object with handles.

③ Click the **Rotate and Skew** modifier (🗗).

Note: See the task "Rotate and Flip Objects" to learn how to rotate an object on the Stage.

④ Click and drag an edge of the object to skew the object shape (⬚ changes to ⬌).

⑤ Release the mouse button.

Flash skews the object.

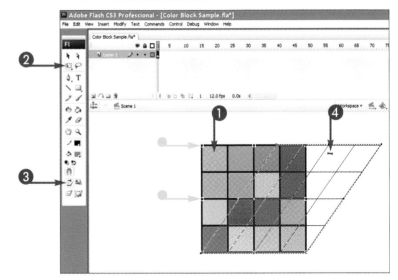

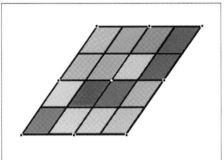

ENVELOPE A SHAPE

1 Select the shape.

2 Click 🔳.

Flash surrounds the object with edit points.

3 Click the **Envelope** modifier (🔲).

4 Click and drag a handle to change the object shape (⬚ changes to ◿).

An outline of the object appears as you drag.

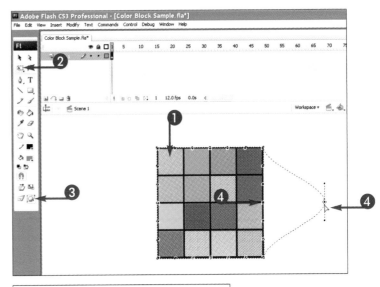

5 Release the mouse button.

Flash reshapes the object.

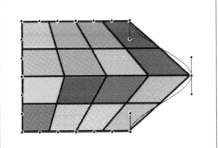

TIPS

How do I distort text in Flash?
Using the Break Apart command, you can break apart the strokes and fills that make up the letters in a word or words, and then use the Envelope modifier to distort the shape of the text. To do so, click in the text box, then click **Modify**, **Break Apart**. Repeat this step two more times, then you can apply the Envelope modifier. See Chapter 5 to learn more about working with the Text tool.

What types of edit points does the Envelope modifier use?
The Envelope modifier uses two types of edit points: regular edit points and tangent handles. Regular edit points are square, and when manipulated can change the corners and sides of an object. Tangent handles are circles that adjust additional points along the edges of a selected object. You can only use the Envelope modifier to change shapes you create in Flash. You cannot use the feature to alter symbols, bitmaps, text boxes, or video objects. You can learn how to use the rotate portion of the feature in the section "Rotate and Flip Objects."

Rotate and Flip Objects

Not every shape or line you draw has to remain as it is on the Stage. You can reorient objects to create different looks. You can spin an object based on its center point, or you can flip an object vertically or horizontally. Both actions enable you to quickly change an object's position in a drawing.

When you rotate an object on the Stage, you use the edit points, also called rotation handles, to reorient the object. When you flip an object, there are no edit points.

Rotate and Flip Objects

① Select the object or shape you want to rotate.

② Click ▦.

③ Click the **Rotate and Skew** tool (↻).

● Flash surrounds the object with edit points, called *handles*.

Note: *See the task "Modify Objects with the Free Transform Tool" to learn how to skew an object on the Stage.*

④ Click and drag a handle to rotate the object (↳ changes to ↻).

● An outline of the object appears as you rotate.

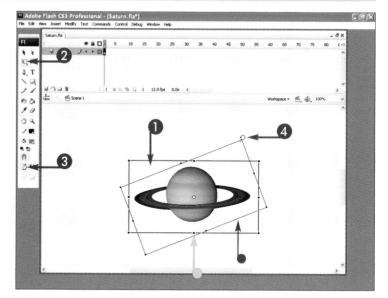

⑤ Release the mouse button.

Flash rotates the object.

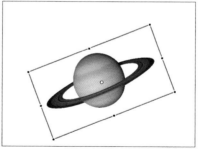

FLIP AN OBJECT

1 Select the object you want to flip.

Note: To learn more about selecting objects, see the section "Select Objects."

2 Click **Modify**.

3 Click **Transform**.

4 Click **Flip Vertical** or **Flip Horizontal**.

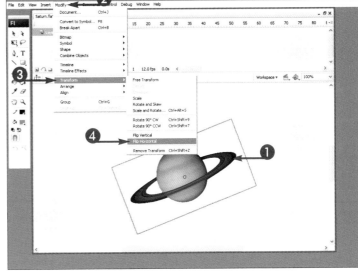

The object flips on the Stage.

Can I change an object's center point?

For most objects, the center point is truly the object's center. But there are times when you want the center point to reference another part of the object. To change an object's center point, select the object, and then click 📷. The center point appears as a tiny circle icon in the middle of the selected object. Click and drag the center point icon to a new location. Note that this only works on overlay-level, not stage-level, objects. See Chapter 2 to learn more about drawing levels.

Can I type a precise degree of rotation?

Yes. You can use the Transform panel to specify an exact rotation. Click **Window**, **Transform** to open the panel. Select the **Rotate** option and type a degree of rotation in the text box. Flash immediately rotates the object on the Stage.

You can use the Eraser tool to erase stray parts of a drawing or object, or you can use it to create new shapes within an object. The Eraser tool has several modifiers you can use to control how the tool works.

Use the Eraser tool to erase strokes and fills on the Stage level. You cannot erase grouped objects, symbols, or text blocks unless you apply the Break Apart command and make the items part of the Stage level rather than the overlay level.

1 Click the **Eraser** tool ( ).

● For a quick erase of entire lines or fills, you can click the **Faucet** modifier ( ) and then click the item you want to erase.

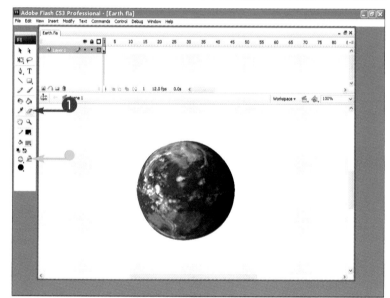

2 Click the **Eraser Shape** modifier ( ).

3 Click a size or shape for the Eraser.

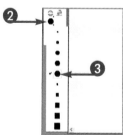

④ Click and drag to begin erasing.

⑤ Release the mouse button when finished erasing.

An eraser path marks everywhere you dragged over the object.

What do the Eraser modifiers do?
You can use one of five modifiers with the Eraser tool:

Erase Normal (⊙): Lets you erase over anything on the Stage

Erase Fills (⊙): Erases inside fill areas but not lines

Erase Lines (⊙): Erases only lines

Erase Selected Fills (⊙): Does just that—erases only the selected fill

Erase Inside (⊙): Erases only inside the selected area

Create a Gradient Effect

You can use gradient effects to add depth and dimension to your Flash drawings. A *gradient* effect is a band of blended color or shading. You can apply a gradient effect as a fill to any shape. By default, the Fill Color palette offers several preformatted gradient effects you can use. This task shows you how to create your own.

① Click **Window**.

② Click **Color**.

The Color panel opens.

Note: *See Chapter 1 to learn how to work with Flash panels.*

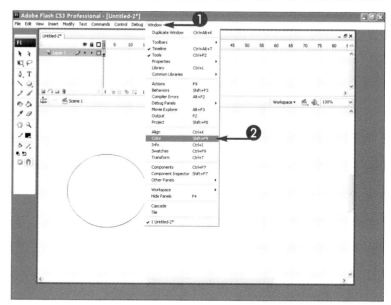

③ Click the **Type** ☑.

④ Select **Linear** or **Radial**.

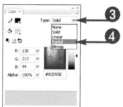

5 Click the color marker you want to change.

6 Click a color.

7 Click a color shade.

● The gradient bar changes color.

Note: *To add another 🔒 to the effect, click below the gradient bar; to remove a 🔒, click and drag it off the panel.*

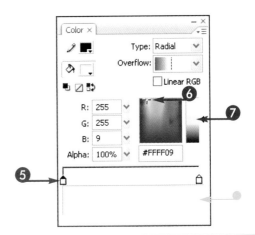

You can continue creating the gradient effect by adding color markers and assigning colors.

● You can click and drag 🔒 left or right to adjust the color intensity bandwidth on the gradient.

8 To save the gradient, click the **Panel Menu** 🔻.

9 Click **Add Swatch**.

The new gradient now appears as a swatch in the color palette.

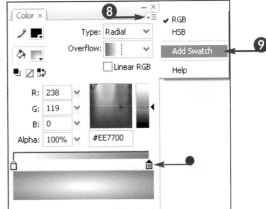

 TIPS

Can I make changes to an existing gradient in the palette?

Yes. You can select an existing gradient effect from the Fill Color palette and make modifications to the colors using the Color panel. You can make changes to the color markers or intensities and save the edits as a new gradient color swatch.

Can I delete a customized gradient effect I no longer need?

Yes. Click **Window**, **Swatches** to display the Swatches panel. Click the gradient effect swatch you want to delete. Click 🔻 at the top of the panel and then click **Delete Swatch**. Flash permanently deletes the gradient effect from all color palettes.

Transform a Gradient Fill

You can use the Fill Transform tool to transform gradient fills. For example, a radiant fill radiates the fill color from the middle of the fill. With one gradient color appearing lighter than the other, it makes the object appear to be highlighted by an off-Stage light source. With the Fill Transform tool, you can change the position of the radiant center point to change the highlight.

Transform a Gradient Fill

1 Assign a gradient fill to an object or shape.

Note: See Chapter 2 to learn how to fill an object.

2 Click the **Free Transform** tool.

3 Click **Gradient Transform Tool**.

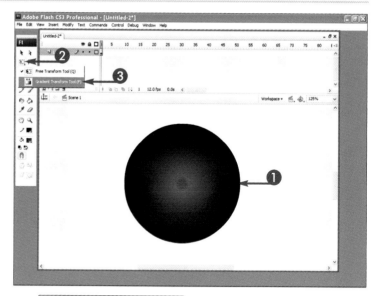

4 Click the fill.

Five edit point controls appear on the fill.

5 Click and drag an edit point to transform the fill.

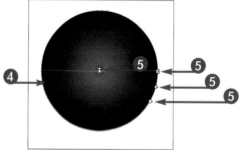

- You can click and drag the Center point to change the position of the gradient's highlight.

- You can click and drag the Width point to change the shape of the gradient effect.

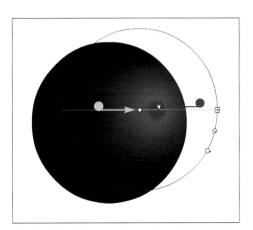

- Click and drag the Rotation point to change the angle of the gradient.

- Click and drag the Size point to change the size or radius of the gradient effect.

- Click and drag the Focal point to change the focal area of the effect.

Note: *The Focal point icon only appears on radial gradient effects.*

6 Click anywhere outside the fill to turn off the Fill Transform feature.

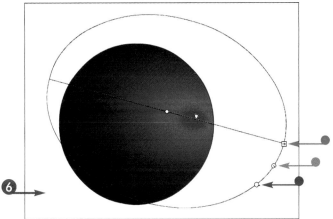

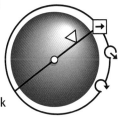

Can I change the size of a linear gradient effect?

No. When you apply the Fill Transform tool to a linear gradient, you only see three edit point controls. A linear gradient uses only the Center, Width, and Rotation edit point controls, allowing you to change the gradient's center, direction or angle, and width.

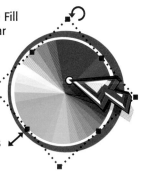

My fill takes up the entire Stage and I cannot see the fill's edit points. How do I view the edit points to transform the fill?

Click the **Magnification** at the top-right corner of the Stage, then click a magnification level. You can also click the **View** menu, click **Magnification**, then click a zoom level to zoom out and see more of the work area.

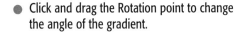

Edit a Color Set

You can customize the colors you use in Flash to create a unique color set to suit the projects you build. Flash comes with a default color set, but you can make new color sets based on the default set by removing colors you do not need for a particular project. You can then save the edited color set as a new color set for use in other Flash projects. You save color sets with the .clr file extension.

Edit a Color Set

REMOVE COLOR SWATCHES

① Click **Window**.

② Click **Swatches**.

The Swatches panel opens.

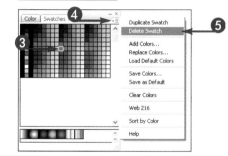

③ To remove a color swatch from the set, click the color.

④ Click the **Panel Menu** button (⊡≡) to display the pop-up menu.

⑤ Click **Delete Swatch**.

⑥ Repeat Steps **4** and **5** to continue removing swatches you do not want as part of your color set.

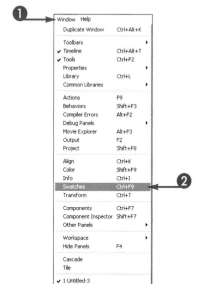

SAVE THE EDITED COLOR SET

⑦ Click 🔻☰.

⑧ Click **Save Colors**.

The Export Color Swatch dialog box appears.

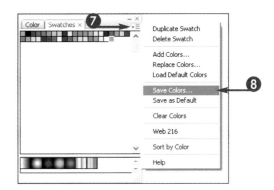

⑨ Type a name for the color set.

● By default, Flash saves the color set in the My Documents folder. You can save the file to another folder by navigating to the appropriate folder.

⑩ Click **Save**.

Flash saves the edited color set.

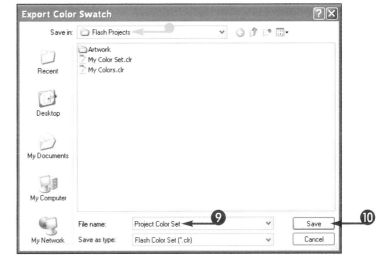

How do I load a color set?

After you create a color set, you can reuse it in any Flash file. Open the Color Swatches panel, click the **Panel Menu** button (🔻☰) in the upper-right corner of the panel, and click **Replace Colors** from the pop-up menu. This opens the Import Color Swatch dialog box. Locate the color set file you want to use, select it, and click **Open**.

Which colors should I use for Web page designs?

Because different computers handle color differently, designers have come up with a Web Safe color palette. The Web Safe palette consists of 216 colors that Web designers find are consistent in both Windows and Mac platforms for all the major Web browser programs. To use the Web Safe palette in Flash, open the Swatches panel, click 🔻☰ in the upper-right corner of the palette, and then click **Web 216**. Using the Web 216 color palette assures that your color selections are suitable for all browsers.

Copy Attributes

You can use the Eyedropper tool to quickly copy attributes from one object to another. Copying attributes rather than reassigning them one at a time can save you time and effort. The Eyedropper tool copies fill and line attributes and enables you to copy the same formatting to other fills and lines.

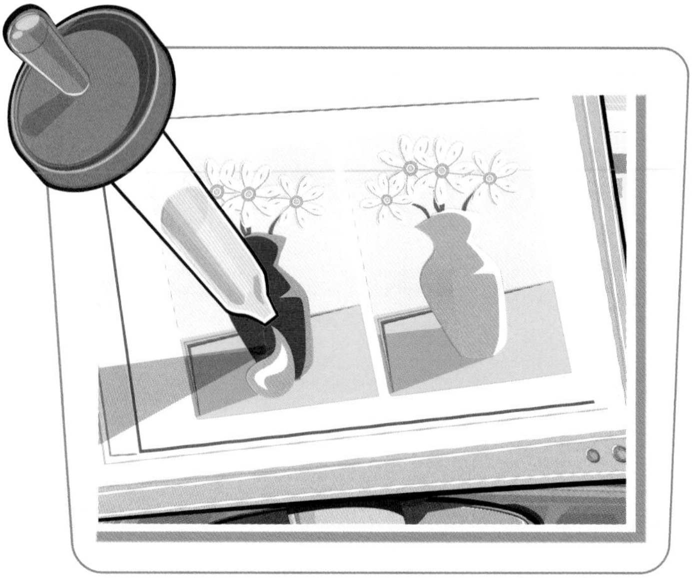

Copy Attributes

1. Click the **Eyedropper** tool.

- The pointer changes to the eyedropper pointer.

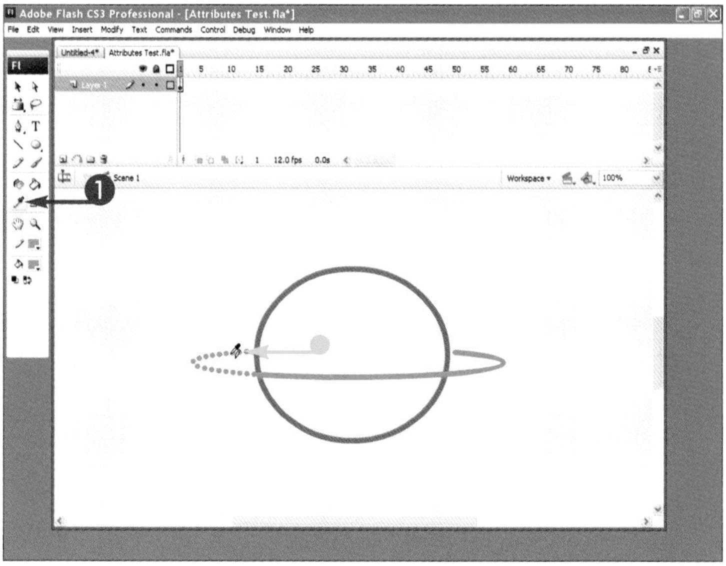

2. Click the line.

- The pointer changes to the ink bottle pointer.

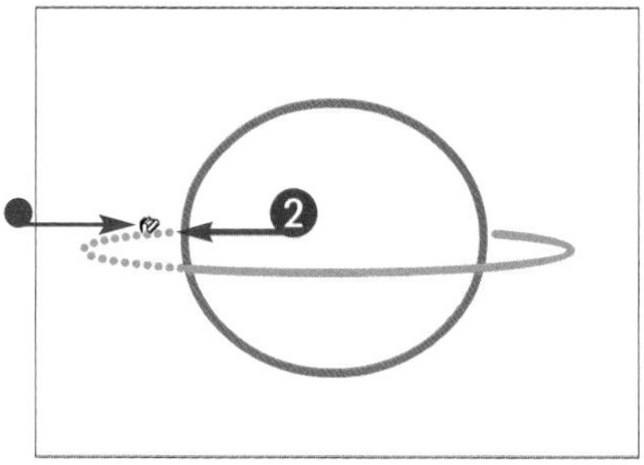

3 Move 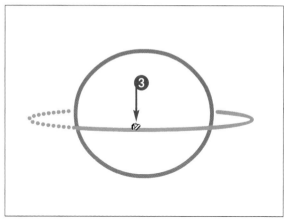 over the line to which you want to copy the attributes.

4 Click the line to which you want to copy.

Flash immediately applies the line formatting.

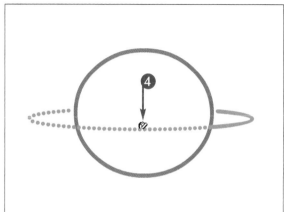

TIPS

Can I copy fill attributes, too?

You can copy fill attributes just like you copy line attributes. When you move  over a fill, a tiny paint brush icon appears next to it to show that you are over a fill. Click to absorb the fill formatting. Move over the fill you want to reformat, and click again. Flash immediately changes the second fill to match the first.

My Eyedropper tool does not work. Why?

When copying line attributes, you cannot use the Ink Bottle on grouped lines. Be sure to ungroup the lines first and then try copying the line attributes to each line. See the section "Group Objects" for more information.

Group Objects

You can work on multiple items at the same time by placing the objects in a group. A group enables you to treat the items as a single unit. Any edits you make affect all items in the group. One of the prime benefits of grouping several objects is that you can move them all at once on the Stage instead of moving one object at a time.

You place grouped objects on the overlay drawing level in Flash. Grouped objects do not interact with objects on the Stage level. See Chapter 2 to learn more about drawing levels.

Group Objects

CREATE A GROUP

① Select all the objects you want to include in a group.

Note: *See the section "Select Objects" to learn more about selecting items on the Flash Stage.*

You can select multiple items by pressing and holding the Shift key while clicking each item.

② Click **Modify**.

③ Click **Group**.

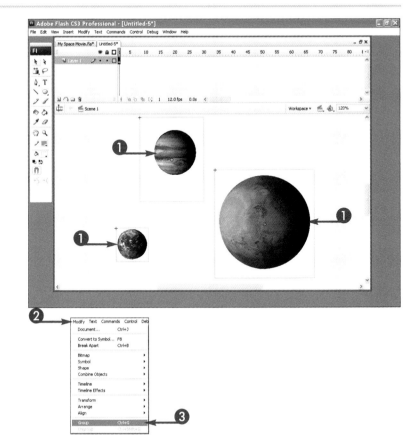

● Flash groups the objects together and surrounds them with a blue box.

UNGROUP A GROUP

① Select the group you want to ungroup.

Note: See the section "Select Objects" to learn more about selecting items on the Flash Stage.

② Click **Modify**.

③ Click **Ungroup**.

Flash ungroups the objects.

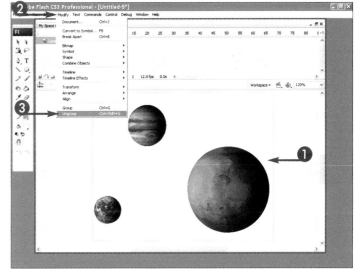

How can I avoid accidentally changing a group?

If you worry about accidentally moving or changing a group, you can lock it. Click **Modify**, **Arrange**, and then **Lock**. To unlock the group again, click **Modify**, **Arrange**, and then **Unlock All**.

Can I have a group of one?

Yes. You can turn one object into a group to move it to the overlay level and keep it from interacting with other objects on the Stage level.

Stack Objects

You can stack objects you add to the Stage to change the appearance of drawings. When placing objects over other objects, you can control exactly where an object appears in the stack. You can place an object at the very back of a stack, at the very front, or somewhere in between.

Stacking only works with grouped objects. Flash places grouped objects – whether the group consists of several objects or just one – on the overlay level, which means that they always appear stacked on top of objects that are located on the stage level.

Stack Objects

① Select the object or group you want to reorder.

Note: *See the section "Select Objects" to learn more about selecting items on the Flash Stage.*

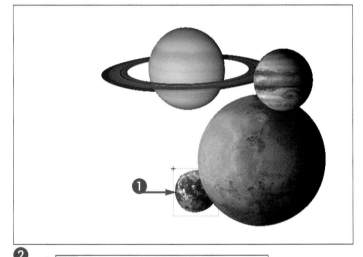

② Click **Modify**.

③ Click **Arrange**.

④ Select an arrangement command.

To send an object to the very back of the stack, click **Send to Back**.

To move an object back, click **Send Backward**.

To bring an object to the very front of the stack, click **Bring to Front**.

To move an object forward, click **Bring Forward**.

The object is relocated in the stacking order.

● In this example, the selected planet moves forward in the stack.

● In this example, the selected planet moves to the back of the stack.

 TIPS

Is there a shortcut for moving an object up or back a layer in a stack?

Yes. You can use keyboard shortcuts to quickly reposition an object in a stack. For the Mac, press ⌘ instead of Ctrl.

Windows	Result
Ctrl + ⬆	Moves the object up one level
Ctrl + Shift + ⬆	Moves the object directly to the top of the stack
Ctrl + ⬇	Moves the object back a level
Ctrl + Shift + ⬇	Moves the object directly to the back of the stack

Can I stack objects located on the Stage level?

No. You cannot apply the stacking commands to objects on the Stage level; if you try, they do not work. Objects you place on the Stage level interact, which means if you move a shape over a line, the line is covered. If you move the shape again, the line is no longer there; it has become a part of the shape. Stacking only works on objects you place on the overlay level. See Chapter 2 to learn more about Stage and overlay levels.

Align Objects

You can control the alignment of objects you add to the Stage, whether they are shapes you draw or graphics you import. You can align objects vertically and horizontally by their edges or centers. You can align objects with other objects, with the edges of the Stage, or even control the amount of space between the objects.

The alignment commands come in handy when you try to position several objects on the Stage, and dragging them around manually does not seem to create the results you want. Although the Flash rulers and grid can help you line things up on the Stage, applying alignment options are much faster and easier.

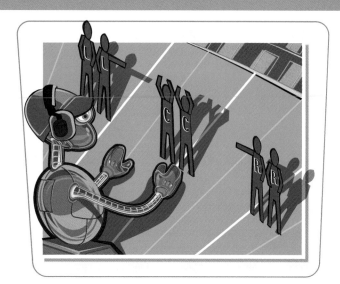

Align Objects

ALIGN OBJECTS WITH OTHER OBJECTS

1 Select the objects you want to align.

You can select multiple items by pressing and holding the **Shift** key while clicking each item.

2 Click **Window**.

3 Click **Align**.

The Align panel opens.

Note: You can also find alignment commands on the Modify menu.

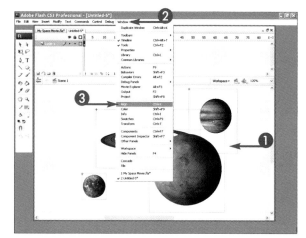

4 Click an alignment option.

Click 🖹 to align objects to the leftmost object.

Click 🖹 to center-align the objects horizontally.

Click 🖹 to align the objects to the rightmost object.

● Flash aligns the objects. In this example, the objects are aligned to the left with the leftmost object.

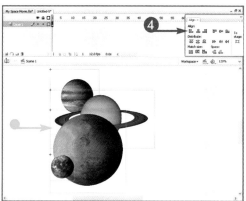

- To align the objects vertically, click a vertical alignment in the Align panel.

  Click 🔲 to align objects to the top.

  Click 🔲 to align the objects vertically centered.

  Click 🔲 to align the objects to the bottom.

- In this example, the selected objects align vertically at the top edge of the topmost object.

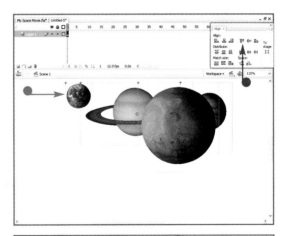

ALIGN OBJECTS WITH THE STAGE

① Select the objects you want to align.

② Open the Align panel.

Note: See the section "Align Objects" to learn how to open the Align panel.

③ Click 🔲.

④ Click an alignment option.

  Flash aligns the objects to the Stage.

- In this example, the selected objects line up on the far-right edge of the Stage.

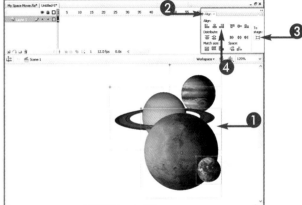

What other options does the Align panel provide?

The Align panel has additional alignment options you can utilize besides basic alignment controls. For example, you can select from the Distribute buttons to distribute objects evenly on the Stage, either vertically or horizontally. You can select from the Match Size buttons to make the selected objects all the same width or height. You can use the Space buttons to ensure that each object is separated by the same amount of spacing in between. Be sure to experiment with the the alignment options to create just the right combination for your own objects.

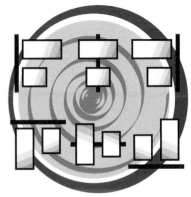

Working with Imported Graphics

Import to Stage

GRAPHICS

Do you want to use artwork from a non-Flash program? By following the steps in these tasks you can import art from other programs to work with in Flash. After you import an image, you can use the Flash tools to make changes to the artwork.

Import Graphics

You can import graphics, including vector or bitmap graphics, from other sources to use in Flash. You can then manipulate imported images with Flash commands. In addition to importing graphics, you can also use the Paste command to paste graphics you cut or copy from other programs.

Bitmap graphics, also called *raster* graphics, are comprised of thousands of pixels. While bitmaps offer a great deal of detail, their file sizes are often quite large. Vector graphics, like those created in Flash, use mathematical equations, or *vectors*, to define the image, making for smaller file sizes.

Import Graphics

IMPORT A GRAPHIC FILE

1 Click **File**.

2 Click **Import**.

3 Click **Import to Stage**.

● To import a graphic directly to the file's library to use later, click **Import to Library** instead.

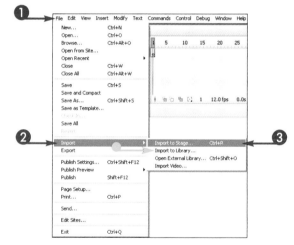

The Import dialog box appears.

4 Navigate to the file you want to import.

5 Click the file name.

● You may need to specify a file type to locate the file you want.

6 Click **Open**.

Flash places the graphic on the Stage as a grouped object.

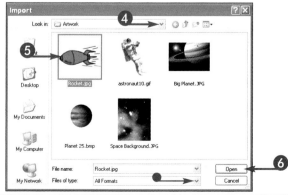

COPY AND PASTE A GRAPHIC

① Open the program and file containing the graphic you want to copy.

② Select the graphic.

● In most programs, selection handles surround the selected object.

③ Click **Edit**.

④ Click **Copy**.

Note: In most programs, you can also press [Ctrl] + [C] to copy a selection.

⑤ Switch back to Flash.

⑥ Click **Edit**.

⑦ Click **Paste in Center**.

Note: You can also press [Ctrl] + [V] to paste a selection.

● Flash pastes the graphic onto the center of the Stage.

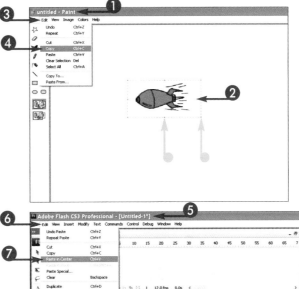

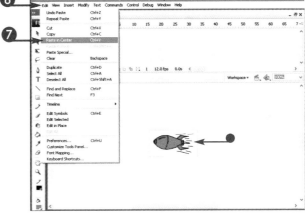

What graphic file types does Flash CS3 support?

Flash supports a wide variety of file types, including GIF, animated GIF, JPG, PNG, BMP, DIB, TGA, TIF, QTIF, WMF, EMF, PDF, PICT, PCT, PNTG, Freehand and Illustrator files, Flash Player files (SWF and SPL), QuickTime Movie (MOV), Photoshop files (PSD), and AutoCAD (DXF) file types.

Can I reuse the bitmap graphic?

When you import a bitmap graphic, Flash immediately adds it to the Flash library for use in other frames in your movie. To view the Library, click **Window**, and then **Library,** or press [Ctrl] + [L] ([⌘] + [L]). See Chapter 7 to learn more about using the Flash Library.

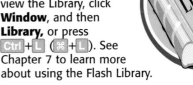

Convert Bitmaps into Vector Graphics

You can use the Trace Bitmap command to convert a bitmap graphic. Turning a bitmap graphic into a vector graphic can minimize the file size and enable you to utilize the Flash tools to manipulate the graphic.

When you apply the Trace Bitmap command, you have an opportunity to adjust several parameters that define the rendering of the image, including how Flash handles the color variances, pixel size translation, and the smoothness of curves or sharpness of corners.

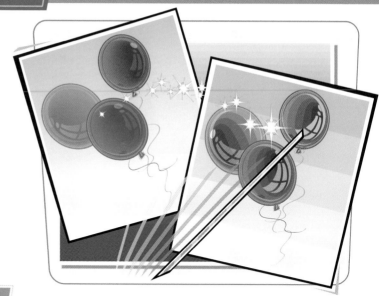

Convert Bitmaps into Vector Graphics

① Select the bitmap graphic you want to convert.

Note: See the previous task to learn how to import graphics. For more on selecting objects on the Stage, see Chapter 3.

② Click **Modify**.

③ Click **Bitmap**.

④ Click **Trace Bitmap**.

The Trace Bitmap dialog box appears.

⑤ Type a value that determines the amount of color variance between neighboring pixels.

A smaller value results in many vector shapes; a larger value results in fewer vectors.

⑥ Type a minimum pixel size for any vector shape.

This value determines the number of surrounding pixels that Flash considers when assigning the pixel color.

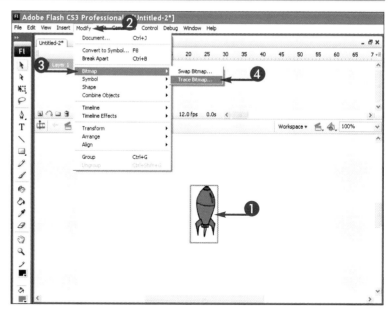

⑦ Click here and select how smoothly Flash traces outlines of the bitmap.

⑧ Click here and select how sharply Flash traces corners.

⑨ Click **OK**.

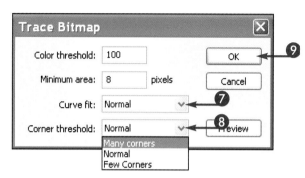

Flash traces the graphic, replacing the bitmap with vector shapes.

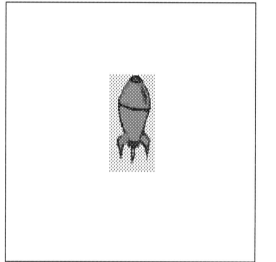

What if my converted graphic does not look like the original?

When applying the Trace Bitmap controls, you may need to experiment with the settings to get the results you want. Start with the default settings. If those do not work, click **Edit**, and then **Undo Trace Bitmap,** and try again, making a few adjustments.

Does converting a bitmap reduce its file size?

Yes, if you do not set the Trace Bitmap threshold settings too low. If the bitmap is a complex drawing with lots of colors and shapes, low threshold settings may result in a larger vector file size. Try to find a balance when adjusting the threshold settings.

You can turn any graphic into an editable image in Flash using the Break Apart command. This command breaks a bitmap image into editable areas, turning individual pixels into vector shapes and gradient fills. You can then select and make changes to the different areas using the Flash drawing tools. This allows you to change the overall appearance of the artwork.

Break Apart a Bitmap

① Select the bitmap image.

② Click **Modify**.

③ Click **Break Apart**.

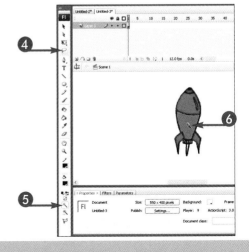

④ Click the **Lasso** tool (🅿).

⑤ Click the **Magic Wand** modifier (🪄).

The ▷ changes to 🅿.

⑥ Click the area you want to edit.

The 🅿 changes to ☀.

To add to the selection, continue clicking.

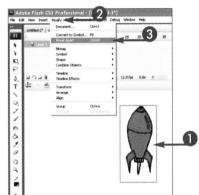

⑦ Click the **Fill Color** palette (■).

The ✷ changes to ✐.

⑧ Click a fill color.

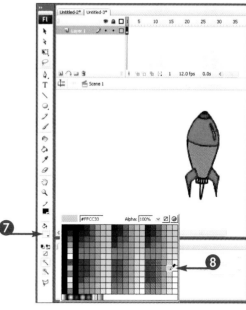

● Flash applies the fill color to all the selected areas.

How do I make the Magic Wand modifier select similar areas in an image?

When you use the Magic Wand modifier for selecting parts of an editable image, Flash selects the pixel you clicked as well as all the surrounding pixels matching the same color. If the Magic Wand fails to select the full range of colors you want, you can adjust the modifier's Threshold setting and try again. You can use the Magic Wand Settings dialog box to change the Threshold and Smoothing settings for selected parts of an image to which the Break Apart command is applied. To activate the feature, click the **Magic Wand Settings** modifier (✎) to open the Magic Wand Settings dialog box. To select similar color areas near the first selected area, increase the number for the Threshold setting. To determine the smoothness of the vector path, select a Smoothing setting.

Turn Bitmaps into Fills

You can turn a bitmap image into a fill for use with Flash drawing tools that use fills, such as the Oval, Rectangle, or Brush. *Fills* are solid colors or patterns that fill a shape. Conventional fills include colors and gradient effects. You can also use a bitmap image, such as a photo, as a fill. Depending on the size of the shape, Flash repeats the image within the shape.

To prepare a bitmap image as a fill, utilize the Break Apart command. This command converts the image into separate pieces. After you separate the image, you can use the Eyedropper tool to duplicate the image as a fill.

Turn Bitmaps into Fills

① Select the bitmap image.

Note: *See Chapter 3 to learn how to select items on the Stage.*

② Click **Modify**.

③ Click **Break Apart**.

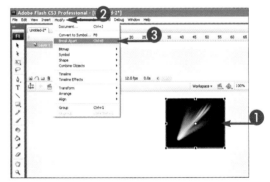

④ Select a drawing tool to create a shape you want to fill.

⑤ Draw an empty shape on the Stage to contain the bitmap fill.

Note: *To learn more about creating shapes, see Chapters 2 and 3.*

You can place the new shape on another layer to help you keep objects organized.

Note: *To learn more about working with layers, see Chapter 6.*

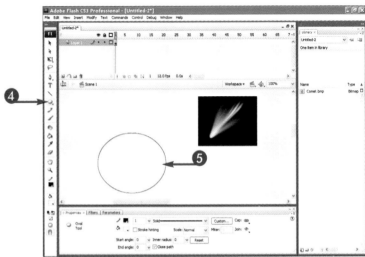

6 Click the **Eyedropper** tool ( ).

The ⌧ changes to ⌧.

7 Click the bitmap image.

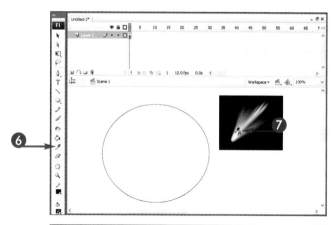

8 Click the object you want to fill.

The bitmap image fills the object.

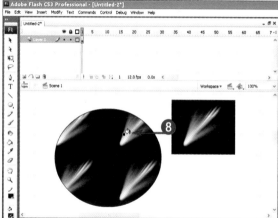

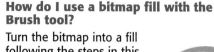

TIPS

What types of edits can I perform on the bitmap fill?

You can edit a bitmap fill just as you can any other fill in Flash, including rotating the image and scaling it to another size.
For example, you might want to create a gradient fill, change the fill color, or reposition the fill area in the graphic. See Chapter 3 to learn more about editing fills in Flash.

How do I use a bitmap fill with the Brush tool?

Turn the bitmap into a fill following the steps in this task. Next, click the **Brush** tool (), select a brush size or shape, and then draw brush strokes on the Stage. Everywhere you draw, Flash uses the bitmap image as your paint color. To learn more about the Brush tool and its options, see Chapter 2.

Working with Text

Does your Flash project need some text? Learn how to add text elements to your drawings with the Flash text tools.

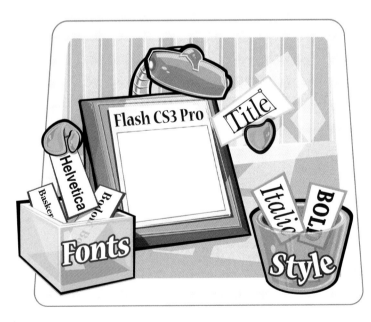

Add Text with the Text Tool

You can use the Text tool to add animated text to a Flash movie or project. You can use three types of text elements: *static*, *dynamic*, or *input* text. Static text, the default text property, does not change—you edit the text the way you want it and it appears the same way in your Flash movie.

You use dynamic text for text fields that you insert into your movie to change and update values. Input text is text that a user types in a field. You often use dynamic and input text with Flash ActionScript.

You can either add text using a single-line text box, or you can use multiple-line text boxes to type lines of text that you want to wrap to other lines.

Add Text with the Text Tool

ADD A SINGLE-LINE TEXT BOX

① Click the **Text** tool (T).

The ⏳ changes to +ᴛ.

② Click in the Stage area.

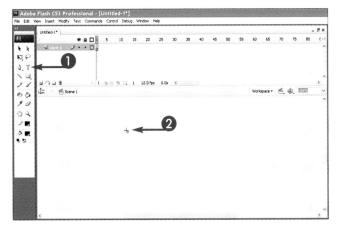

③ Type your text.

● The text appears in a box that enlarges as you type.

● If you click the **Selection** tool (▸), you can double-click a text box to switch to Edit mode and make changes to text.

● If you click T, you can click the text box and make edits.

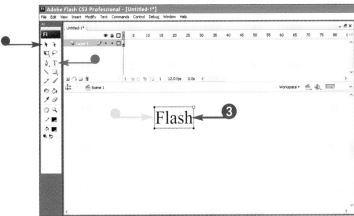

ADD A MULTIPLE-LINE TEXT BOX

1 Click T.

2 Move $+_T$ over the Stage, clicking and dragging the width you want to use for the box.

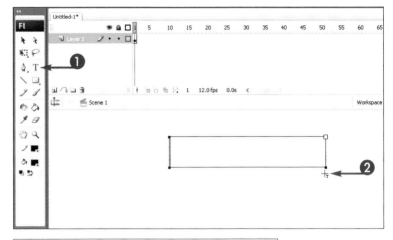

3 Type the text.

The text appears in a box.

Note: See the section, "Format Text" to learn how to assign text attributes.

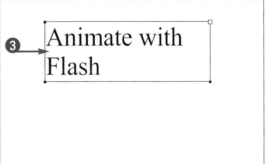

TIPS

What is the difference between single-line and multiple-line text boxes?

When you type text in a single-line text box, text does not wrap. The width of the text box keeps expanding as you type characters. With a multiple-line text box, you specify a width, and when the text reaches the end of the block, it wraps to start a new line, increasing the depth of the text box. To visually discern between the two text box types, look at the icon in the upper-right corner of the text box. Single-line text boxes display a tiny circle icon, and multiple-line text boxes have a tiny square icon.

How do I turn a single-line text box into a multiple-line text box?

Select the text box and move the mouse pointer over ◯ in the upper-right corner of the text box. Drag to the right and release the mouse button. The single-line text box is now a multiple-line text box. Note that you cannot turn multiple-line text boxes into single-line text boxes.

Format Text

You can format text to change the impact or appearance of words and characters. The Property inspector has all the controls for changing text attributes located in one convenient mini-window. You can quickly change the font, font size, font color, and spacing.

The Property inspector panel offers many of the same formatting controls you find in word-processing programs. For example, you can click the Bold button to make your text boldface. See Chapter 1 to learn more about using the Property inspector.

Format Text

CREATE BOLD AND ITALIC

1. Open the Property inspector.

2. Select the text you want to format.

- If you click T, you can click the text box and make edits.

- If you click ↖, you can double-click a text box and make edits.

3. Click the **Bold** button (B) or **Italic** button (I) or both to apply formatting.

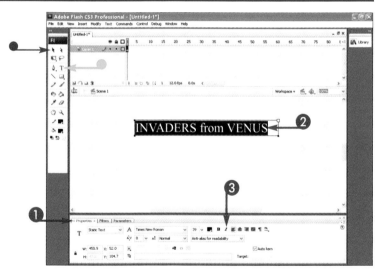

The text changes appearance.

- You can click the **Text (fill) Color** button (■) to open the Color palette and choose another color for the selected text.

- To change the text type from static to dynamic or input, click the **Text Type** ⋁ and click another text type.

Note: See Chapter 12 to learn more about using dynamic and input text with Flash Actions.

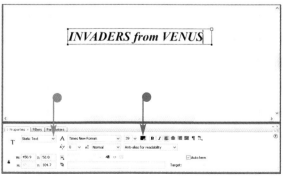

CHANGE TEXT FONT

1 Open the Property inspector.

2 Select the text you want to format.

3 Click the **Font** ⊡.

A list of available fonts appears, along with a sample box.

4 Click a font name.

The text changes font type.

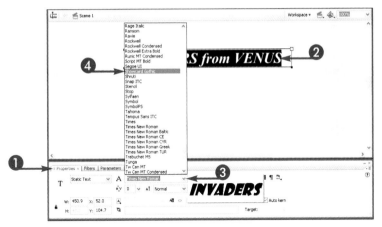

CHANGE THE FONT SIZE

1 Open the Property inspector.

2 Select the text you want to format.

3 Click the **Size** ⊡ and drag ⊡ to a new size setting.

● You can also type the exact size in the Font Size box.

The text changes size.

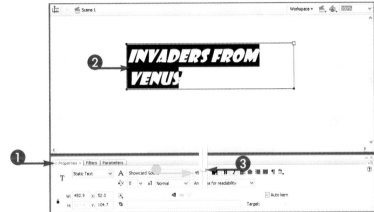

TIPS

Do I have to use the Property inspector panel to format text?

You can also find text formatting controls in the Text menu at the top of the Flash program window. For example, to change the font, click **Text** and then **Font** and then click a font from the menu list that appears. To change the font size, click **Text**, **Size**.

When do I use dynamic or input text?

You can use dynamic and input text boxes to display dynamically updating text in your Flash project, such as user input boxes, text retrieved from a database, or a variable value obtained from a function within your movie or an external script. You commonly use dynamic and input text with Flash actions. See Chapter 12 to learn more about actions and ActionScript.

Align and Kern Text

You can control the position of text within a text box using the alignment options in the Property inspector panel or on the Text menu. Alignment options include setting horizontal controls for the positioning of text, such as left, center, right, or fully justified.

Another way to control the positioning of text is with kerning. *Kerning* **refers to the spacing of characters. By changing the kerning setting, you can create text effects such as word characters condensed together or pulled apart.**

Align and Kern Text

1 Click 🔲.

2 Click the text box.

3 Display the Property inspector.

Note: *See Chapter 1 to learn how to display or hide the Property inspector.*

4 Click an alignment button.

Click 📄 to align text to the left.

Click 📄 to center text.

Click 📄 align text to the right.

Click 📄 to justify text.

The text aligns immediately in the text box.

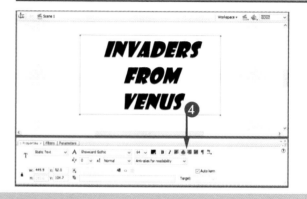

Kern Text

① Click ▸.

② Click the text box.

③ Open the Property inspector.

Note: See Chapter 1 to learn how to display or hide the Property inspector.

④ Click the **Letter Spacing** ▾.

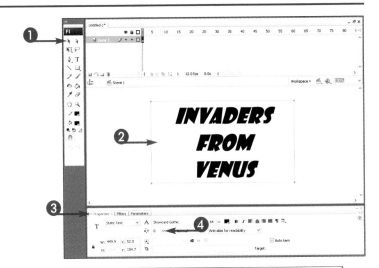

⑤ Click and drag ▭ up to add space between characters or down to remove space.

● Flash immediately kerns the characters in the text box.

TIP

How do I copy attributes from one text box to another?
Follow these steps to copy formatting attributes:

① Click ▸.

② Click the text box containing the text to which you want to copy attributes.

③ Click 🖋 on the Tools panel.

④ Click the text box containing the attributes you want to copy.

Flash immediately copies your attributes.

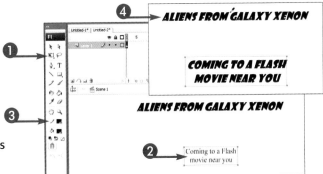

Set Text Box Margins and Indents

You set margins and indents within text boxes for greater control of text positioning. *Margins* define the distance between the edge of the text box and the text inside. You use *indents* to control where a line of text sits within the margins. You can find margin and indent commands in the Format Options dialog box. You can only access this dialog box through the Property inspector panel.

In addition to margin and indent controls, the Paragraph panel also has controls for line spacing. *Line spacing* is the distance between lines of text.

Set Text Box Margins and Indents

① Click 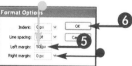.

② Click the text box.

③ Open the Property inspector.

Note: *See Chapter 1 to learn how to work with the Property inspector.*

④ Click **Edit Format Options** (¶).

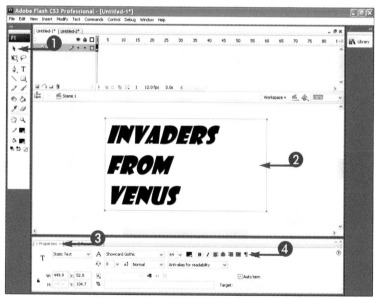

The Format Options dialog box appears.

⑤ Set the left or right margin.

● You can type a value in the margin text box.

● Alternatively, you can click here and drag the ⬜ to the desired position.

The margin immediately changes in the text box.

⑥ Click **OK**.

Set Text Box Indents

1 With the text box selected, click in front of the text line you want to indent.

Note: See the section "Format Text" to learn how to select a text box for editing.

2 Open the Property inspector panel.

Note: See Chapter 1 to learn how to work with the Property inspector.

3 Click ¶.

The Format Options dialog box appears.

4 Type an indent value in the Indent text box.

● Alternatively, you can click here and drag to change the number.

● The indent immediately appears in the text box.

● You can control the spacing between lines by clicking here and dragging up or down.

5 Click **OK**.

Flash applies the new settings.

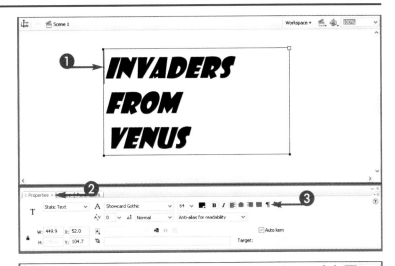

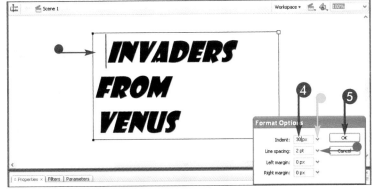

TIPS

How do I change the margin's unit of measurement?

By default, Flash assumes you want to work with pixels as your unit of measurement, but you can change it to the unit of your choice, such as points or inches. Click **Modify** and then **Document**. The Document Properties dialog box appears. You can also press Ctrl+J in Windows (⌘+J on the Mac) to open the dialog box. Click **Ruler Units** and select the appropriate units. Click **OK** to close the dialog box. When you open the Property inspector, the margin values reflect the unit of measurement you defined.

Do I use the Line Spacing slider to set superscript or subscript characters in Flash?

No, you cannot use the **Line Spacing** on individual characters, only entire lines. Instead, to set superscript or subscript characters, first select the text. Next, display the Property inspector. Click the **Character Position**. A list of choices appears. Click **Superscript** or **Subscript**, and Flash immediately applies the attribute.

Move and Resize Text Boxes

You can move text boxes around on the Flash Stage or resize them as needed. Text boxes are as mobile and scalable as any other objects you add to the Stage.

You can resize the text inside depending on the direction you choose to scale the box. Flash overrides any font sizes you have set for the text. If you want the text set at a certain size, you must manually change the font size again after you scale the text box.

Move and Resize Text Boxes

MOVE A TEXT BOX

① Click [▶].

② Click the text box you want to move.

You can also double-click the text box to select it.

③ Move ▷ near a text box border or center of the box (▷ changes to ▶₊).

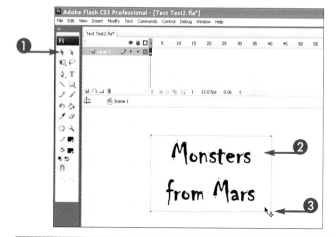

④ Click and drag the box to a new location and release the mouse button.

The text box moves to its new location.

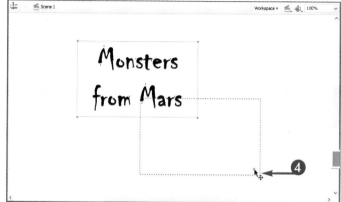

RESIZE A TEXT BOX

1 Click the text box you want to resize.

2 Move the mouse pointer over the text box handle (changes to ↔).

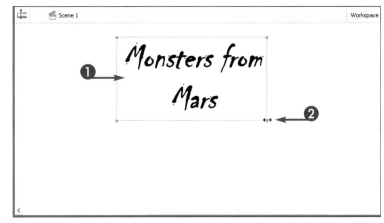

3 Click and drag left or right to resize the text box width.

The text box resizes.

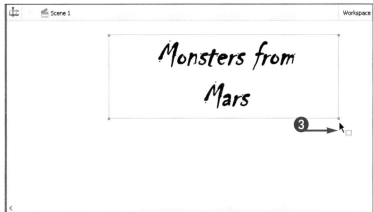

Can I rotate or skew a text box?

Yes. First, select the text box, and then click the **Free Transform** tool (📧). Move the mouse pointer over the corner of the box until it takes the shape of the Rotate icon (↻). Click and drag to rotate the text box. To scale a text box, click 📧, move the mouse pointer over the edge of the selected box until the pointer takes the shape of the Skew icon (↕). Click and drag to skew the box. You can find out more about rotating or resizing objects in Chapter 3.

Can I change the text direction?

Yes. If the text is static text, you can make the text read vertically or even backward. With the text box selected, click the **Change Orientation of Text** button (📧) in the Property inspector panel to reveal a menu of text directions. Click the one you want, and Flash immediately applies the new setting.

You can use the Break Apart command to turn text into graphics and then manipulate the text with the various Flash drawing and editing tools. For example, you can break apart text into separate blocks and distribute them to different layers in your animation, or you can break text apart to make modifications on each character in a word.

Once you apply the Break Apart command to a text block, you can no longer edit the text, such as change the font or font size. For that reason, be sure you apply all the text formatting you want to use before applying the Break Apart command.

Break Apart Text

① Click the text box you want to edit.

② Click **Modify**.

③ Click **Break Apart**.

● Flash breaks apart the text block into mini-character blocks.

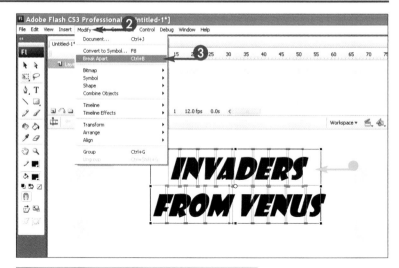

You can now edit the individual letters, which are treated like shapes.

● In this example, the shape character is assigned a new color and position.

You can use the Free Transform tool's Envelope modifier to distort the appearance of text in a Flash project. For example, you can make the text appear as a wave or exaggerate the size of some letters while keeping the other letters the same, or you can make the text seem to follow a path.

In order to use the Envelope modifier, apply the Break Apart command twice to your text box. See the section "Break Apart Text" to learn more about this command. Once you apply this command to a text block, you cannot edit the text formatting again.

Distort Text

① Apply the **Break Apart** command twice to the text box you want to edit.

Note: See the section "Break Apart Text" to learn how to use the Break Apart command.

② Click the **Free Transform** tool (⊞).

③ Click the **Envelope** modifier (▣).

● Edit points appear around the text shape.

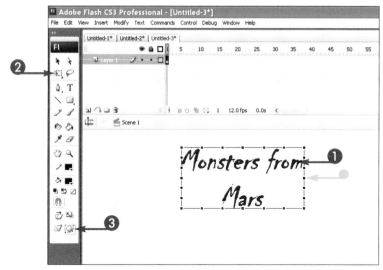

④ Click and drag an edit point to change the text shape (⊵ changes to ⊳).

An outline of the change appears as you drag.

● Flash modifies the text shape.

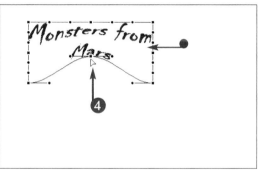

Working with Layers

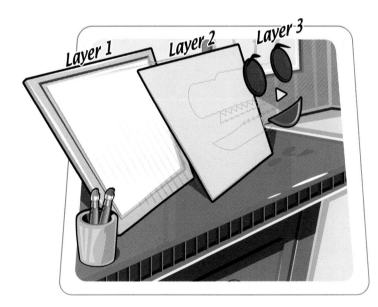

Are you ready to organize parts of your drawing or animation? This chapter shows you how to work with the Flash layers.

Add and Delete Layers

When you create a new movie or scene, Flash starts you out with a single layer and a Timeline. You can add layers to the Timeline, or delete layers you no longer need. Additional layers do not affect the file size, so you can add and delete as many layers as your project requires.

Layers can help you keep track of related items in your movie. For example, you might want to place all the objects you use for a logo on a single layer, and all the objects for a product illustration on another layer.

ADD A LAYER

1 Click the layer in the Timeline that you want to appear below the new layer.

2 Click the **Insert Layer** button (▣).

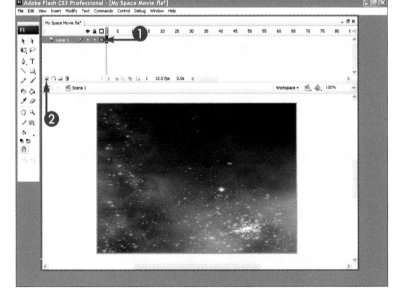

● A new layer immediately appears.

Flash adds the same amount of frames to the new layer to match the layer with the longest frame sequence.

Note: See Chapter 8 to learn more about frames.

DELETE A LAYER

1 Click the layer you want to delete.

2 Click the **Delete Layer** button ( ).

You can delete more than one layer by clicking the first layer you want to remove, and then pressing Ctrl (Windows) or ⌘ (Mac) while clicking other layers and then clicking .

● The layer disappears from the Timeline.

Note: If you accidentally delete the wrong layer, you can click the Edit menu and click Undo Delete Layer.

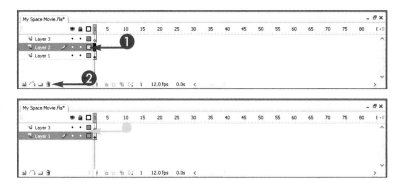

Why would I use layers?

Layers Can Organize

The bigger your project, the more elements it is likely to contain. Rather than placing all of these elements in a single layer, which make them more difficult to locate and edit, you can insert them into separate layers and name each layer with a descriptive name that tells what is in the layer.

Add Depth

Layers are similar to transparent sheets of paper stacked one on top of another. Flash stacks layers from top to bottom. Each layer lets you see through to the layer below. As you add more layers, existing layers move down in the stack to appear behind new layers. For example, you might place a background on the bottom layer and add other objects to subsequent layers to create a feeling of depth.

Create Guides and Masks

Guide layers can assist you with the layout and positioning of objects on other layers. Mask layers enable you to hide elements in underlying layers from view. You create a hole, as it were, in the mask layer that lets you view layers below.

You can define the aspects of any given layer through the Layer Properties dialog box, a one-stop shop for controlling a layer's name, function, and appearance. The more you work with layers in Flash, the more necessary it is to change layer properties.

By naming layers, you can more easily keep track of their contents and position. You also have the option of hiding the layer to get its contents out of the way. To keep the layer's contents safe from editing, you can lock the layer.

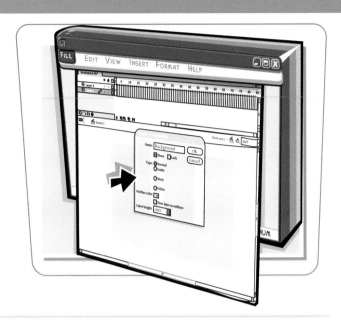

Set Layer Properties

1 Click the layer for which you want to set controls.

Note: Flash automatically selects all objects associated with the selected layer.

2 Click **Modify**.

3 Click **Timeline**.

4 Click **Layer Properties**.

*Note: You can also right-click over the layer and click **Properties** to open the Layer Properties dialog box.*

The Layer Properties dialog box appears.

5 Type a distinctive name for the layer in the **Name** text box.

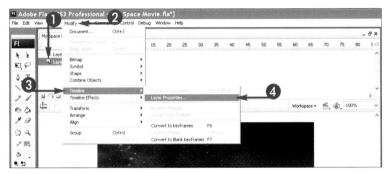

⑥ Change the desired layer property.

● To make the layer visible in the Timeline, leave the **Show** check box checked.

● To lock the layer to prevent changes, select the **Lock** check box (☐ changes to ☑).

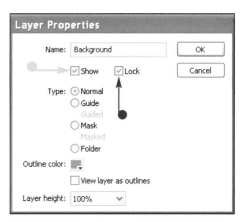

● You can select a layer type.

● To enlarge the layer height, you can click ☑ and select a percentage. An enlarged height is useful for viewing sound waveforms in the layer.

⑦ Click **OK**.

The layer properties change to your specifications.

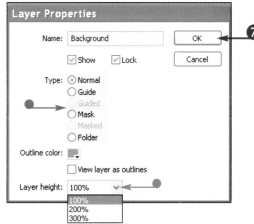

What are layer types?

By default, all layers you add to the Timeline are *normal,* which means all the objects on the layer appear in the movie. Objects you place on guide layers do not appear in the movie. A regular *guide* layer can be used for reference points and alignment. A *guided* layer is a layer linked to a regular guide layer. A *mask* layer hides any layers linked to it. You can also place layers into folders to keep your movie organized. To change the layer type, click a type in the Layer Properties dialog box (○ changes to ⊙). To learn more about layer folders, see the task "Organize Layers into Folders."

Work with Layers in the Timeline

Flash makes it easy to control layers in the Timeline. You can quickly rename a layer, hide a layer, or lock a layer to prevent unnecessary changes without having to open a separate dialog box. The Timeline has buttons and toggles that you can use to control a layer with a quick click.

In addition to controlling layer status, you can also quickly name layers in the Timeline by typing new labels directly on the layer name list.

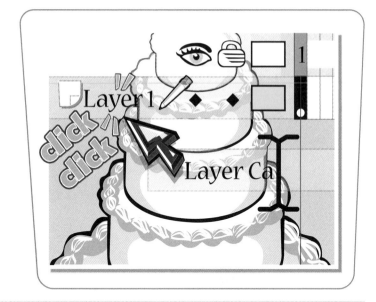

Work with Layers in the Timeline

RENAME A LAYER

① Double-click the layer name.

② Type a new name.

③ Press **Enter** (**Return**).

The layer's name changes.

HIDE A LAYER

① Click ⊡ beneath the 👁 column.

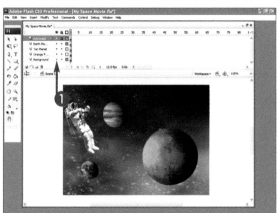

changes to ⊠ and all the objects on the layer become invisible.

To make the layer objects visible again, you can click ⊠ under the eye icon column (⊠ changes to •).

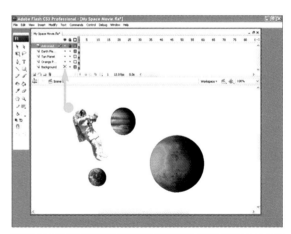

LOCK A LAYER

1 Under the 🔒 column, click the layer's bullet (• changes to 🔒).

Flash locks the layer and you cannot edit the contents.

To unlock a layer, click the layer's padlock icon (🔒 changes to •).

TIPS

How can I tell which objects are on which layer?

You can choose to view layer contents as outlines, making it easy to distinguish the objects from other layers. Click ☐ under the square icon column (☐ changes to ▢). All objects on the layer are now outlined in the same color as the square you clicked.

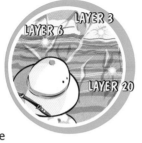

Can I enlarge the size of a layer?

All layers you add to the Timeline use a default size; however, you can enlarge a layer to better view its contents. To enlarge the layer height, right-click the layer name and click **Properties** to open the Layer Properties dialog box. Click the **Layer Height** ▾ and choose a percentage. Click **OK**.

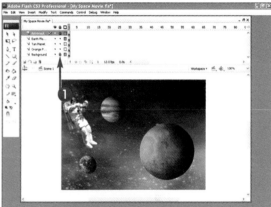

Stack Layers

To rearrange how objects appear in your Flash movie, you can stack layers. Layers act like sheets of transparent plastic. Depending on the placement of the layers, objects can appear in front of or behind objects on other layers. Stacking layers in this manner creates the illusion of depth in your movie.

You can change the order of a layer by moving it up or down in the layer list on the Timeline. The layer at the top of the list appears at the top of the stack, while the layer at the bottom of the list appears at the bottom of the stack.

Stack Layers

① Click the layer you want to move.

Note: Flash automatically selects all objects associated with the selected layer.

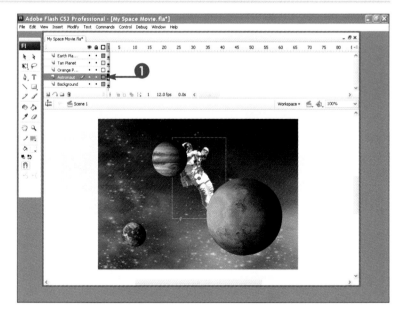

② Drag the layer up or down to its new location in the stack.

● An insertion bar appears, showing where the dragged layer will rest.

③ Release the mouse button.

● The layer assumes its new position.

● In this example, the layer moves up in the stacking order. Any objects on the layer now appear on top of the other layer objects.

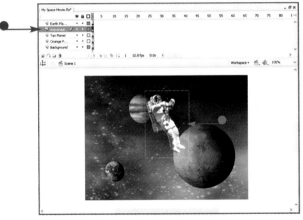

● In this example, the layer moves down in the stacking order. Any objects on the layer now appear to be beneath other top layer objects.

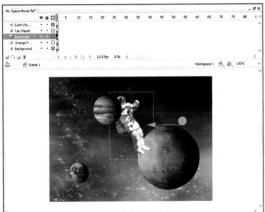

TIPS

How can I see more layers at a time in my Timeline?

You can resize the Timeline to see more of your layers. Move the ⌖ over the bottom border of the Timeline until it becomes a ⬍. Click and drag the border down to increase the size of the Timeline. This should enable you to see more of the layers in the Timeline.

I cannot see all my layers. Why?

The more layers you add to the Timeline, the longer the list of layer names. Not all the layers stay in view. Use the scroll bar at the far-right end of the Timeline to scroll up and down the layer list and view other layers. You can also use the Flash layer folders to organize layers in the Timeline. See the section "Organize Layers into Folders" to learn more.

Organize Layers into Folders

You can use layer folders to further organize the numerous layers you use in a Flash movie project. Layer folders act just like the folders found on your computer's hard drive. For example, you can place related layers into one layer folder on the Timeline. This makes it much easier to find a layer for editing later. Layer folders are identified in the Timeline by tiny folder icons next to the folder names.

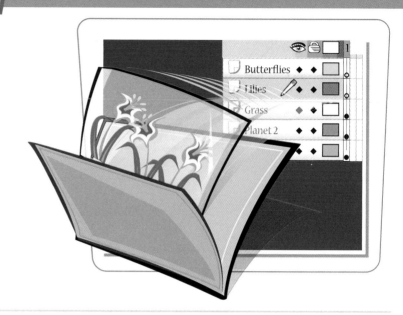

Organize Layers into Folders

CREATE A FOLDER

① Click the **Insert Layer Folder** button (□).

● Flash adds a layer folder to the Timeline.

● You can also click the **Insert** menu and click **Timeline** and then **Layer Folder**.

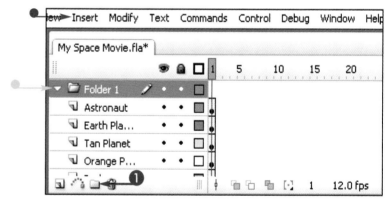

ADD A LAYER TO A FOLDER

① Click the layer you want to move into a folder.

② Drag the layer over the folder.

③ Release the mouse button.

The layer is moved to the layer folder and indented slightly in the list to indicate it appears in a folder.

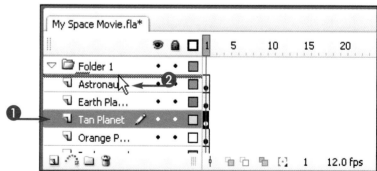

RENAME A FOLDER

1 Double-click the layer folder name you want to rename.

2 Type a new name.

3 Press **Enter** (**Return**).

The layer folder is renamed.

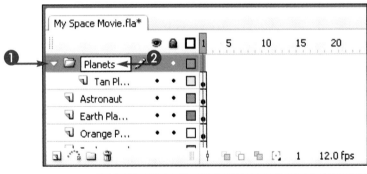

COLLAPSE A FOLDER

1 Click the layer folder's **Expand** icon (▷).

▷ changes to ▽.

Layers associated with the folder are now hidden.

You can click the layer folder's **Collapse** icon (▽) to view the folder's contents again.

▽ changes to ▷.

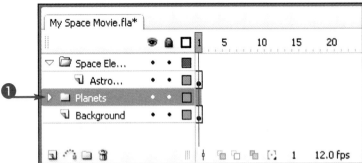

 TIPS

How do I remove a layer from a folder?

Display the layer folder's contents, then click and drag the layer you want to remove from the folder and drop it elsewhere on the Timeline. To remove the layer completely from the Timeline, click the layer name and click 🗑.

Can I lock a layer folder?

Yes. You can lock and hide layer folders just as you can lock and hide layers. Locking a folder locks all the layers included within the folder. Click the folder layer's bullet (• changes to 🔒). Flash locks the folder and any layers associated with the folder.

Add Guide Layers

You can use guide layers to help you position objects. There are two types of guide layers in Flash: *plain* and *motion*. A plain guide layer can help you position objects on the Stage, but it does not appear in your final movie. Use plain guide layers to assist you in lining things up.

You use a motion guide layer to animate an object to a path on the Flash Stage. A motion guide layer links to an object on another layer. Flash exports motion guide layers with the movie, but the guide layers are not visible in the movie.

Add Guide Layers

ADD A PLAIN GUIDE LAYER

1 Click the layer that you want to appear below the new guide layer.

2 Click ⬛.

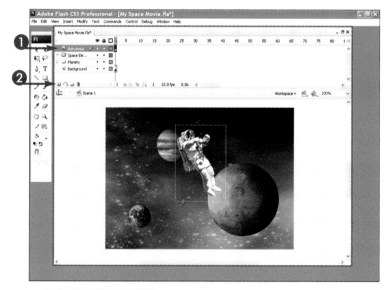

Flash adds a new layer to the Timeline.

3 Right-click the new layer name.

4 Click **Guide**.

● The layer becomes a guide layer, noted by its ◈ icon. You can place objects on the layer or use it to create a layout.

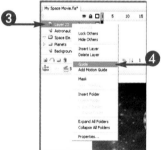

ADD A MOTION GUIDE LAYER

1 Click the layer that you want to link to a motion guide layer.

2 Click the **Add Motion Guide** icon ().

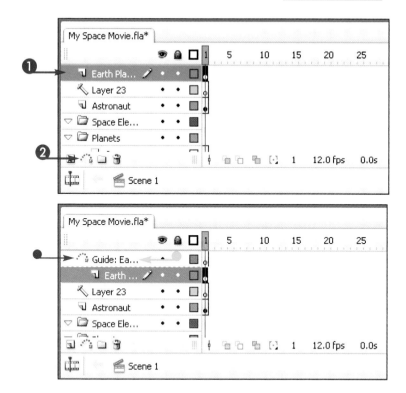

Flash adds the motion guide layer to the Timeline and links it to the layer you selected.

You can distinguish a guide layer by its unique icon .

How exactly does a motion guide layer work?

Flash links motion guide layers to layers containing objects that you want to animate along a given path. The motion guide layer contains the path and you can link it to one or more layers. The motion guide layer always appears directly above the layer (or layers) to which it links. To learn more about animating in Flash, see Chapter 8.

Can I lock my guide layer in place?

Yes. In fact, it is a good idea to always lock guide layers and motion guide layers in place so you do not accidentally move anything on them. To lock a layer, click ⊡ on the Timeline. To unlock the layer again, click ⓐ. See the section "Work with Layers in the Timeline" to learn more about using the layer toggles.

Create
Mask Layers

You can use mask layers to hide various elements on underlying layers. A mask is much like a stencil you tape to a wall. Only certain portions of the underlying layer appear through the mask design, while other parts of the layer are hidden, or *masked*. Flash links masked layers to layers and exports them in the final movie file.

Mask layers appear with a unique icon on the Timeline. You can only link a mask layer to the layer directly below it. Mask layers can only contain one fill shape, symbol, or object to use as a window.

Create Mask Layers

ADD A MASK LAYER

① Click the layer to which you want to add a mask.

② Click ⬜.

A new layer appears.

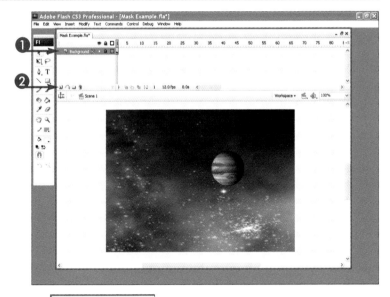

③ Right-click the new layer's name.

④ Click **Mask**.

Flash marks the layer as a mask layer, locks it against any changes, and links it to the layer below.

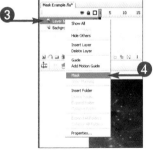

CREATE A MASK

1 Unlock the mask layer (🔒 changes to ▪).

Note: To unlock a layer, see the section "Work with Layers in the Timeline."

2 Draw a fill shape on the Stage over the area you want to view in the layer below.

● In this example, several rectangle fill shapes are used as a window-like mask.

Note: See Chapter 2 to create a fill shape.

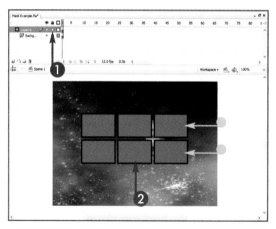

3 Lock the mask layer.

Note: To lock a layer, see the section "Work with Layers in the Timeline."

● You can now see the masking effect.

Note: Anything appearing outside the fill shape is masked in the masked layer.

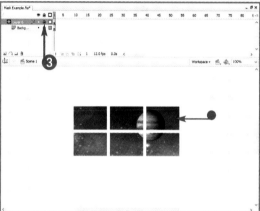

TIPS

If you cannot see the mask effect, you probably unlocked the layer. You must first lock the mask layer in order to see the mask effect. You can also see the effect if you run the movie in test mode; click the **Control** menu and click **Test Movie**. The Flash Player window opens and runs the movie. Click the window's ⊠ to return to the Flash program window.

What sort of fill should I draw for my mask shape?

You can use any kind of fill color or pattern to create the mask shape. Regardless of what makes up your fill, Flash treats the shape as a window to the linked layer (or layers) below. For that reason, you might consider using a transparent fill rather than a solid so you can see through the fill to the layer below and position it correctly on the Stage.

Customize the Timeline

You can customize the Timeline and change its appearance. You can use the Panel Menu to access customizing controls. For example, you may want the Timeline docked in another area of the program window. You can also control the size of the frames within the Timeline. For example, you may prefer to enlarge the frames to better see the type of content each contains. This is especially helpful if your frames contain any note text or sound waveforms.

Customize the Timeline

CHANGE THE TIMELINE POSITION

① Click the **Panel Menu** button (⊟).

② Click **Placement**.

③ Click a placement option.

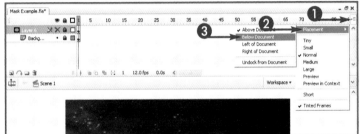

Flash docks the Timeline in the selected position.

● In this example, the Timeline is docked at the bottom of the document window.

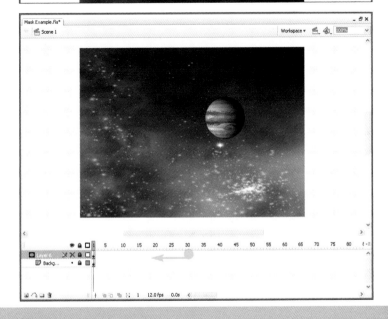

CHANGE FRAME SIZE

1 Click the **Panel Menu** button (▤).

2 Click a frame size.

● You can click the **Short** option to decrease the height of the frame cell rows.

● Turn off interval frame tinting by deselecting this option.

Flash changes the frame size.

● In this example, large frames now appear in the Timeline.

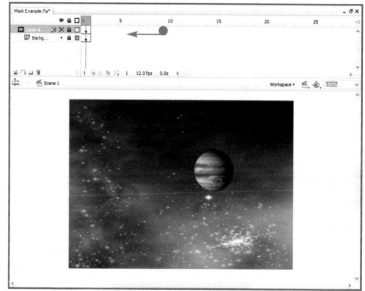

 TIPS

Can I drag the Timeline on the screen?

Yes. To move the Timeline freely and position it anywhere on-screen, simply click and drag the Gripper area — the two dotted vertical lines that appear in the upper-left corner of the Timeline (▥). To dock the Timeline again, click and drag it to the top of the program window. To prevent the Timeline from docking along with the other open panels, press and hold the **Ctrl** key while dragging.

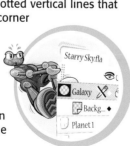

What do the Preview and Preview in Context options do?

From the **Panel Menu**, click **Preview** to display thumbnail images of the frame contents scaled to fit the Timeline frames. Click **Preview in Context** to display thumbnail images of each full frame. Both options require a change in the Timeline appearance in order to view the frame contents. To learn more about using frames in animation, see Chapters 8 and 9.

Working with Flash Symbols and Instances

Are you ready to start using drawn object or imported artwork in your Flash movie? This chapter teaches you how to use Flash symbols and store them in the Library.

Understanding Symbols and Instances

In Flash, a *symbol* is a reusable element you can store in the Flash Library. You can repeatedly use a symbol throughout your movie by inserting an *instance* of the symbol in the frame in which you want it to appear. An instance is merely a copy of the original symbol.

Flash Symbols

A *symbol* is any graphical element you store in the Flash Library. A symbol can be an object you draw with the Flash drawing tools, a movie clip, or a graphic created in another program. Symbols can also be sound clips or buttons.

Flash Instances

Anytime you insert a copy of the symbol into your project, you are inserting an *instance*. The instance references the original so the file size is not greatly affected by how many times you reuse a symbol.

Types of Symbols

You can reuse symbols to create animations in your Flash movies. Every time you reuse a symbol, you must specify how you want the symbol to behave. Flash classifies symbols, or *behaviors*, into three types: graphics, buttons, or movie clips.

Graphic Symbols

Graphic objects, such as those you create in Flash with the drawing tools, can be reused for creating animation in the Flash Timeline.

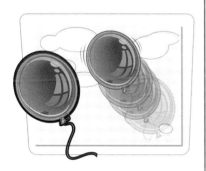

Button Symbols

You can save interactive buttons, also called *rollover buttons*, as symbols and reuse them by associating different actions to the same button.

Movie Clips

Movie clip symbols are simply mini-movies that reside inside the main Flash movie file. Movie clips utilize timelines that are independent of the main movie's timeline.

Using the Flash Library

A Flash project can contain hundreds of graphics, sounds, interactive buttons, video, and movie clips. The Flash Library can help you organize these elements. For example, you can store related symbols in the same folder, create new folders, or delete folders and symbols you no longer need.

Every time you import a graphic image into a Flash file, convert a graphic element into a symbol, or add a new sound to a frame, Flash adds it to the file's Library. In effect, the Library is a compendium of your movie's contents. You can use the Library panel to view and manage your movie elements.

Using the Flash Library

OPEN THE LIBRARY PANEL

1 Click **Window**.

2 Click **Library**.

Note: You can also press **F11** to quickly open the Library panel.

● The Library panel appears.

Note: By default, the Library panel is docked on the right side of the screen.

● You can click the **Collapse to Icons** button (▶▶) to reduce the panel to an icon.

● You can click the **Minimize** button (▬), or click the top of the panel to minimize the Library panel.

You can maximize the panel again by clicking the **Expand Dock** button (▬), the **Maximize** button (▭), or click the panel name to expand the Library.

● You can click the **Wide Library View** button (▭) to display a fuller version of the Library panel.

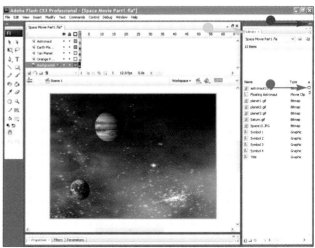

- You can return the panel to the narrow, default state by clicking the **Narrow Library View** button ([⬚]).

- You can click the **Panel Menu** button ([▾≡]) to display a pop-up menu of commands related to Library tasks and items.

- You can preview an item in the Library by clicking the item.

Note: *You can manipulate the Library panel just like you can any other panel in Flash. See Chapter 1 to learn how to work with panels.*

③ Click the **Close** button ([×]).

Flash closes the Library panel.

Note: *You can leave the Library panel open as long as you need it, and you can drag it around the program window to move it out of the way.*

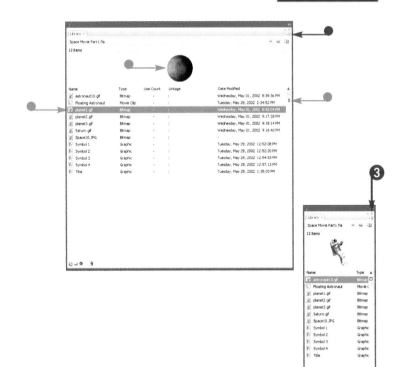

Can I use symbols from another movie's Library?

You can easily insert symbols into your current project from another file's library. Click **File**, **Import**, and then **Open External Library**. The Open as Library dialog box appears. Click the file name, and then click **Open**. The Library panel opens, listing the other file's symbols. Click and drag the symbol you want to use onto the Stage.

How do I place a symbol from the Library onto the Stage?

From the Library panel, locate the symbol you want to use, and then click and drag it from the Library and drop it onto the Stage. The symbol is added to the Stage. You can then move or edit the symbol as needed, or use it in animation effects.

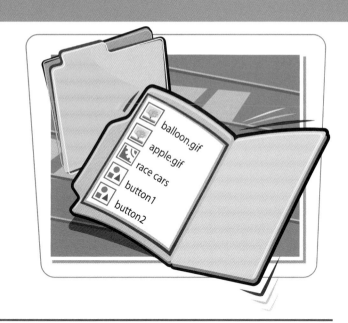

To organize all of your symbols, you can store them in folders. The Library folders display like any other folder on your computer system. Open the folder to view its contents or hide the contents and view only the folder name. When you open a folder, you can see every symbol it contains. The icons next to the symbol name in the Library panel indicate the symbol type.

Using the Flash Library *(continued)*

CREATE A NEW FOLDER

1 Open the Library panel.

2 Click the **New Folder** button (⬜) at the bottom of the Library panel.

● You can also click ▾☰ and click **New Folder**.

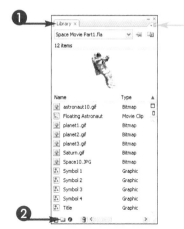

3 Type a name for the folder.

4 Press Enter (Return).

Flash creates a new folder

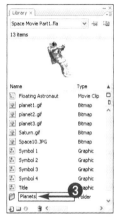

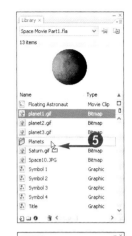

⑤ Click and drag the item you want to place in the new folder.

⑥ Release the mouse button.

The item moves into the folder.

● To view a folder's contents, you can double-click the **Folder** icon ().

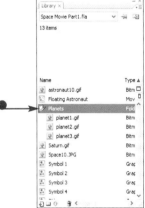

How do I rename a folder?

Double-click the folder name in the Library panel to highlight the folder name. Type a new name, press Enter (Return) and Flash applies the new name. You can use this same technique to rename symbols in the Library window.

Can I delete a folder I no longer need?

Yes, but make sure it does not contain any symbols you want to keep or are currently using in the file. After you delete a folder, Flash deletes its contents, along with any instances you use in your animation. To delete a folder, click it, and then click the **Delete** icon (🗑) at the bottom of the Library panel. Flash warns you that you are about to permanently delete the folder and its contents. Click **Yes** and the folder is removed.

Create a Symbol

You can easily turn any object you draw on the Flash Stage into a symbol you can reuse throughout your project. You can also convert any existing drawing or graphical element into a symbol. When you save an item as a symbol, Flash stores it in the file's Library. When you reuse the symbol, you are using an *instance* or copy of the original symbol.

There are three types of behaviors you can assign to a symbol: graphic, movie clip, or button. The behavior you assign depends on what you want to do with the symbol.

Create a Symbol

CONVERT AN OBJECT TO A SYMBOL

1 Select all the objects on the Stage you want to convert into a symbol.

Note: To select objects, see Chapter 3.

To select multiple objects, you can press and hold down **Shift** while clicking on each object.

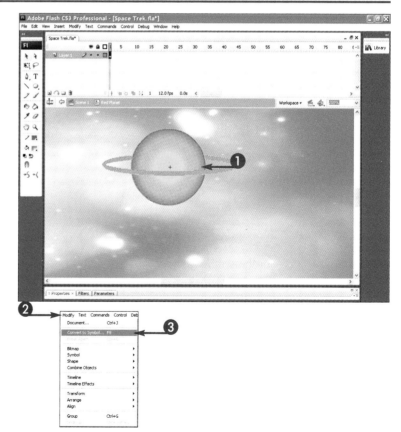

2 Click **Modify**.

3 Click **Convert to Symbol**.

*Note: You can also press **F8** to quickly convert to a symbol.*

The Convert to Symbol dialog box appears.

4 Type a unique name for the symbol.

5 Select a behavior type to assign to the symbol (○ changes to ◉).

6 Click **OK**.

Flash adds the symbol to the file's Library.

PREVIEW THE SYMBOL

1 Open the Library panel.

Note: See the section "Using the Flash Library" to learn how to open the Library panel.

2 Click the symbol name.

● The symbol appears in the top section of the Library panel.

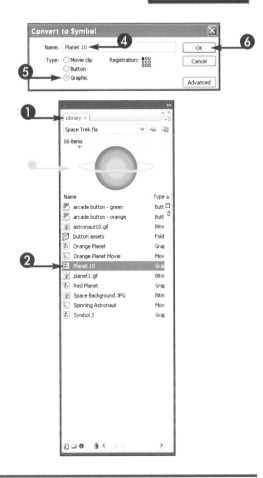

TIPS

How to I create a symbol from scratch?

Rather than converting an object into a symbol, you can switch to symbol-edit mode and create a new symbol. Click **Insert** and then **New Symbol**. Type a name for the symbol and assign a behavior, such as Graphic, and then click **OK**. Flash immediately switches you to symbol-edit mode and you can use the drawing tools to create a new symbol. The symbol's name appears above the Stage area. To save the symbol and exit symbol-edit mode, click the Scene name link to the left of the symbol name.

Can I create a duplicate symbol?

Yes. For example, you might want to copy a symbol and change it ever so slightly in one frame of your Flash movie. From the Library panel, right-click the symbol you want to duplicate. Click **Duplicate**. Type a new name and assign a behavior. Click **OK**. Now you can edit the copy of the symbol without affecting the original.

Insert an Instance

To reuse a symbol in your Flash project, you can place an *instance* of it on the Stage. An instance is a copy of the original symbol. The copy references the original instead of redrawing the object completely. This method of referencing a vector object for reuse is much more efficient than copying an object over and over again in a file.

Ordinarily, when copying an object, you are copying the entire set of instructions that tells the computer how to draw the object. With the Flash method, the symbol instance merely points to the original symbol without needing a complete set of instructions for re-creating the object. This greatly decreases the movie's file size.

Insert an Instance

① Click the frame and layer where you want to insert the instance.

Note: To learn more about frames, see Chapter 8. To learn more about layers, see Chapter 6.

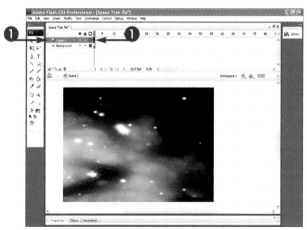

② Open the Library panel.

Note: See the section "Using the Flash Library" to learn how to open the Library panel.

③ Click the symbol's name.

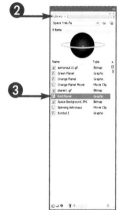

④ Click and drag the symbol from the Library panel.

⑤ Drop the instance where you want it to appear.

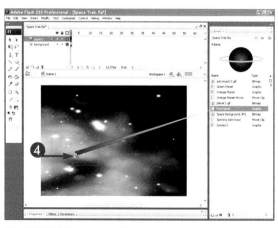

An instance of the symbol now appears on the Stage.

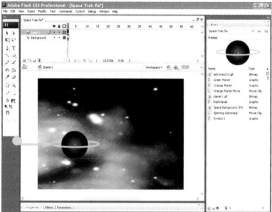

 TIPS

Can I replace one instance with another?

Yes. First, click the symbol you want to replace, and then open the Property inspector panel. Click the **Swap** button to open the Swap Symbol dialog box and select the replacement symbol you want to use. See the task "Swap Symbols" later in this chapter to learn more about this technique. See Chapter 1 to learn more about viewing the Property inspector.

Flash does not let me place an instance in a regular frame. Why not?

You can only place an instance in a keyframe in the Flash Timeline. You are not allowed to place instances in regular frames. To learn more about how frames work in the Timeline, see Chapter 8.

Modify an Instance

After you place a symbol instance on the Stage, you can change the way it appears without changing the original symbol. For example, you can change its color or make it appear transparent.

When you make changes to an instance in the Property inspector panel, you use several tools to modify its properties. You can change the object's behavior by turning a graphic symbol into a movie clip or into a button. You can also experiment by fine-tuning an instance's color effects.

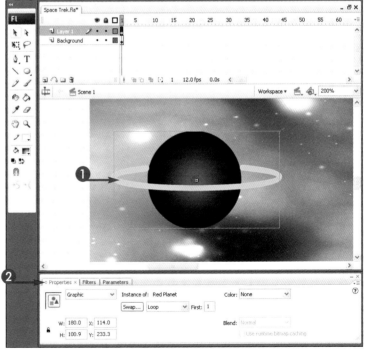

Modify an Instance

① Click the instance you want to modify.

② Open the Property inspector panel.

Note: See Chapter 1 to learn more about using the Property inspector.

③ Click the **Color** ▾.

④ Click **Advanced**.

⑤ Click **Settings**.

The Advanced Effect dialog box appears.

⑥ Click ⊙ next to a color and drag ⊡ to a new color setting.

● The selected object changes color as you drag the slider.

You might want to experiment with the various color settings to achieve the color effect you want.

⑦ Click **OK**.

● Flash applies the new settings.

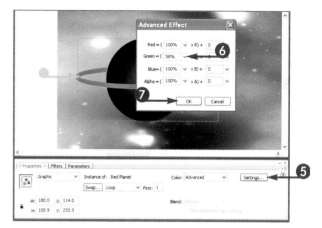

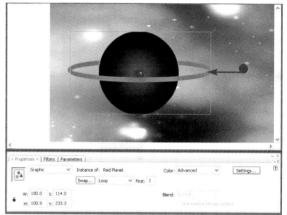

How do I make the instance transparent?

To make an instance appear transparent, change its Alpha setting. Follow Steps **1** to **3** in the section "Modify an Instance." Open the Advanced Effect dialog box and click and drag the **Alpha** slider (⊡) to the transparency level you want to apply. Click **OK** to apply the effect.

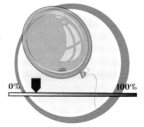

Can I name an instance?

You can name a movie clip or button instance and use the name in your action variables. Click inside the **Instance Name** text box in the Property inspector panel and type a name. This only works for movie clip or button instances. You cannot name graphic instances. See Chapter 10 to learn more about Flash actions.

Edit Symbols

You can edit symbols you have stored in the Library. For example, you might need to change a symbol slightly, such as adjusting a line or shape. You can make changes to the original symbol and Flash automatically updates all instances of it in your movie. This can save you considerable time and effort.

You can edit symbols in Symbol Edit mode or in a new window. When in Symbol Edit mode, Flash locks the other objects on the Stage to prevent accidental changes. When you edit in a new window, only the symbol you want to edit appears.

Edit Symbols

EDIT A SYMBOL IN SYMBOL EDIT MODE

1 Double-click the symbol you want to edit.

Flash switches to Symbol Edit mode.

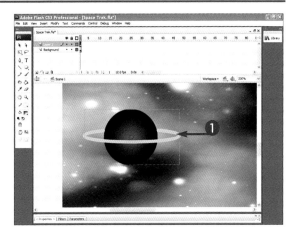

● If the symbol name appears at the top of the Stage, you know you are in Symbol Edit mode.

2 Edit the symbol as needed.

You can use the Flash drawing tools to make changes to the object, such as changing the fill color or adjusting a line segment.

Note: *See Chapter 3 to learn more about editing objects.*

3 Click the scene name to return to Movie Edit mode.

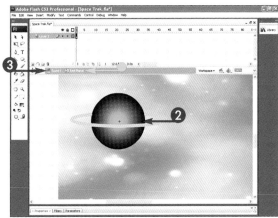

EDIT A SYMBOL IN A NEW WINDOW

① Click the **Edit Symbols** button ([icon]).

② Click the symbol you want to edit.

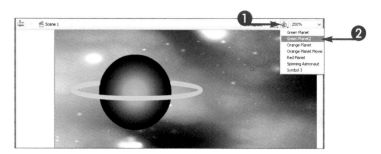

Flash opens a new window for editing the symbol.

③ Edit the symbol as needed.

You can use the Flash drawing tools to make changes to the object, such as changing the fill color or adjusting a line segment.

Note: See Chapter 3 to learn more about editing objects.

④ Click the scene name to return to Movie Edit mode.

Flash closes the window and returns to the main movie.

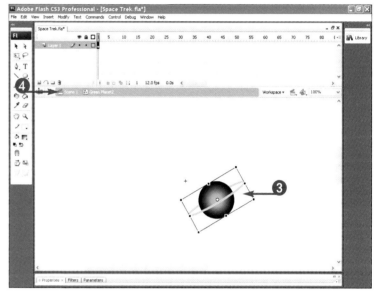

TIPS

How do I remove a symbol I no longer want?

First, make sure you do not use the symbol anywhere in your Flash movie. When you delete a symbol, Flash removes any instances of the symbol. Open the Library panel and select the symbol you want to remove. Click [icon]. Note that after you delete a symbol, you cannot undo the action. To continue, click **Delete**; Flash permanently removes the symbol from the file's Library.

Flash does not let me edit my symbol. Why not?

Depending on the complexity of the symbol, you may need to first apply the Break Apart or Ungroup command. The Break Apart command breaks the symbol down into its most basic construction — lines and fills. You can then edit a single line or fill. The Ungroup command ungroups a grouped object. You can find the Break Apart and Ungroup commands on the Modify menu. See Chapter 3 to learn more about using these commands.

Swap Symbols

You can replace a symbol instance with another from the Flash Library. When you apply the Swap Symbol command, you can keep all the modifications you assigned to the selected instance and apply them to the new symbol you insert in its place.

Swap Symbols

① Click the frame and symbol you want to edit.

② Open the Property inspector.

③ Click the **Swap** button.

The Swap Symbol dialog box appears.

● A bullet denotes the current symbol.

④ Click the symbol you want to swap.

⑤ Click **OK**.

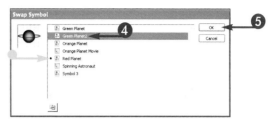

● Flash swaps the symbols.

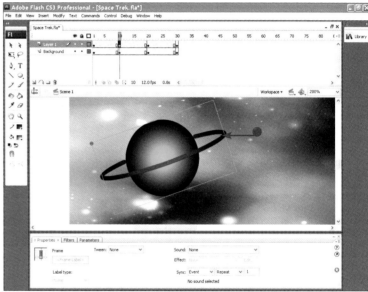

What if I want to make further edits to the swapped symbol?

You can click the **Duplicate Symbol** button ( ) in the Swap Symbol dialog box to make a copy of the symbol you are inserting as the swapped symbol. This allows you to make changes to the duplicate without affecting the master version of the symbol. If you attempt to edit a swapped symbol in Symbol Edit mode, Flash applies the edits to the original or master

symbol as well.

I am using symbols from different files, but the Library panel keeps changing. How do I keep the source panel in view?

You can click the **Pin Current Library** icon ( ) on the source Library panel to keep it active and in the same place. You can now continue to view files from other Library panels, but the source panel remains in place, ready

Creating Basic Animation in Flash

Are you ready to start animating? Whether you want to make an object move across the screen, build a detailed cartoon, or simply animate a company logo, the Flash animation tools can help you create all kinds of animations to use on the Web or in other Flash projects. This chapter shows you how to use frames and create simple animations.

Introduction to Animation

One of the most exciting aspects of Flash is its animation features. You can animate objects, synchronize the animation with sounds, add backgrounds, animate buttons, and much more. After you complete a Flash animation, you can place it on a Web page or distribute it for others to view.

How Do I Use Animations?

You can use Flash animations to present a lively message or to simply entertain. Animations you create in Flash can make a Web site come to life. For example, you can create a cartoon to play in your site's banner, or animate buttons for the user to click. You can also create animations for mobile phones, company presentations, and more. With the Flash animation tools, you have complete control over your movies.

How Do Animations Work?

Animation is simply a change that occurs between two or more frames in a movie. The change can be the placement of an object that moves slightly from one area on the screen to another, or it can be a change in color, intensity, size, or shape of an object. Any change you make to an object makes the object appear to be animated during playback of your movie.

Animation History

In the early days of animating, cartoonists and other animators painted objects and scenes on *cels*, which are transparent sheets of celluloid. The cels were stacked to create an image. A movie camera then took a snapshot of that image to create a single frame. The animators reused some of the cels for the next frame, such as backgrounds, and changed other cels to create an object's movement across the foreground.

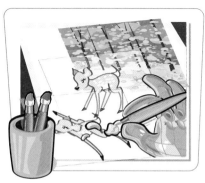

Animation in Flash

Flash uses similar principles to create animations today. Instead of transparent cels, you add content to frames and layers, then stack the layers to create depth. Anytime you want the content to change, you can add keyframes to the Timeline and vary the position or appearance of the content. When the animation, or movie, is played back, the content appears to move.

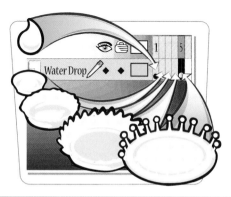

Frame-by-Frame Animation

Frame-by-frame animation is just as its name implies, creating the effect of movement by subtly changing the content's appearance from frame to frame. This type of animation method gives you a great deal of control over how the content changes across the Flash Timeline. You determine how much of a change appears from one frame to the next. Frame-by-frame animations increase the overall file size.

Tweened Animation

The other method of animating in Flash is called *tweened animation*. With tweened animation, you tell Flash to calculate the in-between frames from one keyframe to the content change in the next keyframe. Flash then draws the in-between phases of change to get from the first keyframe to the next. This in-between framing is where the term "tweened" comes from. Tweened animation is faster, easier to edit, and consumes less file size.

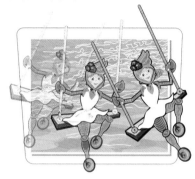

Introduction to Frames

You can use frames to create the illusion of motion and change across time. Frames are the backbone of your animation effects. When you start a new Flash file, it opens with a single layer and hundreds of placeholder frames in the Timeline. You can insert frames to each layer you add to the Timeline. Before you start animating objects, you need to understand how frames work.

Frame Rates

The number of frames you use in your Flash movie combined with the speed at which they play determines the length of the movie. By default, new Flash files you create use a frame rate of 12 frames per second, or 12 fps. You can set a frame rate higher or lower than the default if needed.

Frame Types

You can work with several different types of frames in the Flash Timeline: placeholder frames, keyframes, static frames, and tweened frames. Frames appear as tiny boxes in the Timeline. By default, the frames appear in Normal size; however, you can use the Timeline Options Menu to change the appearance of frames in your Timeline.

Placeholder Frames

A *placeholder frame* is merely an empty frame. It has no content. When your movie reaches an empty frame, it stops playing. With the exception of the first frame in a new layer, the remaining frames are all placeholders until you assign another frame type.

Keyframes

A *keyframe* defines a change in animation, such as an object moving or taking on a new appearance. By default, Flash inserts a blank keyframe for you in the first frame of every new layer you add to the Timeline. When you add a keyframe, it duplicates the content from the previous keyframe. This technique makes it easy to tweak the contents slightly to create the illusion of movement between frames.

Static Frames

Static or regular frames display the same content as the previous frame in the Timeline. Static frames must be preceded by a keyframe. Static frames are used to hold content that you want to remain visible until you add another keyframe in the layer.

Tweened Frames

One way to create animation in a movie is to allow Flash to calculate the number of frames between two keyframes to create movement. Called *tweening*, Flash determines the in-between positions of the animated object from one keyframe to the next and spaces out the changes in the tweened frames between the two keyframes.

See Chapter 9 to find out more about tweening effects.

Set Movie Dimensions and Frame Rate

You can specify the size and frame rate of a movie before you begin building the animation. A movie's dimensions refer to its vertical and horizontal size on the Flash Stage. The movie's frame rate determines the number of frames per second, or *fps*, that the animation occurs. Taking time to set the movie dimensions and speed now can save you time and prevent headaches later.

Set Movie Dimensions and Frame Rate

① Click **Modify**.

② Click **Document**.

You can also double-click the frame rate on the Timeline to open the Document Properties dialog box.

The Document Properties dialog box appears.

③ Type the number of frames per second you want the movie to play in the **Frame rate** text box.

Note: If you use a higher fps setting, slower computers might not be able to play back your movie properly.

④ Type a width value in the **width** text box.

⑤ Type a height value in the **height** text box.

Note: *The allowable dimensions in Flash are 1-2,880 pixels in size.*

⑥ Click **OK**.

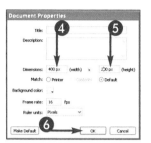

● The Flash Stage adjusts to the new dimensions you assigned.

● The new frame rate appears here.

● You can click the **Magnification** ☑ to choose another view to see the new dimensions you set.

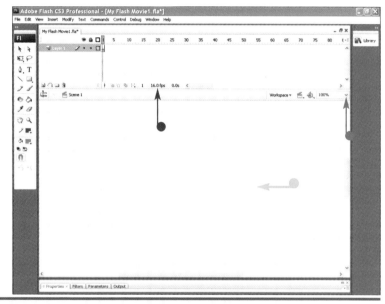

What is a good frame rate for my movie?

The frame rate controls how quickly Flash displays images in a movie. If the images are displayed too fast, they appear as a blur. If the images are displayed too slowly, they appear jerky. The default frame rate of 12 fps works well for most projects. The maximum rate you should set is 24 fps, unless you are exporting your movie as a QuickTime or Windows AVI video file, which can handle higher rates without consuming computer processor power. If you set a higher frame rate, slower computers struggle to play at such speeds. If you are confident your target audience uses a high bandwidth and the latest version of the Flash Player, you can utilize a higher frame rate.

Can I vary the frame rate throughout my movie?

No. Once you set a frame rate, that rate is in effect for the entire movie. You can, however, vary the speed of animation sequences by adding or removing frames. If a sequence seems to go too fast, you can add regular frames between the keyframes to slow it down. See the next section to learn more about frames, or see the section "Adjust the Animation Speed with Frames."

Add Frames

You can add frames to add content and length to your movie. When you add a new layer or start a new file, Flash starts you out with one keyframe in the Timeline and lots of placeholder frames. Adding more frames is as easy as adding pages to a document.

You can add regular frames, keyframes, and blank keyframes, and you can add more than one at a time. Add keyframes to define changes in the animation's appearance. Add regular frames to repeat the content of the keyframe preceding them.

Add Frames

ADD A REGULAR FRAME

1 Click a frame on the Timeline where you want to insert a new frame.

Note: See Chapter 1 to learn more about the Flash Timeline.

2 Click **Insert**.

3 Click **Timeline**.

4 Click **Frame**.

Note: You can also right-click over a frame and choose which type of frame you want to add from the pop-up menu.

Note: You can also press F5 to quickly insert a regular frame.

● Flash inserts a regular frame.

If you add a regular frame in the midst of existing regular frames, all the frames to the right of the insertion move over to make room for the new frame.

● In this example, a regular frame is added increasing the number of frames for the Orange Planet layer to 21.

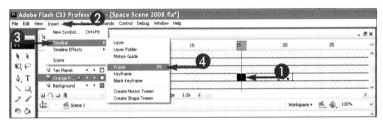

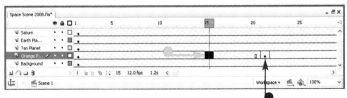

ADD A KEYFRAME

1 Click the frame on the Timeline that you want to turn into a keyframe.

Note: If you have trouble selecting a single frame within a group of frames, press `Ctrl` *(*`⌘`*) while clicking the frame.*

2 Click **Insert**.

3 Click **Timeline**.

4 Click **Keyframe**.

Note: You can also right-click over a frame and choose which type of frame you want to add from the pop-up menu.

Note: You can also press `F6` *to quickly insert a keyframe.*

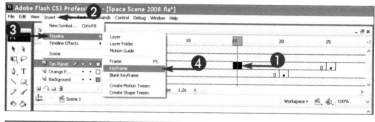

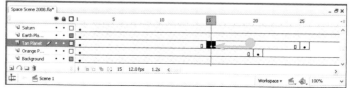

● Flash inserts a keyframe, marked by a bullet in the Timeline.

If the frame you select in Step **1** is a regular frame, Flash converts it to a keyframe.

If the frame is an empty frame, Flash inserts regular frames in between the last regular frame or keyframe up to the frame you clicked in Step **1**.

 TIP

How can I tell which frames are which in the Timeline?
You can identify Flash frames by the following characteristics:

● Keyframes with content appear with a solid bullet (●) in the Timeline.
● In-between frames that contain content appear tinted or grayed on the Timeline.
● Flash places a hollow box (□) preceding a keyframe.
● Blank keyframes — keyframes that have no content added yet — appear as hollow bullets (○).
● Flash highlights selected frames in black.
● Empty frames appear white.

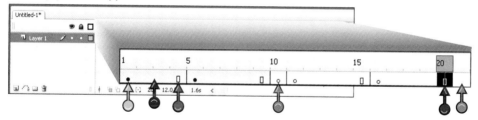

Add Frames
(continued)

You can add a blank keyframe when you want to start brand-new content in your movie. Unlike a default keyframe, which copies the content from the previous keyframe in the sequence, a blank keyframe is completely without content.

You can also add multiple frames. For example, perhaps you are creating an animation sequence that needs to be extended a bit in the Timeline in order to play more slowly in playback. Rather than insert one regular frame at a time, you can insert multiple frames, such as five frames at once.

Add Frames *(continued)*

ADD A BLANK KEYFRAME

1 Click a frame on the Timeline where you want to insert a blank keyframe.

2 Click **Insert**.

3 Click **Timeline**.

4 Click **Blank Keyframe**.

Note: You can also right-click over a frame and choose which type of frame you want to add from the pop-up menu.

Note: You can also press F7 *to quickly insert a blank keyframe.*

Flash inserts a blank keyframe.

● A hollow box precedes the blank keyframe.

● In this example, a blank keyframe is inserted into frame 20.

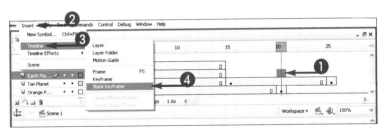

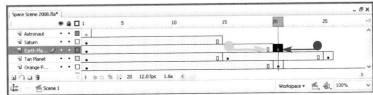

ADD MULTIPLE FRAMES

 Select two or more frames by clicking them.

To select multiple frames, click the first frame in the range, press **Shift**, and click the last frame in the range.

Note: See the section "Select Frames" to find out more about selecting frames.

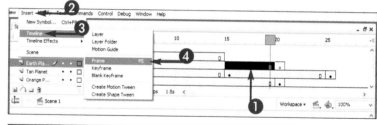

② Click **Insert**.

③ Click **Timeline**.

④ Click **Frame** to insert regular frames, or click **Keyframe** or **Blank Keyframe** to make the new frames all keyframes.

● Flash inserts the same number of new frames and lengthens the by the same number of frames.

TIPS

Can I change the size of the Timeline frames for better viewing?

Yes. By default, the frames appear in Normal size. You can change them to Tiny or Small to fit more frames in the Timeline view, or try Medium or Large to make the frames easier to see. The Preview options let you see thumbnails of frame content in the Timeline. Click the **Panel Menu** button (⊟), then click a frame size.

Can I resize the Timeline to view more layers?

Yes. You can click and drag the bottom border of the docked Timeline to increase its size. You can also change the docking of the Timeline. For example, you may prefer to move it to the bottom of the screen. To change the Timeline placement, click the **Panel Menu** button (⊟), click Placement, and choose a docking option. To learn more about using the Flash Timeline, see Chapter 1.

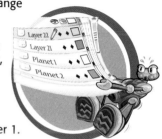

Select Frames

You can select frames in the Flash Timeline in order to add content or to edit the frames. You must also select frames in order to remove them from the Timeline. You can use a couple of selection techniques when working with frames.

When you select a single frame containing content, it appears highlighted in the Timeline, and the frame number appears in the Timeline's status bar. The playhead also appears directly above the selected frame.

Select Frames

SELECT A SINGLE FRAME

1 Click the frame to select it.

Flash highlights the frame in the Timeline.

Note: See the section "Understand Frames" in this chapter to find out more about frame types.

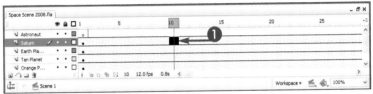

SELECT MULTIPLE FRAMES

1 Click the first frame in the range of frames you want to select.

2 Press and hold **Shift** and click the last frame in the range.

● Flash selects all the frames in between.

To select all the frames between two keyframes, double-click anywhere between the two keyframes.

To select multiple frames, press and hold the **Ctrl** key (**⌘**) while clicking frames.

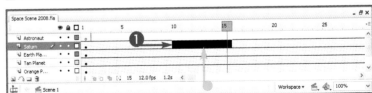

You can use the Property inspector panel to define properties for frames, such as labels and tweening status. Frame labels, for example, help you immediately recognize a frame's contents. You can also use labels to organize frames with actions, animation effects, sounds, and so on.

When you select a tweening status, additional options appear in the Property inspector panel. See Chapter 9 to learn more about creating tweened animations.

Properties
Frame   Diver 6
Tween   None
        Motion
        Shape

Modify Frame Properties

① Click the frame you want to modify.

② Open the Property inspector panel.

You can press `Ctrl`+`F3` (`⌘`+`F3`) to open the panel.

Note: *See Chapter 1 to learn how to display the Property inspector.*

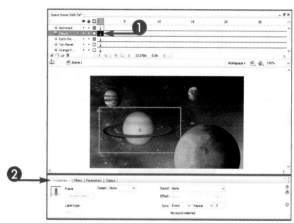

③ Type a label for the frame.

● The label appears in the Timeline.

● To specify another type of label, such as a comment, click here and select a type.

④ Click the **Tween** ☑ to change the frame type, such as assigning a tweening status.

The new frame type is assigned.

Note: *See Chapter 9 to learn more about tweening.*

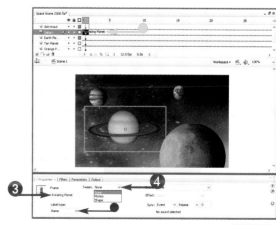

Delete or Change the Status of Frames

You can remove frames you no longer need or change them to a type of frame that you do need. You can remove regular frames to make an animation sequence appear to move more quickly. Or you might make a drastic change in your animation and decide you no longer need a particular keyframe in the sequence.

Instead of removing a keyframe completely, you can turn it into a regular frame. Using the Clear Keyframe command you can remove the frame's keyframe status and demote it to a regular frame. If you change a keyframe's status, all in-between frames are altered as well.

Delete or Change the Status of Frames

DELETE FRAMES

① Click the frame, or range of frames, you want to delete.

② Click **Edit**.

③ Click **Timeline**.

④ Click **Remove Frames**.

Note: To select a single frame within a group of frames, press Ctrl *(* ⌘ *) while clicking the frame.*

Note: You can also right-click the selected frame and click ***Remove Frames***.

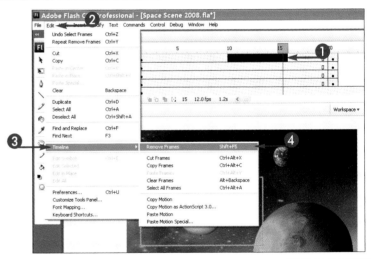

● Flash removes the frame and any existing frames to the right move over to fill the void.

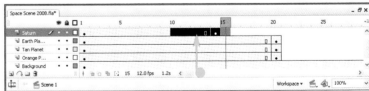

DEMOTE A KEYFRAME

1 Right-click the keyframe you want to change.

2 Click **Clear Keyframe**.

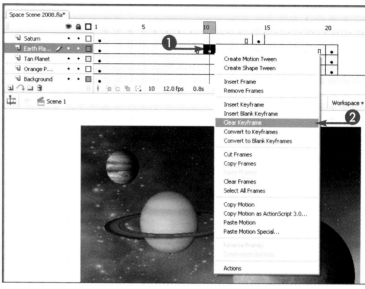

Flash converts the frame to a regular frame, and changes the frame to match the previous keyframe's contents.

Note: *You cannot change the status of the first keyframe in a layer.*

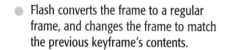

 TIPS

Can I delete a keyframe?

Yes. To remove a keyframe completely from the Timeline, select the keyframe and all the in-between frames associated with it, then apply the **Remove Frames** command; otherwise, the **Remove Frames** command does not work properly to remove the keyframe.

If I delete a frame, is the frame label removed as well?

Yes. Any time you remove a frame from the Timeline, any associated frame labels are removed as well. See the section "Modify Frame Properties" to learn more about frame labels.

Create Frame-by-Frame Animation

You can create the illusion of movement in a Flash movie by changing the placement or appearance of the Stage content from keyframe to keyframe in the Flash Timeline. This type of animation is called, appropriately, *frame-by-frame animation.*

You can add an animation sequence to any layer in your movie, and you can use one sequence right after another. For example, you might start your movie with a fade-in animation of your company logo, then jump to a completely different animation detailing a new product or service.

Create Frame-by-Frame Animation

1 Click the first keyframe in the layer you want to animate.

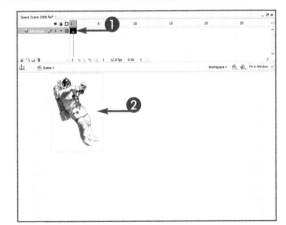

2 Place the object you want to animate on the Flash Stage.

You can add an instance of a symbol from the Library to animate, or you can use the drawing tools to create an object.

Note: *See Chapter 7 to learn more about creating symbols and using instances. See Chapter 2 to learn how to use the drawing tools.*

3 Click the next frame in the Timeline where you want to continue the animation.

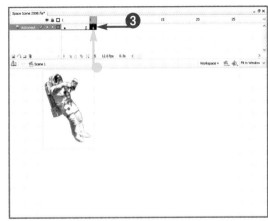

Note: *You can continue the animation in the very next frame or space the animation out with a few regular frames in between.*

4 Add a keyframe.

You can press F6 to quickly add a keyframe.

● Flash inserts a keyframe that duplicates the previous keyframe's contents.

⑤ Change the object slightly to animate.

● You can move the object a bit on the Stage, or change the object's appearance, such as color or size.

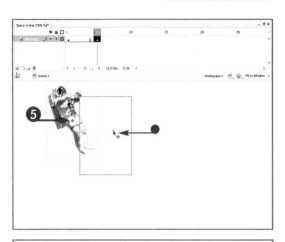

⑥ Click the next frame in the layer and add a keyframe.

You can press **F6** to quickly add a keyframe.

● Flash inserts a keyframe that duplicates the previous keyframe's contents.

⑦ Change the object slightly again.

You can move the object a bit more on the Stage or change the object's appearance.

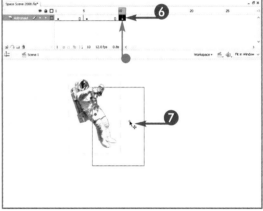

 TIPS

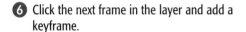

Can I add in-between frames to the animation?

Yes. To slow down the animation sequence, especially if the changes between keyframes are happening too fast to see very well, just add regular frames between keyframes in your frame-by-frame animation. To add in-between frames, click a keyframe. Click **Insert**, **Timeline**, and then click **Frame**, or press **F5**. Flash adds a regular frame behind the keyframe. You can keep adding more regular frames to achieve the effect you want. When you play back the movie, the animation appears to slow down a bit in its movement.

When should I use frame-by-frame animation or tweening?

Although the frame-by-frame animation technique is more labor intensive, it can help you create smooth animation actions. Use frame-by-frame animation when you want to create a subtle change in content. Use the tweening technique when your animations require more labor efficiency. See Chapter 9 to learn more about tweening.

You can create all kinds of animation effects using frame-by-frame animation techniques. For example, a simple circle shape can become a bouncing ball if moved strategically around the Stage in each frame of the movie.

The example in this section shows how to create the illusion of a floating astronaut by moving the astronaut slightly down the Stage in each keyframe. By the last keyframe, the astronaut reaches the bottom.

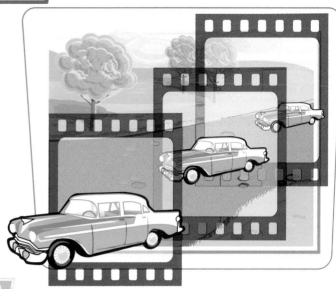

Create Frame-by-Frame Animation *(continued)*

⑧ Click the next frame in the layer to which you want to change the animation and add a keyframe.

You can press F6 to quickly add a keyframe.

● Flash inserts a keyframe that duplicates the previous keyframe's contents.

⑨ Change the object again so it varies from the previous keyframe.

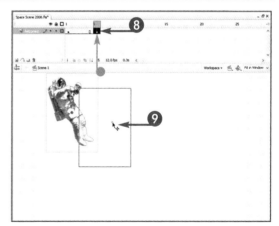

⑩ Click the next frame in the layer and add a keyframe.

You can press F6 to quickly add a keyframe.

● Flash inserts a keyframe that duplicates the previous keyframe's contents.

⑪ Change the object again.

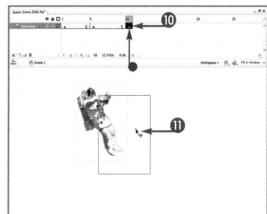

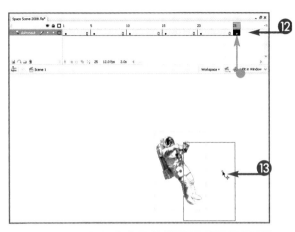

⑫ Click the next frame in the layer and add a final keyframe.

You can press **F6** to quickly add a keyframe.

● Flash inserts a keyframe that duplicates the previous keyframe's contents.

⑬ Change the object again for the final keyframe in the animation sequence.

⑭ Click the first keyframe in the layer.

Note: You can also click and drag the playhead to the first frame of any layer and press **Enter** *(* **Return** *) to play the movie.*

⑮ Press **Enter** (**Return**).

Flash plays the entire animation sequence.

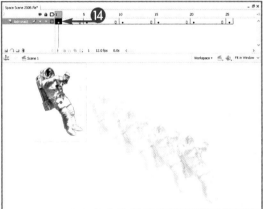

How do I edit a symbol as I create the animation?

To make changes to a symbol, select the keyframe where you want to introduce a change. To open the symbol in Symbol Edit mode, double-click on the symbol. Make your edits, and then click the Scene name to return to Movie Edit mode. You can switch back and forth between edit modes as needed when creating your animation sequence.

How do I know where to reposition an object on the Stage?

To help you control how an object moves around the Stage, turn on the gridlines by clicking the **View** menu, and then clicking **Grid**, **Show Grid**. With the grid turned on, you can more clearly see the placement of objects on the Stage. To turn off the grid marks, click **View**, **Grid**, **Show Grid**.

Onion-Skinning an Animation

You can use the onion-skinning feature to quickly assess the positioning of objects in surrounding frames in your movie. By viewing the placement of objects in other frames, you can more clearly determine how you want to position the object in the frame in which you are working.

The name *onion-skinning* refers to the effect of seeing the contents of other frames as shaded layers — like the translucent layers of an onion — in context to the current frame. Onion-skinning offers two modes of display: dimmed content or outlined content.

Onion-Skinning an Animation

TURN ON ONION-SKINNING

1 Click a frame.

2 Click the **Onion Skin** button (⬚) at the bottom of the Flash Timeline.

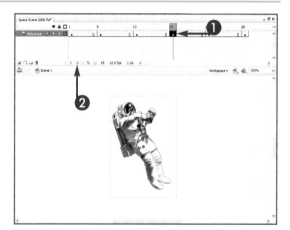

● Flash displays dimmed images from the surrounding frames and places onion-skin markers at the top of the Timeline.

● To turn off onion-skinning, you can click ⬚ again.

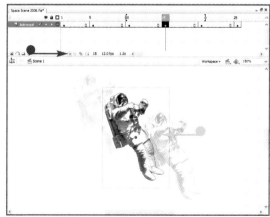

TURN ON ONION-SKINNING OUTLINES

① Click a frame.

② Click the **Onion Skin Outlines** button (□) at the bottom of the Flash Timeline.

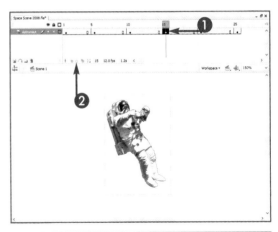

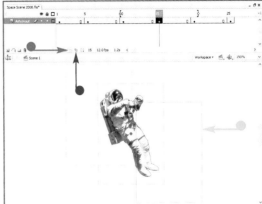

● Flash displays outlines of the objects from the surrounding frames and places onion-skin markers at the top of the Timeline.

● To make the content of the onion-skin frames editable, click the **Edit Multiple Frames** button (□).

● To turn off onion-skinning, you can click □ again.

 TIPS

Can I edit the onion-skinned frames?

No. You cannot edit the onion-skin frames unless you click the Edit Multiple Frames button (□). When you make the other frames editable, you can select and move the onion-skinned objects to fine-tune the animation sequence.

Can I play back my movie with the onion-skin feature on?

Yes. However, the onion-skinning turns off while the movie plays. Click in the first frame of your movie and press `Enter` (`Return`). Flash plays the movie on the Stage. When it reaches the last frame, the onion-skin feature resumes its active state again.

continued

The onion-skinning features can help you better gauge the changes needed to create your animations. You can control which frames appear in onion-skin mode using the onion-skin markers that appear on the Timeline. You can also opt to control the markers using the Modify Onion Markers pop-up menu.

When you activate the Modify Onion Markers button, the pop-up menu displays several choices for controlling markers on the Timeline.

Onion-Skinning an Animation *(continued)*

MOVE THE ONION-SKIN MARKERS

1 To view more or less frames with onion-skinning, you can click and drag an onion-skin marker left or right.

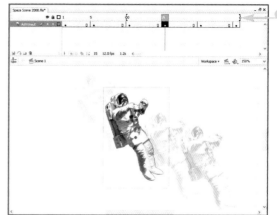

Flash adds or subtracts the additional frames from the view.

● In this example, moving the marker displays more frames.

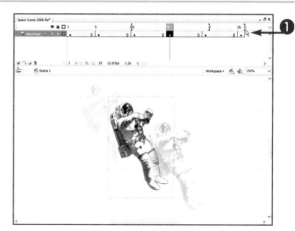

CHANGE THE MARKER DISPLAY

① To change how the onion-skin markers appear on the Timeline, click the **Modify Onion Markers** button (□).

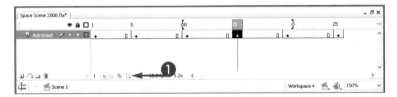

The Modify menu appears with options for changing the marker display.

② Click the marker setting you want to apply.

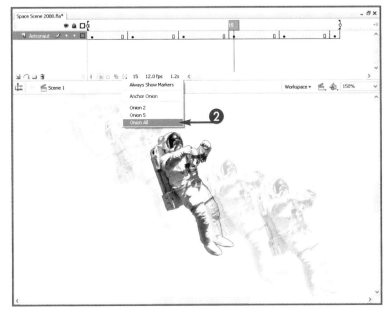

What are my options for modifying the onion-skin markers?

When you click □, the pop-up menu displays several choices for controlling markers on the Timeline. Click **Always Show Markers** to leave the markers on even when onion-skinning is turned off.

Click **Anchor Onion** to lock the markers in place, even as you view frames at the other end of the Timeline.

Click **Onion 2** or **Onion 5** to display the corresponding number of frames before and after the current frame.

Click **Onion All** to onion-skin all the frames.

Always Show Markers

Anchor Onion

Onion 2
Onion 5
Onion All

Preview a Flash Animation

You can click on an animation sequence one frame at a time to see each frame's contents, but a faster way to check the sequence is to play the movie. You can use the built-in Flash Player window to see the movie without all the surrounding Flash tools. Test Movie mode lets you see the movie as your audience will see it.

Another quick way to test the movie is to move the playhead to the first frame and press Enter. Flash plays your movie directly on the Stage.

① Click **Control**.

② Click **Test Movie**.

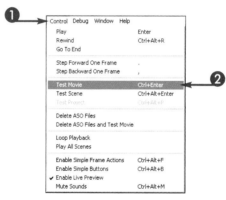

● Flash exports your movie to the Flash Player and plays the animation.

You can stop the animation from playing by pressing Enter (Return).

You can resume playing by pressing Enter (Return).

③ To return to the Flash Editor window, click the **Close** button (☒).

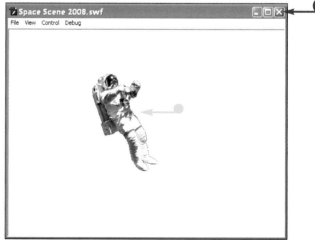

You can use regular frames in your movie to adjust the speed of an animation sequence. Although a movie's frame rate is constant throughout the movie, you can slow or speed up an animation by adding or subtracting frames. Adding regular frames to an animation sequence extends the length of time the sequence plays back.

If a particular section of your animation seems to happen too quickly during playback, you can slow it down a bit if you insert regular frames between two keyframes. By adding in-between frames rather than keyframes, you do not increase the movie's file size.

Adjust the Animation Speed with Frames

① Click the keyframe you want to add frames to or click a regular frame from between two keyframes.

② Click **Insert**.

③ Click **Timeline**.

③ Click **Frame**.

You can also press F5 to add a regular frame.

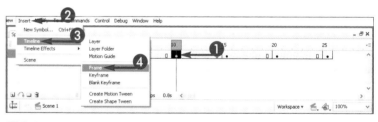

● Flash adds a regular frame after the keyframe.

Because adding just one regular frame is not always enough, repeat Steps **2** and **3** as needed to add more frames to the sequence.

To test the animation, click the first frame in the Timeline and press Enter (Return).

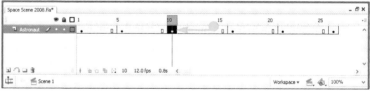

Move and Copy Frames

You can move and copy frames in your animation sequence to change the way in which it plays. For example, you may want to move a keyframe up or back in the Timeline, or copy multiple regular frames to place between two keyframes.

You cannot copy frames like you copy other objects in Flash; you must use the Copy Frames and Paste Frames commands found in the Edit menu. Using the standard Copy and Paste commands do not work.

Move and Copy Frames

MOVE A FRAME

① Click the frame to select it.

Flash highlights the frame in the Timeline.

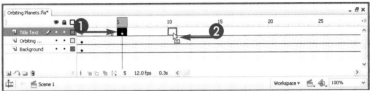

② Drag the frame to a new location in the Timeline.

③ Drop the frame in place.

● The frame moves.

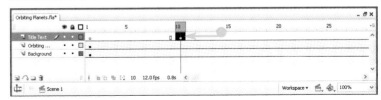

COPY A FRAME

① Click the frame to select it.

Flash highlights the frame in the Timeline.

② Click **Edit**.

③ Click **Timeline**.

④ Click **Copy Frames**.

You can also right-click the frame and click **Copy Frames**.

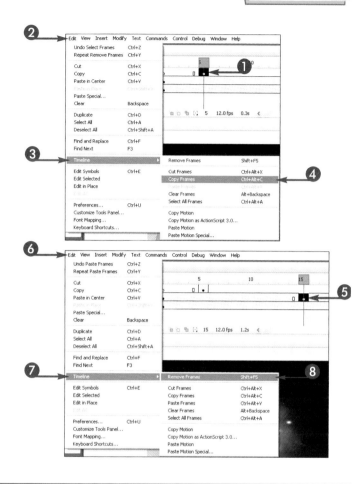

⑤ Click a frame where you want to place the copy.

⑥ Click **Edit**.

⑦ Click **Timeline**.

⑧ Click **Paste Frames**.

You can also right-click the frame and click **Paste Frames**.

Flash pastes the copied frame into the selected frame and any copied frame content appears on the stage.

 TIPS

Can I use the drag-and-drop technique to copy frames?

Yes. First select the frame or frames you want to copy. Press and hold the Alt (Option) key and then drag the frame (or frames) and drop it into the new location on the Timeline. Flash duplicates the frames.

Can I click and drag an end keyframe to extend an animation?

Yes. Dragging an end keyframe in your animation sequence can quickly lengthen or shorten an animation, depending on which direction you drag. For example, you can drag a keyframe to the right a couple of frames and Flash automatically adds in-between frames for you. This extends your animation sequence.

Create Scenes

You can create scenes in your movie to organize your animation sequences. Scenes are blocks of the animation frames turned into their own independent Timelines. Rather than scrolling around long Timelines and trying to keep track of where you are, you can break your movie into smaller, manageable scenes that you can work with individually.

The current scene's name appears at the top of the Timeline. During playback, the scenes are played in the order in which they are listed in the Scene panel.

Create Scenes

OPEN THE SCENE PANEL

1. Click **Window**.

2. Click **Other Panels**.

3. Click **Scene**.

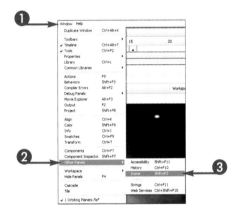

ADD A NEW SCENE

The Scene panel opens.

4. Click the **Add Scene** button (＋).

You can also click the **Insert** menu and then click **Scene** to add a scene.

● Flash adds a scene to the panel, and the Timeline switches to the new scene.

● To rename the scene, double-click the scene name, type a new name, and then press Enter (Return).

You can add frames and create an animation sequence for the scene.

● You can click the Close button (✕) to close the panel.

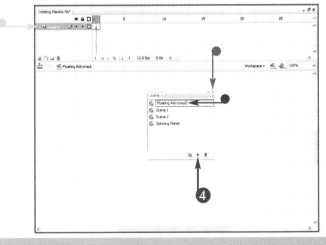

SWITCH BETWEEN SCENES

1 Click the **Edit Scene** button ().

Flash displays a pop-up menu listing all the available scenes.

2 Click the scene you want to view.

● If the Scene panel is open, you can also click the scene name you want to view.

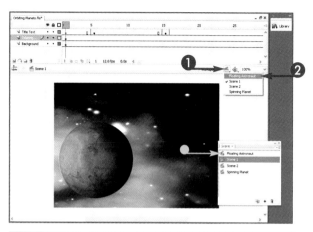

● Flash switches to the scene you selected.

Scene names always appear at the top of the Stage.

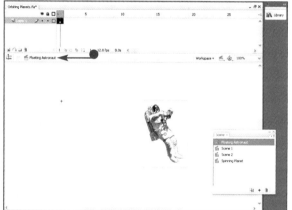

TIPS

How do I rearrange the scene order?

You can move scenes around using the Scene panel. Open the Scene panel to display a list of all the available scenes (Steps **1** through **3** in this section). Click the scene you want to move, then drag it to a new location in the list. As soon as you finish dragging, the scenes are reordered.

How do I delete a scene?

Open the Scene panel, select the scene you want to remove and click the **Delete** button (). Flash removes the scene from the panel.

Save an Animation as a Movie Clip

You can save an animation sequence as a movie clip that you can use again elsewhere in your movie. When you save an animation sequence, Flash saves it as a movie clip symbol. Movie clip symbols are just one of the three symbol types you can create in Flash. Movie clips utilize their own timelines apart from the main movie Timeline.

As with graphic and button symbols, you can place a movie clip symbol on the Stage for any frame. When Flash reaches that frame during playback, it plays the movie clip animation.

Save an Animation as a Movie Clip

1 Select all the frames included in the animation sequence.

Note: See the section "Select Frames" to learn how to select frames in the Timeline.

2 Click **Edit**.

3 Click **Timeline**.

4 Click **Copy Frames**.

You can also right-click the frames and click **Copy Frames**.

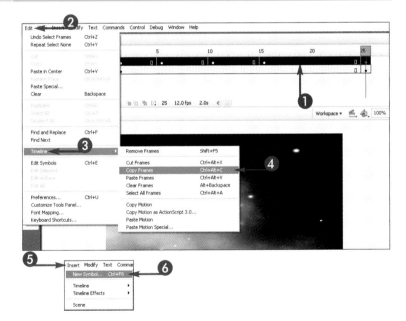

5 Click **Insert**.

6 Click **New Symbol**.

The Create New Symbol dialog box appears.

7 Type a name for the symbol.

8 Select the **Movie clip** behavior type (○ changes to ⊙).

9 Click **OK**.

Flash switches you to Symbol Edit mode.

10 Make sure Frame 1 is selected.

11 Click **Edit**.

12 Click **Timeline**.

13 Click **Paste Frames**.

You can also right-click the frames and click **Paste Frames**.

● Flash copies the animation into the movie clip's Timeline. Flash saves the animation in the Flash Library as a movie clip.

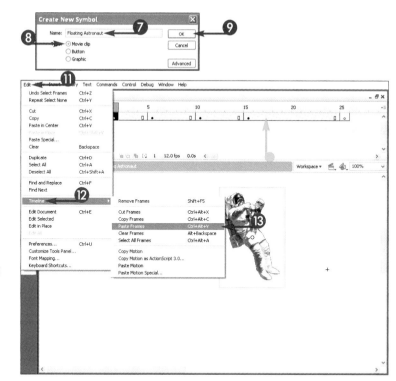

How do I place a movie clip in my movie?

You can place movie clips into your movie just as you place any other item saved in the Flash Library. Click the frame where you want to insert the clip, open the Library panel, and drag the movie clip onto the Stage. You can turn any animation effect, including frame-by-frame motion and shape tweens, into movie clips.

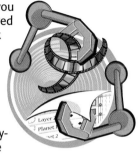

How do I save an existing clip as a new clip?

You can use the Convert to Symbol command. You may do this if you want to alter the clip slightly and use it again elsewhere. Right-click the clip and click **Convert to Symbol**. In the Convert to Symbol dialog box, make sure the symbol type is set to Movie clip. Then type a new name for the clip and click **OK**. The clip is added to your movie's Library.

Using Movie Explorer

You can use the Movie Explorer panel to view and organize different elements in a scene. Each scene element is listed in a navigable tree hierarchy, including instances, actions, movie clips, sound files, and more. You can choose what objects to view or hide. You can also search for a specific object.

You can also use Movie Explorer to see the construction of other developers' Flash files. As you expand and collapse the list, you can view various elements using the Show buttons, which act as filters for the list display. For example, you can view the ActionScript assigned to an object to learn how the action works.

Using Movie Explorer

① Open the scene you want to view.

② Click **Window**.

③ Click **Movie Explorer**.

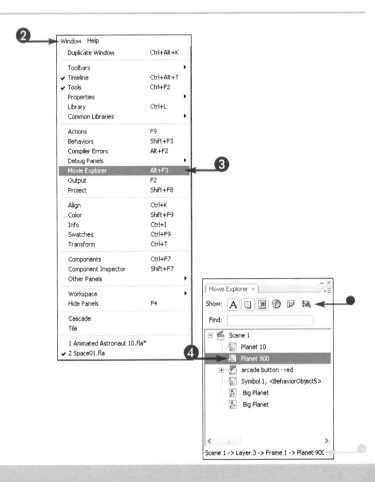

Flash opens the Movie Explorer panel.

④ Click the object you want to view.

● Flash displays the full path to the object here.

● You can click these buttons to change which objects are displayed in the navigation tree.

● You can expand or collapse the hierarchy by clicking **Expand** (⊞) or **Collapse** (⊟).

● To search for a specific item in your movie, type the object name here and press Enter (Return).

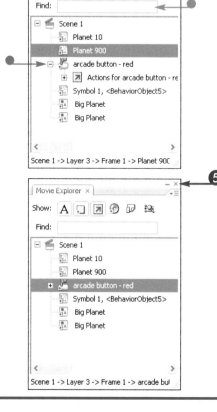

⑤ When finished, click the panel's **Close** button (⊠).

Flash closes the panel.

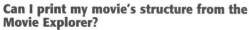

TIPS

What hierarchal order does the Movie Explorer panel display?

The panel always displays scene elements in a certain order, and depending on what objects you choose to view or hide in the hierarchal tree, the objects are always listed in this order. At the top of the tree is the scene name, followed by layers, frames, objects within frames, and symbol definitions. Using the Show buttons, you can control which objects appear in the list. For example, when studying another developer's Flash file, you might choose to view just the ActionScript elements.

Can I print my movie's structure from the Movie Explorer?

Yes. First use the Show buttons to display just the objects you want to appear in the list. Next, click the **Panel Menu** button (▾≡) and click **Print**. This opens the Print dialog box, and you can set any printing options before printing the hierarchal tree.

Creating Animation by Tweening

Flash includes built-in animating techniques that make it easy to create complex animations. This chapter shows you how to create animation using motion and shape tweening.

Create a
Motion Tween

Flash can help you animate moving objects when you apply a motion tween. A *motion tween* is when you define two points of movement in the Timeline with two keyframes, and then let Flash calculate all the in-between frames necessary to get from point A to point B. Motion-tweened animations take up much less file space than frame-by-frame animations.

You can motion tween only symbols or grouped objects, and you can tween only one symbol per layer in a timeline.

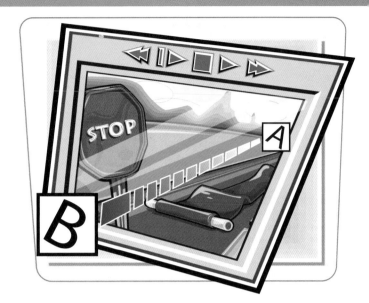

Create a Motion Tween

ADD KEYFRAMES AND SYMBOL

① Insert a keyframe where you want to start the motion tween.

Note: See Chapter 8 to learn about adding frames.

② Place the symbol you want to animate on the Stage.

● The symbol's position should be the starting point of the animation effect, such as a corner or side of the movie area.

Note: Chapter 7 explains how to work with symbols.

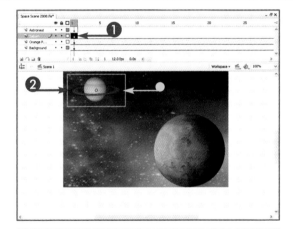

③ Click the last frame you want to include in the motion tween.

④ Insert a keyframe.

You can press F6 to quickly insert a keyframe.

Note: See Chapter 8 to learn more about keyframes.

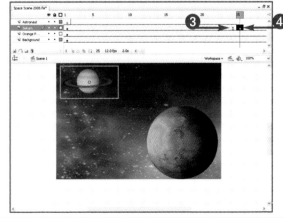

5 Move the symbol to the position on which you want the motion tween to end (for example, the other side of the Stage).

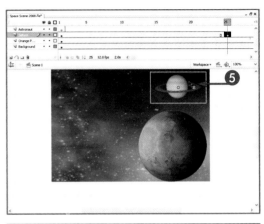

6 Double-click a frame between the two keyframes that make up your motion tween to select the frames.

Note: See Chapter 8 to find out how to select frames.

7 Open the Property inspector panel.

You can press `Ctrl`+`F3` (`⌘`+`F3`) to quickly open the Property inspector.

Note: See Chapter 1 to learn more about the Property inspector panel.

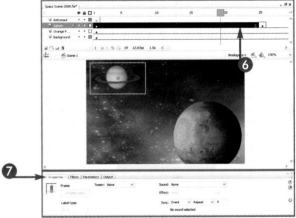

TIPS

Can I make an object move on or off the Stage?

Yes. You can place an object off the Stage area and animate it onto and across the Stage, then off the other side. For example, start the animation effect with the object located outside the left Stage area and end the effect with the same object outside the right Stage area. Anything that appears off the Stage area is not visible in the final movie.

What is the difference between a shape tween and a motion tween?

You can create two types of tweened animations in Flash: *motion tween* or *shape tween*. Use motion tweening to make Flash calculate the changes for an object moving around the Stage. Use shape tweening to make Flash calculate the changes between an object that morphs into another object.

continued

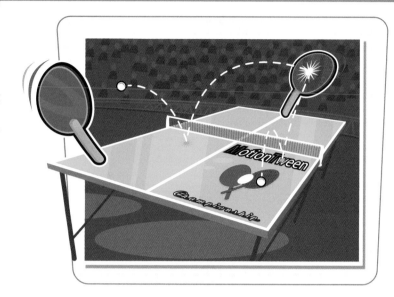

You can assign as many motion tween segments as you like throughout your movie, or you can make your animation one long motion tween. Motion tweening works best for objects you want to move around the Flash Stage.

The number of in-between frames is determined by your placement of the second keyframe in the sequence. You should allow five or more frames between your reference keyframes to create a smooth motion tween effect.

Create a Motion Tween *(continued)*

CREATE A TWEEN EFFECT

⑧ Click the **Tween** ☑.

⑨ Click **Motion**.

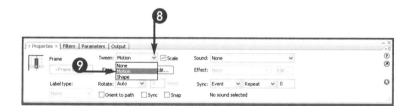

Flash calculates the in-between changes the symbol must undergo to move from the first keyframe to the next keyframe.

● Flash adds a motion tween arrow (⟐⟶) from the first keyframe in the tween effect to the last keyframe in the tween effect.

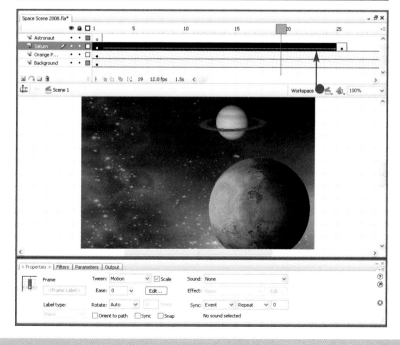

TEST THE TWEEN EFFECT

10 To view a motion tween in action, click in the first frame of the motion tween.

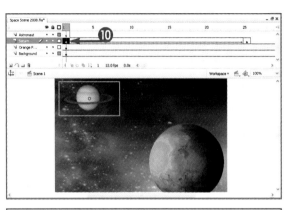

11 Press Enter (Return).

Flash plays the animation sequence.

● You can click the title bar of the panel to hide the Property inspector and free up more on-screen space for viewing the animation.

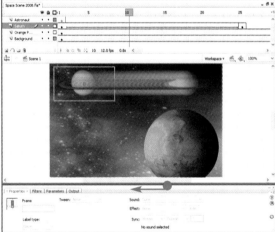

Can I create a motion tween as I go?

You can start a motion tween without defining the end keyframe in the sequence. Start by adding a keyframe and placing the symbol you want to animate on the Stage. Click the **Insert** menu and click **Create Motion Tween**. Add as many frames as you want to the sequence. A dotted line appears in the frames, indicating a motion tween in the making, but not yet complete. In the final frame of the sequence, move the symbol on the Stage to where you want the animation to end. Flash automatically assigns keyframe status to the frame and marks the in-between frames with an arrow to show the motion tween is complete.

Can I undo a motion tween?

You can turn off the frame's tween status in the Property inspector panel. Select the frames containing the tween, click the **Tween** ⌄ in the Property inspector panel, then click **None**. Resetting the tween status to None removes all the Flash calculations between the keyframes and the object no longer moves across the Stage.

Create a Spinning Tween

You can create an animation effect that makes a symbol appear to spin. Using two identical keyframes and a motion tween, you can tell Flash to rotate the symbol in the in-between frames to create a spinning effect during playback.

The rotated object starts and ends up at the same spot, so the two keyframes that begin and end the effect remain the same. You specify which direction to spin the object and Flash calculates all the incremental changes that must occur in the in-between frames to create the spinning effect.

Create a Spinning Tween

CREATE THE TWEEN EFFECT

① Insert a keyframe where you want to start the spin motion tween in the Timeline.

You can press F6 to quickly insert a keyframe.

② Place the symbol you want to animate on the Stage.

Note: *It is a good idea to place animations on a separate layer from the movie background. See Chapter 6 to learn more about working with layers.*

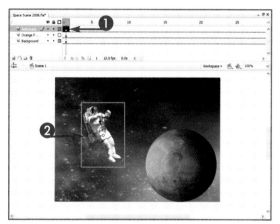

③ Click the frame in which you want to conclude the motion tween.

For example, you can complete the spin effect 20 frames later.

④ Insert a keyframe.

You can press F6 to insert a keyframe.

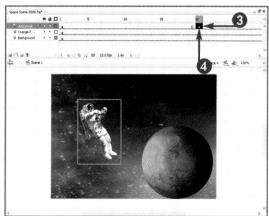

5 Double-click a frame between the two keyframes that make up your motion tween to select the frames.

Note: See Chapter 8 to learn how to select frames.

6 Open the Property inspector panel.

You can press `Ctrl`+`F3` (`⌘`+`F3`) to quickly open the Property inspector.

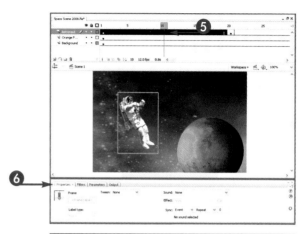

7 Click the **Tween** ☑ to view tweening types.

8 Click **Motion**.

● Flash adds a motion tween arrow (`>———`) to the selected frames.

Does it matter in which direction the symbol spins?

No. You can set a rotation direction in the Property inspector, or you can tell Flash to set a direction for you. If you let Flash pick a direction, it chooses the rotation that involves the least amount of change from frame to frame creating a smoother animation. To instruct Flash to handle the rotation, leave the **Auto** option selected for the **Rotate** setting.

How do I make the motion tween continue past the end keyframe?

If you plan to continue the motion tween, make sure you select the end keyframe along with the start keyframe and in-between frames. See Chapter 8 to learn how to select frames. To stop a motion tween, click the last keyframe in the sequence, then assign **None** using the **Tween** setting in the Property inspector.

continued

You can use the Rotation controls to spin items. By assigning a motion tween effect, Flash takes care of the hard work of differing each frame in the sequence for you. You can specify how many times the symbol rotates between the two keyframes, and exactly which direction it goes.

The steps in this section show an example of a ringed planet as a spinning object. You can apply the same principles to other objects you create or add to the Flash Stage. If you prefer to control your own rotation, you manually rotate the object in each keyframe yourself.

Create a Spinning Tween *(continued)*

SELECT A SPIN ROTATION

⑨ Click the **Rotate** ☑ to view rotation types.

⑩ Click a rotation direction for the spin.

You can choose **CW** to spin the symbol clockwise.

You can choose **CCW** to spin the symbol counterclockwise.

⑪ Type the number of times you want the rotation to occur.

Flash calculates the in-between changes the symbol must undergo to move from the first keyframe to the next keyframe.

● You can click the panel's title bar to hide the Property inspector.

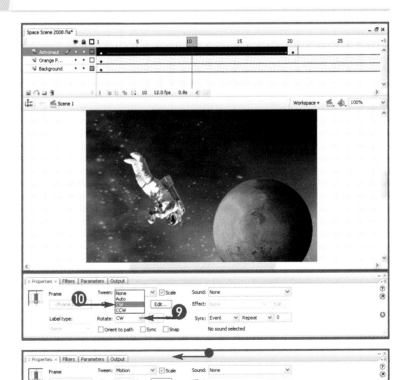

VIEW THE SPIN

⑫ To view a motion tween in action, click in the first frame of the motion tween.

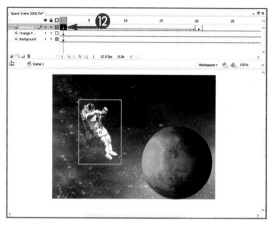

⑬ Press `Enter` (`Return`).

● Flash plays the animation sequence on the Stage.

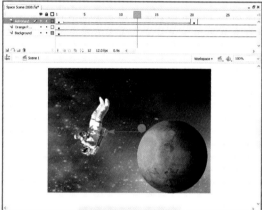

TIPS

What does the Auto rotate setting do?

You can choose **Auto** from the **Rotate** menu in the Property inspector panel to have Flash determine the rotation for you. The Auto selection rotates the selected object in the direction using the least amount of motion.

Can I control how quickly the object starts spinning?

Yes. Use the **Ease** setting in the Property inspector panel to speed up the start of your motion tween's spinning effect. You can click and drag the **Ease** slider up to accelerate the spin or down to slow it down.

Create a Growing or Shrinking Tween

You can use the motion tween technique to create an animation that changes size. For example, you can make a symbol seem to grow or shrink in size. You define two keyframes, one of which includes the symbol scaled to a new size. Flash fills in all the in-between frames with the incremental changes needed to create the illusion of growth or shrinkage.

You can use the same scaling tools from the Flash drawing tools to resize symbols for animation effects.

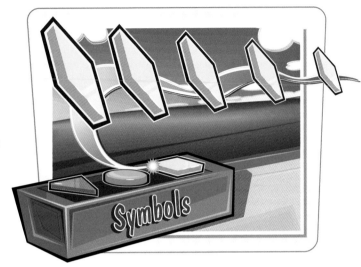

Create a Growing or Shrinking Tween

CREATE THE TWEEN EFFECT

① Insert a keyframe where you want to start the motion tween.

You can press F6 to insert a keyframe.

② Place the symbol you want to animate on the Stage.

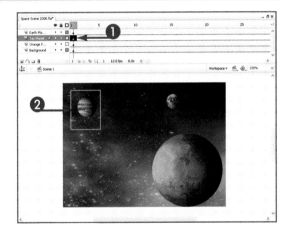

③ Click the frame in which you want to conclude the motion tween.

④ Insert a keyframe.

RESIZE THE SYMBOL

5 Select the symbol, and if necessary, place it where you want it to appear.

In this example, the animation ends mostly off-screen in the work area after appearing on the Stage.

6 Click the **Free Transform tool** (⬚).

7 Click the **Scale modifier** (⬚).

Flash surrounds the object with edit points, called *handles*.

8 Click and drag a handle to resize the symbol.

9 Double-click a frame between the two keyframes that make up your motion tween.

Note: *Select both the start and end keyframes in the tween before applying Motion tween status to continue the tween status.*

10 Open the Property inspector.

You can press Ctrl+F3 (⌘+F3) to quickly open the Property inspector.

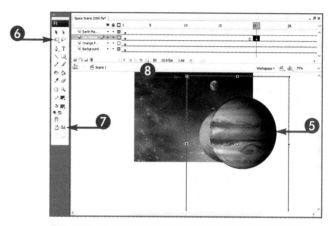

 TIPS

How can I tell what size changes take place in my motion tween?

You can use the Onion Skin tool to see the changes in the frames that surround the current frame. Click the **Onion Skin** button (⬚) at the bottom of the Timeline. Click and drag the onion skin markers left or right to include other frames in the view. See Chapter 8 to learn more about how to use this feature.

Which Scale edit point should I drag?

When resizing an object on the Stage, you can use any of the edit points, called *handles*, to drag the object to a new size. Depending on the point you drag, the object resizes in different directions. For best results, drag a corner edit point.

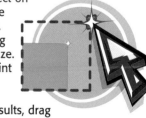

continued

You can use the Scale option in the Property inspector to make symbols seem to grow or shrink. The speed at which this occurs depends on how many frames you insert between the two defining keyframes.

You can experiment with the number of regular frames to create just the right animation speed. For example, if your motion tween uses five in-between frames, adding five more slows down the tween effect. This means the object seems to grow or shrink at a slower pace.

Create a Growing or Shrinking Tween *(continued)*

⓫ Click the **Tween** ☑ to view tweening types.

⓬ Click **Motion**.

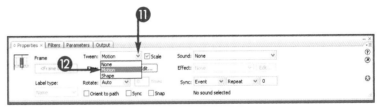

● Flash adds a motion tween arrow (▷——▶) from the first keyframe in the tween effect to the last keyframe in the tween effect.

⓭ Select the **Scale** check box (☐ changes to ☑) if it is not selected already.

● You can click the panel's title bar to hide the Property inspector.

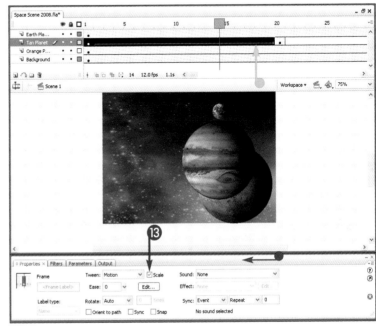

VIEW THE ANIMATION

⑭ To view a motion tween in action, click the first frame of the motion tween.

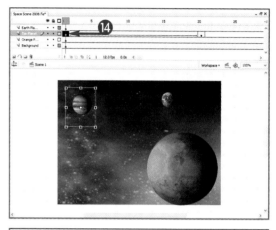

⑮ Press Enter (Return).

● Flash plays the animation sequence.

TIPS

My symbol does not grow or shrink very much. Why not?

For a maximum tween effect, you need to make the final symbol in the tween sequence much smaller or larger than the symbol shown in the first keyframe. Allow plenty of regular keyframes in between the two anchor keyframes. See Chapter 8 to learn more about adding frames to the Timeline.

How do I make my object shrink back again to its original size?

You can copy the entire sequence and apply the Reverse Frames command to make the object seem to shrink again after growing. See the section "Using Reverse Frames" later in this chapter to learn how to apply this command to your motion tweens.

Original size

Animate Symbols Along a Path

You can make a symbol follow a path in your Flash movie. Using the motion tween technique and a *motion guide layer*, you define points A and B in the sequence, draw a line that tells Flash exactly where you want the symbol to move, and then Flash calculates all the in-between frames for you.

A *motion guide layer* is a special layer used to define the motion tween path. Using the drawing tools, you draw on the Stage exactly where you want the symbol to go. The symbol follows your path. The motion guide layer is not visible when you export the movie.

Animate Symbols Along a Path

CREATE AND SELECT A TWEEN LAYER

1 Create a motion tween animation.

Note: See the section "Create a Motion Tween" earlier in this chapter to learn how to make a motion tween animation sequence.

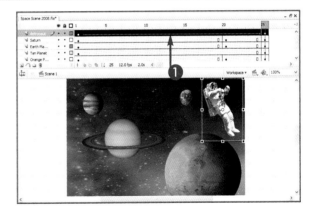

2 Select the layer containing the motion tween.

Note: See Chapter 6 to learn more about working with layers.

3 Click the **Add Motion Guide** button( ).

Flash adds a motion guide layer directly above the layer containing the motion tween.

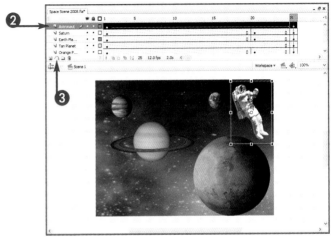

④ Click the motion guide layer's first frame.

⑤ Click the **Onion Skin** button (▣).

⑥ Click and drag the onion skin markers to include all the frames in the motion tween.

Note: *See Chapter 8 to learn more about the onion-skinning feature.*

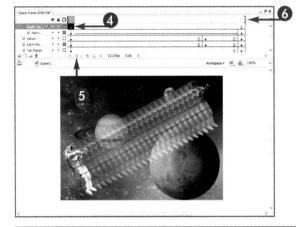

DRAW THE MOTION PATH

⑦ Click the **Pencil tool** (✐).

Note: *See Chapter 2 to learn how to draw with the Pencil tool.*

⑧ Draw a path from the center of the first motion tween symbol to the center of the last motion tween symbol.

Note: *If you do not draw your path from center to center, the symbol cannot follow the motion path.*

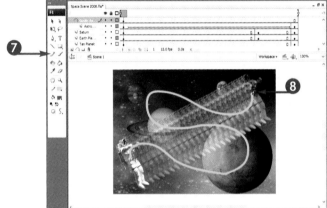

TIPS

Does it matter which line color or thickness I use to draw the motion path?

No. You can use any line color or attributes for the motion path. To make the line easy to see, consider using a thicker line style in a bright color. Be sure to set the line attributes in the Property inspector before you start drawing the path.

What drawing tools can I use to define a path?

You can use any of the following drawing tools to add a path to the motion guide layer: Pencil, Brush, Line, Oval, or Rectangle. For example, to make a symbol follow a perfect loop around the Stage, use the Oval tool to draw the motion path, creating a circular line for the path to follow.

continued

You can make your motion tween follow any type of path, even if it falls out of the movie area's boundaries. Starting and ending your path directly in the center of the symbol you are animating is very important. Do not stop your path line when you reach the edge of the object; continue it on to the middle of the object.

You must also make sure that you select the Snap option in the Property inspector. This feature sticks the symbol to the path, much like a magnet. If the Snap feature is not turned on, the symbol may not properly follow the path you have established.

Animate Symbols Along a Path *(continued)*

9 Hide the Motion Guide layer.

● You can lock the layer to keep from accidentally changing the path.

Note: See Chapter 6 to learn more about hiding and locking layers.

10 Click 🔲 to turn off the onion skin feature.

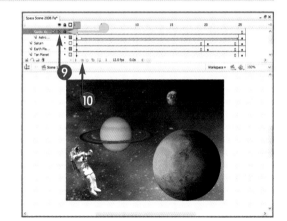

11 Select the layer containing the motion tween.

● Flash selects all the layer's frames.

12 Open the Property inspector.

You can press Ctrl + F3 (⌘ + F3) to quickly open the Property inspector.

13 Select the **Snap** option (☐ changes to ✓).

● To make the symbol orient itself to the path, select the **Orient to path** option (☐ changes to ✓).

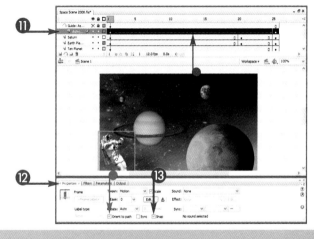

VIEW THE ANIMATION

- You can hide the Property inspector panel to view more of the Stage area.

⑭ Click in the first frame of the motion tween.

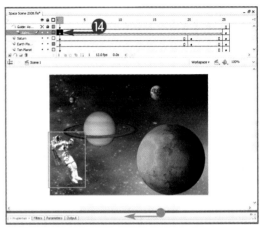

⑮ Press Enter (Return).

- Flash plays the animation sequence along the motion path.

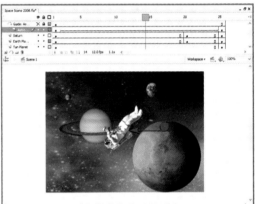

 TIPS

What does the Orient to path option do?

To make your symbol orient itself to the motion path you have drawn, select the **Orient to path** check box in the Property inspector. This option aligns the symbol to the path, regardless of which direction the path goes. Sometimes, the effect makes the symbol's movement seem unnatural. To remedy the situation, you can insert extra keyframes in the animation sequence and rotate the symbol to where you want it on the path. Flash recalculates the in-between frames for you. To learn more about rotating objects, see Chapter 3. To learn how to rotate animated symbols, see the section "Create a Spinning Tween" earlier in this chaper.

Can I rename a motion guide layer?

Yes. You can rename any layer you add to the Flash Timeline. For example, you might want to give the layer a distinct name that describes its contents or path to help you quickly see the layer's purpose. To rename a layer, simply double-click the layer name, type a new name, and press Enter (Return). To learn more about using layers in Flash, see Chapter 6.

Set Tween Speed

You can control a tweened animation's speed by using the Ease control. Found in the Property inspector panel, the Ease control enables you to speed up or slow down the tween effect.

You may have learned in some of the previous sections that you can slow down or speed up an animation sequence by subtracting or adding frames. The addition or subtraction of regular frames between two keyframes does not affect tween speed.

Set Tween Speed

1 Select the frames containing the motion tween you want to adjust.

2 Open the Property inspector.

You can press **Ctrl** + **F3** (**⌘** + **F3**) to quickly open the Property inspector.

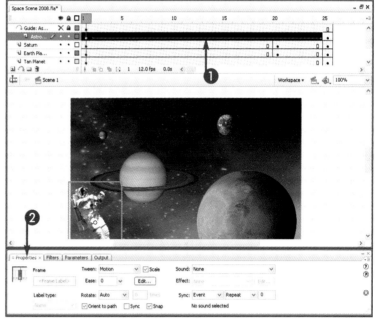

3 Click and drag the **Ease** slider (⬜) to a new setting.

Drag the slider up to accelerate the tween speed or down to decelerate the tween speed.

A zero value indicates a constant rate of speed.

Note: To test the new speed, click the first frame in the motion tween and press **Enter** (**Return**).

Adjust Symbol Opacity

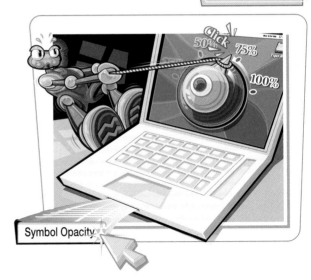

You can control the opacity of an animated symbol instance using the Alpha setting control. For example, you may want the symbol to appear to fade out at the end of a motion tween or fade in at the beginning of the animation.

You can find the Alpha setting in the Property inspector. The Alpha setting allows you to change the opacity or *alpha value* of an instance. Transparency is measured in a percentage range, with 100 percent being completely visible, or saturated, and 0 percent being completely transparent.

Symbol Opacity

Adjust Symbol Opacity

① Click the keyframe containing the symbol you want to change.

② Open the Property Inspector.

   You can press `Ctrl`+`F3` (`⌘`+`F3`) to quickly open the Property inspector.

③ Click the symbol you want to edit.

④ Click the **Color** `▾`.

⑤ Click **Alpha**.

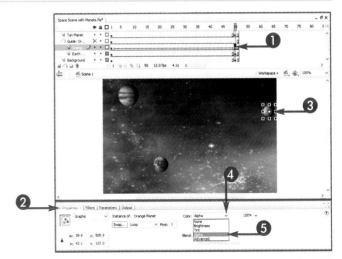

The Alpha setting option appears.

⑥ Click and drag the **Alpha** slider up or down to increase or decrease symbol opacity.

● Flash applies the changes to the symbol.

Note: *To test the new alpha setting, click the first frame in the motion tween and press* `Enter` (`Return`).

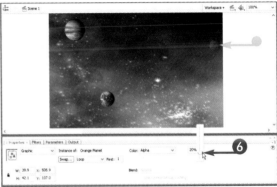

Create a Shape Tween

You can create a shape tween to morph objects in an animation. Shape tweens enable you to create dynamic animations that change from one form to an entirely different form over the course of several frames. For example, you can morph a circle shape into a square or turn your company logo into a graphic depicting a product.

Unlike other animations you create in Flash, shape tweening does not require the use of symbols or groups. You can animate any object you draw with the Drawing tools using the shape tween effect.

Create a Shape Tween

CREATE THE TWEEN EFFECT

1 Select the frame in which you want to start a shape tween.

2 Draw the object you want to animate in Frame 1.

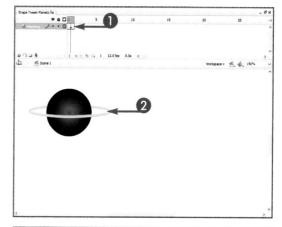

3 Click the frame in which you want to end the shape tween effect.

4 Insert a blank keyframe.

You can press F7 to quickly insert a blank keyframe.

Note: *See Chapter 8 to learn how to use Flash frames.*

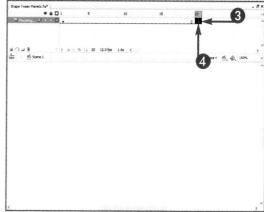

⑤ Draw the shape into which you want your image to morph, such as a variation of the first frame's shape or an entirely different shape.

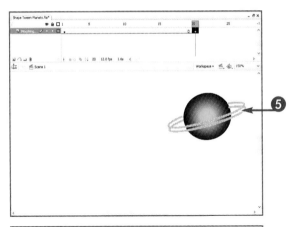

⑥ Click a single frame in the middle of the tween sequence, or select all the frames that make up your shape tween.

Note: See Chapter 8 to learn how to select frames.

⑦ Open the Property inspector.

You can press `Ctrl`+`F3` (`⌘`+`F3`) to open the Property inspector.

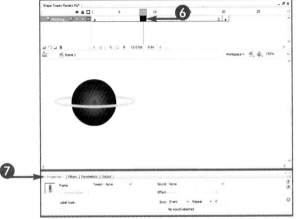

 TIPS

How is a shape tween different from a motion tween?

With a motion tween, you can animate only symbols, grouped objects, or text blocks. With a shape tween, you can animate any object you draw on the Stage. You do not have to save it as a symbol first or group it in order for Flash to create in-between frames. You cannot shape tween a symbol or group. Although a motion tween is good for moving objects from one point to another, you should use a shape tween when you want to morph the object into another object entirely.

Can I change the shape tween color or transparency?

Yes. You can use the Color tool on the Tools panel or in the Property inspector to make changes to the shape's color. You can also adjust the opacity using the Alpha setting. Display the color palette and click and drag the **Alpha** slider (⬜) at the top of the palette to change the opacity of the stroke or fill. To learn more about using the color tools in Flash, see Chapters 2 and 3.

continued

You can use as many shape tweens as you want in an animation, and you can start one right after the other in the Timeline. For best results, tween one shape at a time in your Flash movie. Doing so gives you greater control over the object and the tween effect.

The Property inspector offers two types of blends: Distributive or Angular. If you apply a Distributive blend, Flash smoothes out the straight lines and sharp corners as your shape morphs. If you choose an Angular blend, Flash keeps all the sharp angles and lines intact during the tween.

Create a Shape Tween *(continued)*

MORPH THE SHAPE

⑧ Click the **Tween** ☑ to view tweening types.

⑨ Click **Shape**.

Flash shades the selected frames green in the Timeline and adds a tween arrow from the first keyframe to the last.

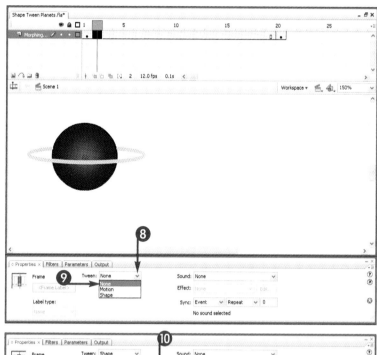

⑩ Click the **Blend** ☑ to view blend types.

⑪ Click a blend type.

You can use the Distributive blend to smooth out lines in the in-between frames.

You can use the Angular blend to keep the sharp corners and straight lines that occur during the morph effect.

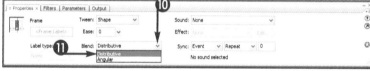

VIEW THE ANIMATION

● You can click the Property inspector title bar to hide the panel and view more of the Stage.

⑫ To view a shape tween in action, click the first frame of the shape tween.

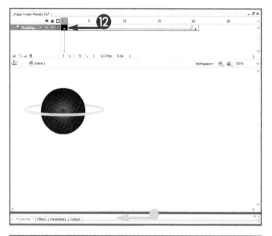

⑬ Press **Enter** (**Return**).

● Flash plays the animation sequence.

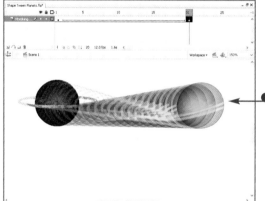

Can I use a symbol from my movie's Library?

Yes, but you must convert it first. You cannot shape tween symbols, but you can take a symbol and break it apart into objects that the shape tween effect can morph. To turn a symbol into an object, add the symbol to the Stage, then click **Modify**, **Break Apart**. Depending on how many groups of objects comprise the symbol, you may need to select the command several times to reach the last level of ungrouped objects.

What kind of changes can I apply to shape tweens?

You can use shape tweens to change the appearance of an object you draw, including color, size, shape, position, and more. The only change you cannot perform on a shape tween object is to make it follow a motion path or rotate a specified number of times.

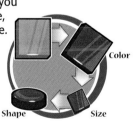

Using Shape Hints

You can have more control over the morphing process during a shape tween by using shape hints. A shape hint is a marker that identifies areas on the original shape that match up with areas on the final shape and mark crucial points of change. Shape hints are labeled *a* through *z*, and you can use up to 26 shape hints in a shape tween.

Use shape hints when you are morphing a particularly complex shape. By assigning shape hints to the object you are morphing, you can help Flash figure out points of change.

① Create a shape tween animation.

Note: See the section "Create a Shape Tween" earlier in this chapter for details.

② Click the keyframe containing the original shape you want to morph.

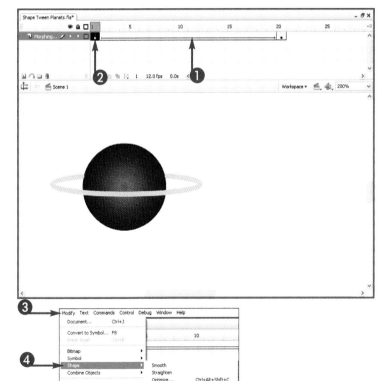

③ Click **Modify**.

④ Click **Shape**.

⑤ Click **Add Shape Hint**.

● Flash adds a shape hint labeled with the letter *a* to the center of the shape.

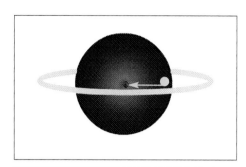

⑥ Click the **Selection** tool (🔖).

⑦ Click and drag the shape hint to a crucial edge of the object Flash may need help with transforming.

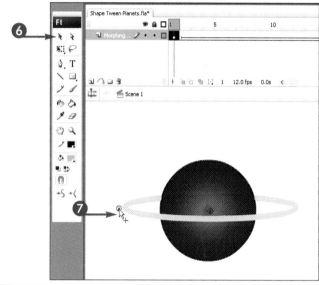

TIPS

What can I do if my shape hints vary their positions between the first keyframe and the last?

Seeing exactly where you place shape hints around an object is not always easy. To help you, make sure you have magnified your view so that you can see where you place the hints. Use the **Magnification** (☑) in the upper-right corner of the Timeline to set a magnification. Next, turn on the onion skin feature and move the onion skin markers to show all the frames within the shape tween. Click the **Onion Skin Outlines** button (🔲) to turn on the outlining feature. See Chapter 8 to learn more about onion skinning.

Can I place shape hints randomly on the object?

No. Shape hints work best when they are in order, allowing the Flash feature to analyze the difficult points on the object. Be sure to place the hints in alphabetical order around the object. You can place hints in a clockwise or counterclockwise pattern.

continued

The more shape hints you add to the shape tween, the smoother the morphing transformation will be. When determining where to place your shape hints, position them at key areas of change around the edges of the shape.

Make sure the shape hints you place around the object in the second keyframe correspond with the same order of shape hints on the object in the first keyframe.

Using Shape Hints *(continued)*

⑧ Repeat Steps **3** to **7** to continue adding shape hints to other areas on the shape that can assist Flash with morphing the final shape design.

Note: *For best results, arrange shape hints around the shape's edge in alphabetical order going clockwise or counterclockwise.*

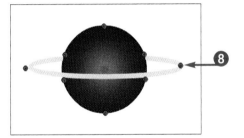

⑨ Click the last keyframe in the shape tween.

● In this example, shape hints have been added to the final shape and stacked in the middle of the shape.

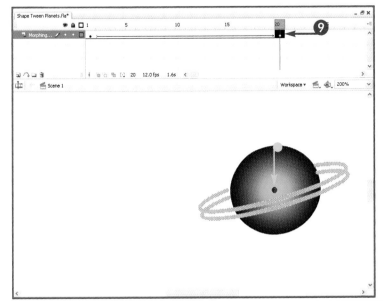

10 Click and drag each shape hint to the correct position around the final shape.

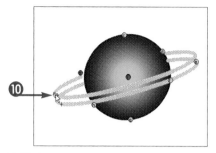

You can adjust the shape hints in the final frame as needed.

● Clicking the **Onion Skin** button (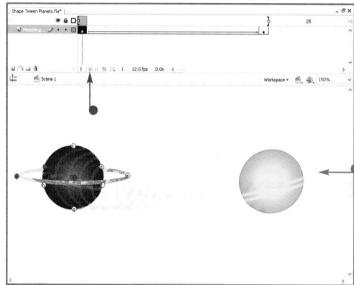) lets you see how the in-between frames morph the shape as directed by the shape hints.

● To view the animation, click the first keyframe and press Enter (Return).

TIPS

How do I remove a shape hint?

To delete a shape hint, click and drag the shape hint completely off the Stage area. To rid the keyframe of all the shape hints, click **Modify, Shape**, and then **Remove All Hints**.

Is there a quicker way to add shape hints?

Yes. Press and hold Ctrl + Shift (⌘ + Return) while pressing H on the keyboard. This adds a shape hint to the Stage.

Using Reverse Frames

You can reverse the order of your animation sequence with the Reverse Frames feature. The feature literally reverses the order of frames in your movie. For example, if you create a motion tween that makes a symbol grow in size, you can reverse the frame sequence to create the opposite effect in the second half of the animation.

The Reverse Frames feature allows you to save time creating an animation by reusing frames in your movie. This saves you from having to create another animation sequence for the backward effect.

Using Reverse Frames

① Select all the frames included in the animation sequence for which you want to create a reverse effect.

Note: Be sure to include the end keyframe in your selection. See Chapter 8 to learn more about selecting frames.

② Click **Edit**.

③ Click **Timeline**.

④ Click **Copy Frames**.

⑤ Click the frame where you want to insert the copied frames.

⑥ Click **Edit**.

⑦ Click **Timeline**.

⑧ Click **Paste Frames**.

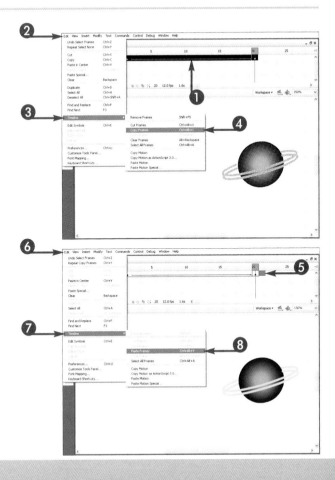

9 Select the newly copied frames.

If you have trouble selecting the copied frames, press and hold `Shift` + `Ctrl` while clicking the frames.

10 Click **Modify**.

11 Click **Timeline**.

12 Click **Reverse Frames**.

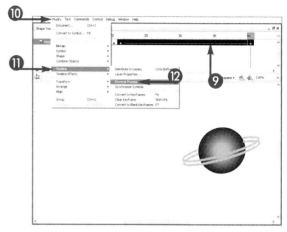

● Flash reverses the tween effect.

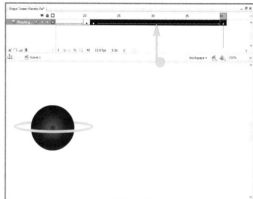

How else can I activate the Reverse Frames command?

Right-click the frames and a pop-up menu appears with frame-related commands, including the Reverse Frames, Copy Frames, and Paste Frames commands.

Insert Frame
Remove Frames
Cut Frames
Copy Frames
Paste Frames
Clear Frames
Select All Frames
Reverse Frames

How do I undo a reverse?

You can immediately undo the Reverse Frames command if you click **Edit** and then **Undo**. Make sure you do this immediately after you realize you are not happy with the animation results.

You can use mask layers to hide various elements on underlying layers in your Flash movies. In addition, you can animate a mask layer using any of the Flash animation techniques, such as a motion path or shape tween.

For example, you might draw an oval fill shape that acts as a peephole to the layer below the mask, and animate the peephole to move around the movie. The "hole" lets you see anything directly beneath, but the remainder of the mask layer hides anything that lies out of view of the "hole."

Animate a Mask

1 Click the mask layer you want to animate.

Note: See Chapter 6 to learn how to create a mask layer.

2 Click the lock icon (🔒) to unlock the mask layer.

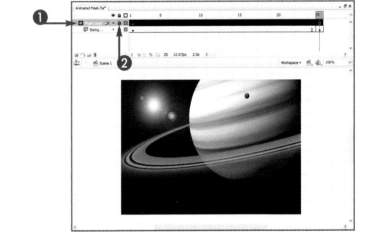

3 Apply a motion or shape tween to the mask.

If the mask object is a graphic symbol, you can apply a motion tween.

If the mask object is a fill shape, you can apply a shape tween.

Note: See the section "Create a Motion Tween" or "Create a Shape Tween" to learn how to create an animation sequence.

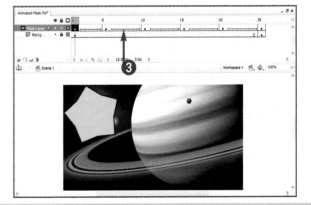

④ Click ⦿ to lock the mask layer.

⑤ Click ⦿ to lock the layer below the mask.

Note: See Chapter 6 to learn how to unlock layers.

Flash masks the underlying layer.

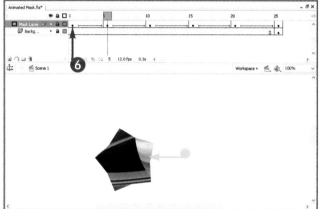

VIEW THE ANIMATION

⑥ To view the animated mask, click the first frame of the sequence.

⑦ Press Enter (Return).

● Flash plays the animation sequence.

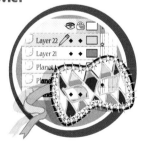

TIPS

Flash will not let me create a motion tween in my mask layer. Why not?

You can only assign a motion tween to a mask that you create from a symbol, instance, or object group. You cannot use more than one symbol as a mask. You must assign a shape tween to a fill shape. Check and make sure you know what type of object you are using as a mask and then assign the appropriate motion tween type.

Can I use the mask to mask out other layers in my movie?

Yes. Any layers placed directly under the mask layer, between the original linked layer and the mask layer, are also masked.

Distribute Objects to Layers

You can use the Distribute to Layers command to quickly distribute objects to different layers in your movie and then animate each object separately. For example, you might use this technique to animate individual letters in a company logo or animate a group of graphic objects with individual motion tweens.

The Distribute to Layers command can help you create a variety of layered animation effects. Used in conjunction with the Break Apart command, you can create individual pieces of a whole and animate them separately.

Distribute Objects to Layers

① Click the **Selection** tool (⬚).

② Click the object you want to break apart into separate layers.

③ Click **Modify**.

④ Click **Break Apart**.

Flash breaks apart the object.

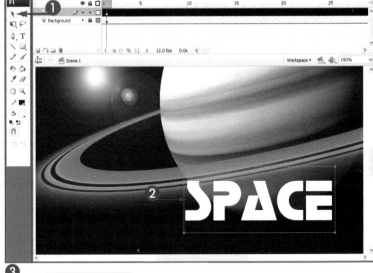

5 Click **Modify**.

6 Click **Timeline**.

7 Click **Distribute to Layers**.

Note: You must select all objects you want to distribute to layers before applying the command. If you clicked elsewhere on the Stage after using the Break Apart command, you must select all the objects again.

Flash distributes each object to a separate layer.

● In this example, Flash places each letter on a layer and names the layer accordingly.

You can now animate each object separately from the rest.

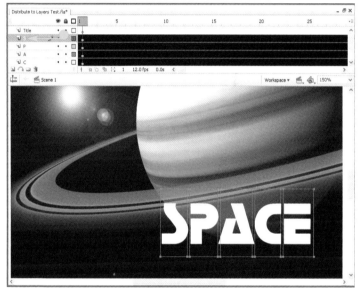

 TIPS

How do I tell which object is on which layer?

Use the Show All Layers As Outlines column for each layer to help you color coordinate what object is on what layer. Click the layer you want to identify, then click ☐ under the Outline column. Flash changes ☐ to ☐ and highlights the object in the designated color. See Chapter 6 to learn more about using layers.

Can I use a shortcut to distribute objects to layers?

Yes. If distributing characters from a text box to layers, you can right-click the text box and click **Break Apart**, then right-click again and click **Distribute to Layers**.

CHAPTER 10

Adding Special Effects

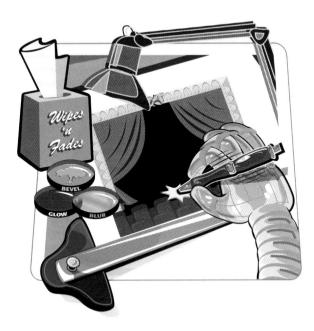

You can add special effects to your Flash movies to add more visual interest and polish to the presentation. This chapter shows you how to tap into several of the built-in special effects features Flash offers.

You can use filters in your Flash movies to add visual effects and alter the appearance of your movie. For example, you might add a blur to an animated graphic that moves across the screen. You can add filters to text, movie clips, and buttons. You can also use motion tweening to animate a filter. You can use the Filters panel in the Property inspector to add and manage filters you assign. You can assign multiple filters to create unique looks for your movie objects.

The more filters you apply to a Flash file, the more they can affect the performance of your movie in the Flash Player. For best results, keep filters to a minimum, and use the filter's controls to adjust the quality and strength of the filter. Lower settings can improve the playback performance on slower computer systems.

Apply a Filter

ADD A FILTER

1 Click the element to which you want to add a filter.

You can add filters to text objects, movie clips, or buttons.

2 Display the Property inspector.

You can press Ctrl + F3 to quickly open the Property inspector.

Note: *To use filters, the Publish settings must target Flash Player 8 or later. Click File, Publish Settings, and click the Flash tab to change the player Version setting.*

3 Click the **Filters** tab.

4 Click the **Add Filter** button (⊞).

5 Click a filter.

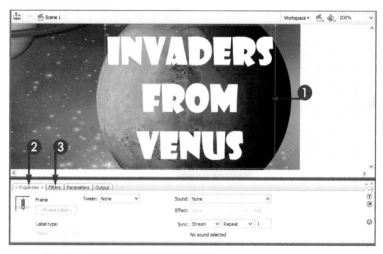

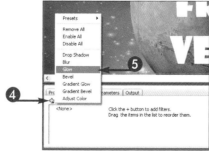

● Flash assigns the filter to the object.

⑥ Depending on the filter you select, make adjustments to the settings until the filter appears to your specifications.

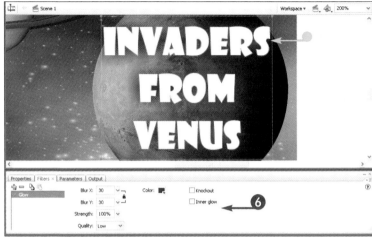

REMOVE A FILTER

① On the Filters tab, click the filter you want to remove.

② Click the **Remove Filter** button (□).

Flash removes the filter.

TIPS

Can I save a filter I have modified to reuse it again later?

Yes. You can store edited filters as presets in Flash and reuse them in your project. First, create and edit a filter just the way you want it, then click the **Add Filter** button (□), click **Presets**, then click **Save As**. The Save Preset As dialog box appears. Type a name for the filter and click **OK**. The next time you want to use it, click □, click **Presets**, and click the name of the filter.

Can I copy a filter to another object in the movie?

Yes. You can use the Copy Filter button in the Filters panel to copy a selected filter to another object. First, select the object containing the filter you want to copy, then click the **Copy Filters** button (□) and click **Copy Selected**. Next, click the object you to which you want to apply the filter and click the **Paste Filters** button (□). Flash pastes the filter.

Apply a Blend Mode

You can use a blend mode to create a composite image in your Flash movie. When you create a composite, you modify the transparency or color interaction of two or more overlapping movie clips. For example, you might place a nearly transparent movie clip over another to create a new visual effect. With more than a dozen blend modes to try, you can create a variety of unique looks for your project.

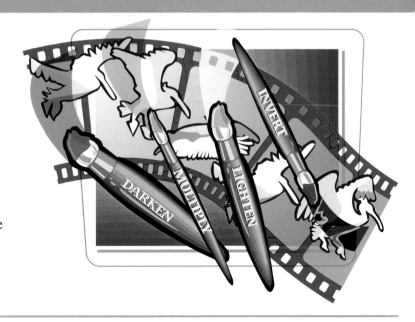

Apply a Blend Mode

APPLY A BLEND MODE

1 Click the movie clip you want to modify with a blend mode.

2 Display the Property inspector.

You can press Ctrl + F3 to quickly open the Property inspector.

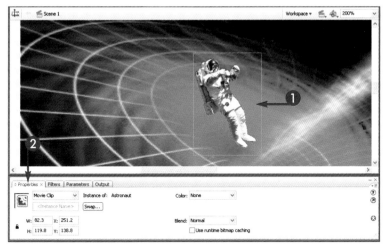

3 Click the **Blend** ▾.

4 Click a blend mode.

Flash immediately applies the effect to the clip.

● In this example, the Difference blend mode is applied.

REMOVE A BLEND MODE

1 Select the clip containing the blend mode.

2 In the Property inspector, click the **Blend** ▾.

3 Click **Normal**.

Flash removes the blend mode.

What can I do with the various blend modes?

With more than a dozen blend modes, it is not always easy to tell what each one does. The following table explains several popular blend modes you can apply.

Blend Mode	Effect
Darken	Compares background and foreground colors and keeps the darker effect
Multiply	Multiplies the base color by the blend color
Lighten	Compares background and foreground colors and keeps the lighter effect
Screen	The blend color is multiplied by the base color and inverted
Overlay	Multiplies the colors based on the base color
Hard Light	Creates the illusion of a spotlight
Invert	Inverts the base color
Alpha	Converts the blend color's alpha transparency value, turning the blend area transparent
Erase	Erases the base color pixels and background image

Assign Timeline Effects

You can use the Flash Timeline effects to add quick and easy animations to objects in your document. For example, you can add a drop shadow or a blur to a graphic object or shape in your movie. Depending on the effect you assign, Flash opens a dialog box offering a variety of settings you can adjust to create just the right effect.

After you create the effect, Flash adds a layer to the Timeline containing the necessary frames to animate the effect. If you need to fine-tune the effect later, you can revisit the effect's dialog box and modify the settings.

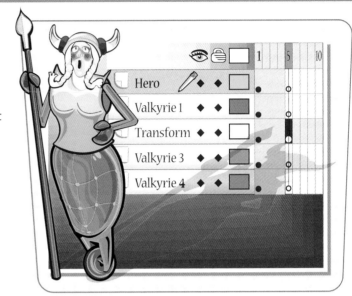

ASSIGN AN EFFECT

① Right-click the object you want to edit.

② Click **Timeline Effects**.

③ Click **Effects**.

④ Click an effect.

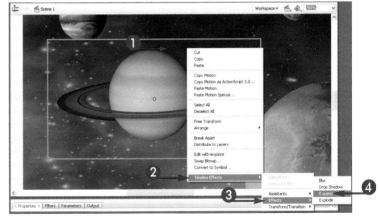

Flash opens the effect's dialog box.

⑤ Edit the settings as needed.

In this example, you can adjust the Explode effect's settings to control the duration, direction, size, rotation, and transparency of the effect.

● Click here to update the preview of the modified settings.

⑥ When finished, click **OK**.

Flash assigns the effect and adds the effect's layer to the main Timeline.

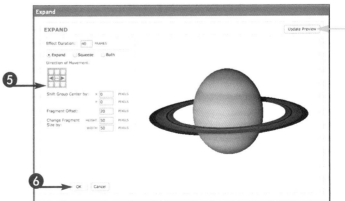

EDIT AN EFFECT

① Right-click the object to which you assigned the effect.

② Click **Timeline Effects**.

③ Click **Edit Effect**.

You can also click the **Modify** menu and click **Timeline Effects**, **Edit Effect**.

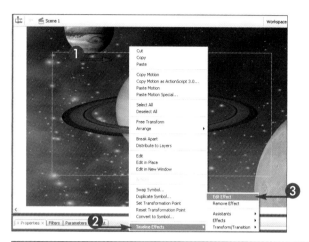

The effect's dialog box appears.

④ Edit the settings as needed.

⑤ Click **OK**.

Flash applies the changes.

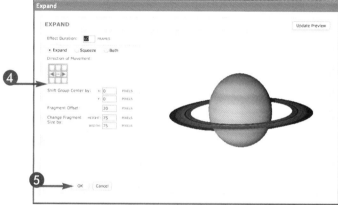

TIPS

How do I remove a timeline effect I no longer want?

To delete an effect, select the object to which the effect is assigned. Next, click the **Modify** menu and click **Timeline Effects**, **Remove Effect**. Flash deletes the effect and the frames associated with the effect. The effect's layer remains in the main Timeline. You can permanently delete the unneeded layer by selecting the layer, and then clicking the **Delete Layer** button (🗑).

What other effects can I create to animate objects?

Flash groups Timeline Effects into three categories: Assistants, Effects, and Tranform/Transition. The Assistants category includes two effects for duplicating an object in a series of rows and columns or carefully spacing duplicates across the Stage. The Effects category includes four effects for animating an object over time. The Transforms/ Transitions category includes effects for creating transitions, wipes, and fades. See the remaining sections in this chapter to learn how to use the transform and transition effects.

Create a Transform Effect

You can add an instant animation effect to an object using the Transform dialog box. For example, you might make an object change transparency over the course of several frames, or transform in color and position as it spins across the screen. Depending on the effect you assign, an effect dialog box opens with settings for controlling position, scale, rotation, spinning, color, transparency, motion ease, and duration of the effect.

You can experiment with all or some of the settings and preview the effect before assigning it to the object on the Stage. Once you apply the transform, Flash adds a layer to the Timeline to create the animation.

Create a Transform Effect

① Right-click the object you want to edit.

② Click **Timeline Effects**.

③ Click **Transform/Transition**.

④ Click **Transform**.

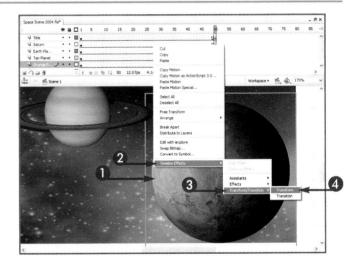

The Transform dialog box appears.

⑤ Edit the settings as needed.

○ Set the duration of the animation here.

● Use these settings to control how much the object moves its position.

● The **Scale** control allows you to change the object's size.

○ You can make the object rotate or spin using these options.

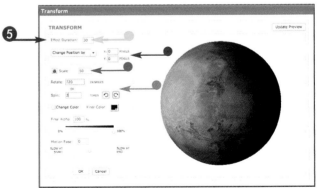

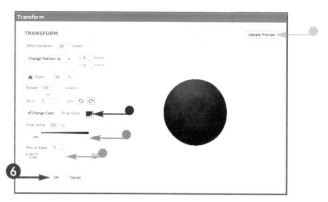

- To make the object change color, click the Change Color control and click here to select a color.

- Click and drag this slider (⬚) to change transparency.

- Click and drag this slider to change motion acceleration.

- You can click here to preview the settings before applying them to the selected object.

6 Click **OK**.

- Flash applies the animation effect and adds a layer to the Timeline.

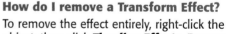
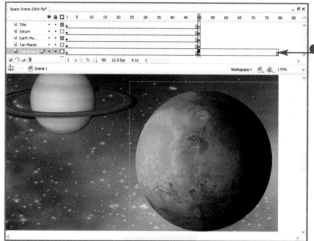

TIPS

How do I make an object fade in for the transform effect?

You can use the alpha value to change the object's transparency setting, thus making it appear to fade in or out. Set the alpha value to zero before applying the Transform Effect command. To do so, select the object and click the Color (▣) on the Tools panel or in the Property inspector. Type a **0** value in the Alpha field. Now you can apply the Transform Effect command and create a fade-in effect.

How do I remove a Transform Effect?

To remove the effect entirely, right-click the object, then click **Timeline Effects**, **Remove Effect**. Flash deletes the animation frames, but leaves the layer created by the effect. To remove the layer, click it and click the **Delete Layer** button (🗑). To edit the effect instead of deleting it, right-click and click **Timeline Effects**, **Edit Effect**.

You can use transition effects to control how one object transitions to another in a movie. Transition effects are just a few of the prebuilt animation techniques you can use to save time and effort. Much like the animated transitions available in Microsoft PowerPoint, you can use Flash transitions to create fades and wipes. You can control the direction of the effect, the duration of the transition, and motion ease.

When you apply a transition, Flash creates a layer in the Timeline specifically for the special effect.

Apply a Transition Effect

① Right-click the object you want to edit.

② Click **Timeline Effects**.

③ Click **Transform/Transition**.

④ Click **Transition**.

The Transition dialog box appears.

⑤ Edit the settings as needed.

● Set the duration of the animation here.

● Use these settings to control the direction of the effect (○ changes to ◉).

● You can choose a fade or a wipe effect, or both (☐ changes to ☑).

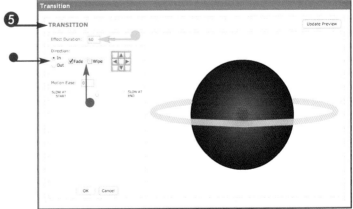

● Click and drag ☐ to change motion acceleration.

   A negative value makes the animation start slowly and end fast, while a positive value does the opposite.

● You can click **Update Preview** to preview the settings before applying them to the selected object.

6 Click **OK**.

● Flash applies the animation effect and adds a layer to the Timeline.

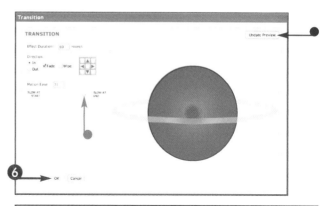

TIPS

Can I edit a transition effect manually?

Yes. However, if you make edits directly to the frames and object in the transition effect layer, you can no longer edit the effect using the Transition dialog box. Flash keeps a copy of the effect in the Library panel. To edit a transition using the original settings, right-click the object, click **Timeline Effects**, **Edit Effect**. This reopens the Transition dialog box, where you can make modifications to the animation.

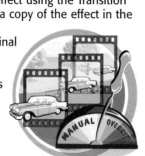

Can I reuse the same transition effect throughout my project?

When you create an effect, Flash places a copy of the effect in the Library panel. You can reuse the effect by placing it on a new layer in the Timeline. If you attempt to make changes to any unused frames in the original transition effect's layer, Flash no longer lets you edit the effect using the Transition dialog box.

Creating Buttons

You can add quick and easy interaction to your Flash movies and projects using buttons. Buttons allow users to activate actions for controlling a movie. This chapter shows you how to add your own interactive buttons and make them stand out with animation effects.

Introduction to Flash Buttons

A popular way to enable users to interact with your Flash movies is through the use of *rollover buttons.* You might create a simple button that changes in appearance when the user rolls the mouse pointer over it, and changes appearance again when the user clicks it. Buttons are commonly employed on Web pages, but you can also use them in other Flash projects you create. You can create buttons in Flash that are static or animated.

Buttons Are Symbols

Buttons are a type of symbol to which Flash assigns *behaviors.* The behaviors are based on what happens when the mouse pointer interacts with the button. You can assign Flash actions to a button that trigger an action or behavior. You can turn any symbol you create in Flash into a button symbol or you can create a new button from scratch.

Button Frames

When you create a button in Flash, it comes with its own Timeline and four distinct frames: Up, Over, Down, and Hit. The four frames make up a mini-movie clip of the button's behavior. A button's timeline does not actually play like other Flash timelines, but rather jumps to the appropriate frame directed by the user's mouse action.

Up Frame

The Up frame is used to display what the inactive button looks like. This is the frame the user sees when the mouse pointer is not hovering over the button. By default, the Up frame has an added keyframe.

Over Frame

The Over frame displays what the button looks like when the mouse pointer moves, or "rolls" over the button. For example, you might make the button turn bright red or emit a sound when the user pauses the mouse pointer over it, thereby alerting the user that the button is active.

Down Frame

The Down frame displays what the button looks like when a user clicks the button. You can use the Down frame to make a button change color or appearance to indicate the user has clicked the button.

Hit Frame

The Hit frame defines the button area or boundary as a whole. This frame is often the same size and shape as the image in the Over and Down frames. The Hit frame differs from the other button frames in that the user never actually sees it.

Create a Button Symbol

You can create button symbols to add interactivity to your Flash movies. Buttons allow users to interact with movies by clicking to start or top an action. You can create new buttons or turn any symbol into a button.

When you create a button, it includes a Timeline with four frames: Up, Over, Down, and Hit. You must assign an image or action to each of the four button states. You can make the image the same in each frame, or you can vary it to create the illusion of movement.

Create a Button Symbol

CREATE A NEW SYMBOL

① Click **Insert**.

② Click **New Symbol**.

Note: *You can also press* `Ctrl` + `F8` *to create a new symbol.*

The Create New Symbol dialog box appears.

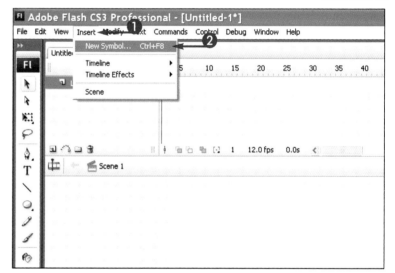

③ Type a name for the new button.

④ Select a button behavior type (○ changes to ◉).

Note: *Depending on how you last used the Create New Symbol dialog box, the Advanced options may appear, offering additional linkage settings and source controls.*

⑤ Click **OK**.

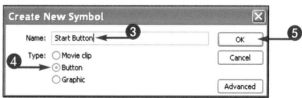

CREATE THE UP STATE

● The button's Timeline opens in Symbol Edit mode with four frames. You can now create each frame's button state.

● By default, Flash selects the Up frame and inserts a keyframe.

6 Create or place the object you want to use as a button on the Stage.

Note: See Chapter 2 to learn more about using the Flash drawing tools. See Chapter 4 to learn how to import graphics.

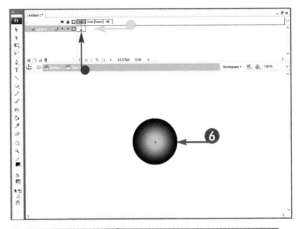

CREATE THE OVER STATE

7 Click the **Over** frame.

8 Insert a keyframe into the frame.

You can right-click the frame and click **Insert Keyframe** or press [F6] to insert a keyframe.

Note: See Chapter 8 to learn more about frames.

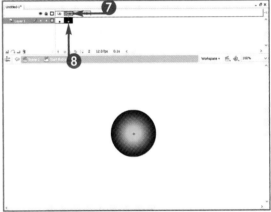

 TIPS

Can I use a button from another file?

Yes. If you have stored a button symbol in another Flash file, you can open the other file's Library and place an instance of the symbol on the Stage. Click **File**, **Import**, and then **Open External Library**. From the Open As Library dialog box that appears, double-click the file you want to access and the associated Library panel opens on-screen. You can then use any button symbol you have stored in the Library.

Does Flash have premade buttons I can use?

Yes. Flash has a library of premade buttons you can choose from. To display the Buttons library, click **Window**, **Common Libraries**, and then **Buttons**. Double-click a folder name to see a list of button types. You can preview a button by clicking its name. You can use a button from the library simply by clicking and dragging it off the Library panel onto the Stage.

continued

When deciding what you want your button to look like, consider your audience. Is it technologically savvy enough to recognize the image you use as a button on-screen, or do you need to keep the button simple and easy to understand? Although it is sometimes tempting to use detailed drawings as buttons, simple geometric shapes are always reliable for a general audience.

Create a Button Symbol *(continued)*

● Flash duplicates the object from the Up keyframe.

  You can make changes to the object, if needed.

● In this example, a text box is added to describe the button.

Note: *See Chapter 3 to learn more about editing objects and Chapter 5 to learn about adding text.*

CREATE THE DOWN STATE

9 Click the **Down** frame.

10 Insert a keyframe into the frame.

  You can right-click the frame and click **Insert Keyframe** to insert a keyframe.

● Flash duplicates the object from the Over keyframe.

  You can edit the object, if needed, such as adding a sound to the frame or a short animation.

Note: *See Chapters 8 and 9 to learn how to create animations. See Chapter 13 to learn how to add sound.*

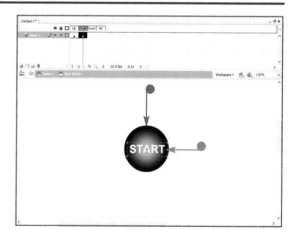

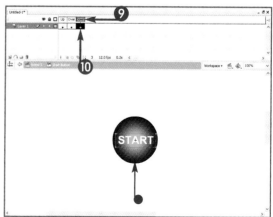

CREATE THE HIT STATE

⑪ Click the **Hit** frame.

⑫ Insert a keyframe into the frame.

You can right-click the frame and click **Insert Keyframe** to insert a keyframe.

● Flash inserts a keyframe that duplicates the Down frame object.

Users cannot see the object contained in the Hit frame.

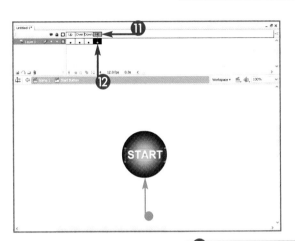

PLACE THE BUTTON ON THE STAGE

⑬ Click the scene name to return to Movie Edit mode.

⑭ Open the Library.

You can press Ctrl + L (⌘ + L) to open the panel.

⑮ Click and drag the button from the Library to the Stage.

● The newly created button appears on the Stage.

To test the button, you can click **Control**, **Enable Simple Buttons**, and interact with the button.

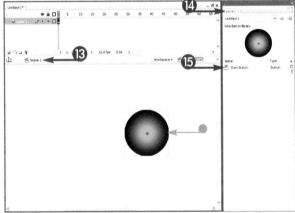

TIPS

What edit mode am I in?

Flash switches you from Movie Edit mode to Symbol Edit mode when you create a button. You can always tell when you are in Symbol Edit mode if you see the name of the symbol to the right of the scene name at the top of the Stage. To exit Symbol Edit mode, click the scene name. You can also exit by pressing Ctrl + E (⌘ + E).

How do I preview a button?

By default, Flash buttons are disabled so you can easily work with them. You can quickly enable them any time you want to test a button. In Symbol Edit mode, click the button's Up frame, and then press Enter. Watch the Stage as Flash plays through the four button frames. Any changes made to frames appear during playback.

You can preview the button in Movie Edit mode by pressing Ctrl + Alt + B and moving the mouse pointer over the button and clicking it to see the rollover capabilities.

Create Shape-Changing Buttons

You can create shape-changing buttons in your Flash movies for added graphical impact. Buttons are a great way to add interactivity to your Flash movies, and shape-changing buttons can make an ordinary button much more dynamic.

Creating a shape-changing button requires four different shapes. The Up, Over, and Down frames can each have a different shape, but the Hit frame requires a shape that encompasses all three of the other shapes. Although a user does not view the Hit frame, it defines a button's size.

Create Shape-Changing Buttons

CREATE A NEW BUTTON

① Start a new button symbol.

Note: See the section "Create a Button Symbol" to create a new symbol.

● Flash switches to Symbol Edit mode, and the button's name appears at the top of the Stage.

● Flash selects the Up frame by default when you switch to Symbol Edit mode.

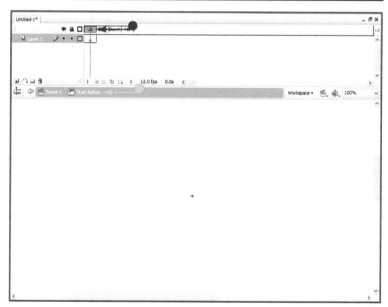

② Click the **Over** frame.

③ Click **Insert**.

④ Click **Timeline**.

⑤ Click **Blank Keyframe**.

You can also right-click the frame and click **Insert Blank Keyframe** or press [F7] to insert a blank keyframe.

Flash inserts a blank keyframe.

⑥ Repeat Steps **3** -**5** to add blank keyframes to the Down and Hit frames.

CREATE THE UP STATE

⑦ Click the **Up** frame to select it.

⑧ Create a new object or place an existing object on the Stage.

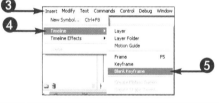

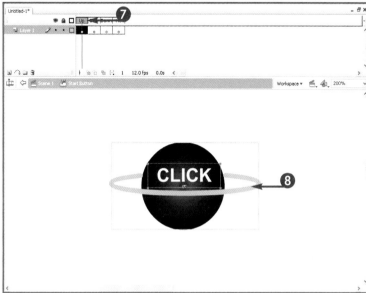

Can I use layers in my button composition?

Yes. The button's timeline works just like the main Timeline in Movie Edit mode. You can add layers to organize various objects. If your button includes a text block, you may want to place it on another layer, or if your button uses a sound, place the clip on a separate layer. See Chapter 6 to learn about layers.

Can I create an invisible button?

Yes. If you create a button with content only on the Hit frame and no content on the other three frames, you can create an invsible button. For example, if you want users to click the screen at the end of a movie, you can make the Hit frame the same size as the Stage and the user can click anywhere in the screen to activate the button.

continued

If a button's image stays the same for all four frames in the button's timeline, users cannot distinguish between its active and inactive states. Changing the button's image for each state gives users some idea of the button's status. They can see a difference when the mouse pointer hovers over a live button or when they click the button.

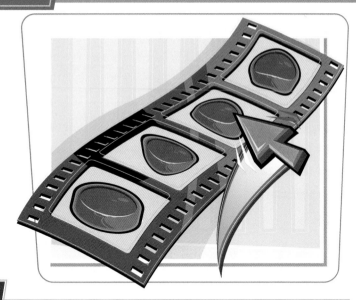

Create Shape-Changing Buttons *(continued)*

CREATE THE OVER STATE

⑨ Click the **Over** frame to select it.

⑩ Create a new object or place an existing object on the Stage to use as the active button state.

The object must differ from the object placed in the Up frame.

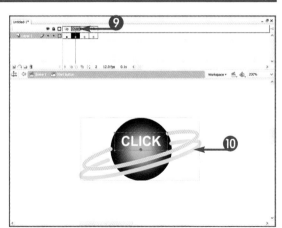

CREATE THE DOWN STATE

⑪ Click the **Down** frame to select it.

⑫ Create another new object or place an existing object on the Stage.

Make this object differ from the other two objects used in the previous frames.

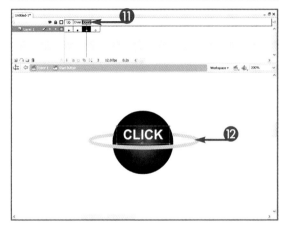

CREATE THE HIT STATE

⑬ Click the **Hit** frame.

⑭ Draw a filled shape large enough to encompass the largest object size used in your button frames.

Note: *If you do not define the Hit frame area properly, the user cannot interact with the button. Users cannot see the Hit frame's contents, but it is essential to the button's operation.*

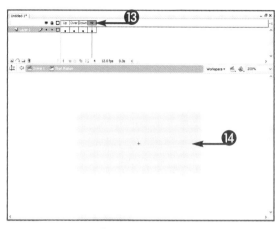

PREVIEW THE BUTTON

⑮ Click the **Up** frame to select it.

⑯ Press `Enter` (`Return`).

● On the Stage, Flash plays through the four button frames and you can see the changing button states.

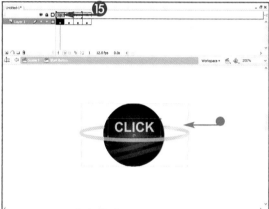

Why do I need to draw a shape in the Hit frame?

Although the Hit frame is invisible to the user, it defines the active area of the button. You must make the object you draw big enough to encompass the largest object in the other button frames. If you do not, a user may click an area of the button that does not activate. If you have trouble guessing how large of an area to define, click the **Onion Skin** icon (⊡) to see outlines of the shapes on all the other frames. Click ⊡ again to turn the feature off.

How do I make changes to a button?

Double-click the button symbol to return to Symbol Edit mode and make changes to the objects in each button timeline frame. For example, you may decide to use a different shape in your shape-changing button. After modifying your button, remember to check the Hit frame to make sure the defining shape size encompasses any new shapes in the other frames.

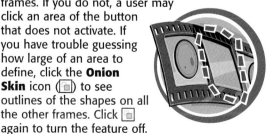

Add Animation to a Button

You can create animation effects for buttons, such as making a button seem to glow when the mouse pointer hovers over it. Spinning, jumping, and flashing buttons are all good examples of animation effects you can apply to help draw the user's attention to interactive buttons.

You can animate buttons by adding movie clips to your button frames. You must first create or import a movie clip and then assign it to a button state. Movie clips utilize their own timelines and play at their own pace. The button remains animated as long as the clip plays.

Add Animation to a Button

INSERT A MOVIE CLIP

1 Click ⬚.

2 Double-click the button to which you want to add an animation.

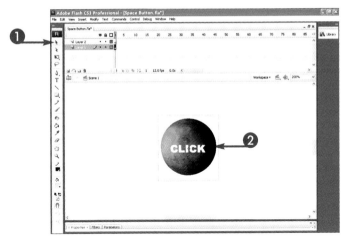

Flash switches you to Symbol Edit mode.

● The button's name appears above the Stage.

Note: See the section "Create a Button Symbol" to learn how to create a button.

3 Click the frame to which you want to add an animation, such as the Up, Over, or Down frame.

Note: The Hit frame is not seen by the user, so it is not useful to animate this frame.

④ Open the Library panel

You can press **Ctrl**+**L** (**⌘**+**L**) to open the Library.

⑤ Click the movie clip that you want to insert.

Note: See Chapters 8 and 9 to learn how to create animations and movie clips in Flash.

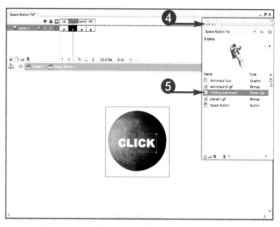

⑥ Drag the movie clip from the Library and place it on the Stage where the button appears.

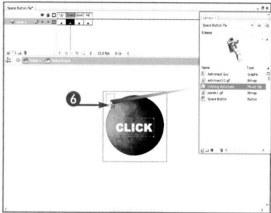

Should I add my movie clip to another layer in my button timeline?

You can utilize as many layers and layer folders as you need with a button to keep the various elements organized, including movie clips you add to the button. To learn more about timeline layers, see Chapter 6.

Is there a limit to the length of a button animation?

No. However, remember that the purpose of your button is for user interaction. When you add a long animation sequence to a button state, you keep the user waiting to complete the action. It is a good idea to keep animation sequences short when applying them to buttons.

continued

You can add an animation to any button state. For example, you might want the user to see a spinning animation when the button is inactive, or you might want the object to spin only when the user rolls over the button with the mouse. The only frame you do not want to animate is the Hit frame because its contents are not visible to the user.

Add Animation to a Button *(continued)*

● Flash inserts an instance of the clip on the Stage.

You can also press [F11] to quickly toggle the Library panel open and closed.

TEST THE MOVIE CLIP

7 Click **Control**.

8 Click **Test Movie**.

Note: *To test the button states within the button timeline, press* [Enter] *(* [Return] *).*

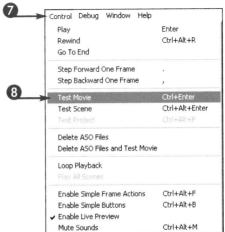

Creating Buttons chapter

The Flash Player window opens.

⑨ Move ▷ over the button to test the animation.

The Flash Player window plays the animation.

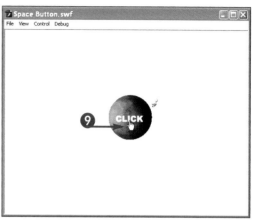

⑩ Click here to close the test window.

The Flash Player window closes.

Can I add sounds to button frames?

Yes. You can add sound clips the same way you add movie clips. For example, you might add a sound to the Down frame that alerts the user to the fact that they have activated the button, or you might add a beeping noise that occurs when the user moves the mouse over the button. A sound wave appears in the frame. See Chapter 13 to learn more about sounds.

How do I preview the animated button in Movie Edit mode?

If you attempt to preview a button in Movie Edit mode by pressing Ctrl + Alt + B (⌘ + Option + B) to activate the Enable Simple Buttons command, you will not be able to see your animation. Instead, you see the first frame of the movie clip. To see the fully animated button, you must click **Control**, **Test Movie**.

Assign Button Behaviors

You can assign all kinds of behaviors to buttons you create. Behaviors are built-in ActionScript that you can assign to make your Flash projects interactive. Buttons already utilize built-in actions, such as moving immediately to the Down frame when a user clicks the button. You can add other behaviors, such as a Play action that starts a movie clip playing when the user clicks the button.

In the case of buttons, you can assign frame behaviors that determine how the user interacts with the button. You add frame behaviors in Movie Edit mode, not Symbol Edit mode, and you add them to the frame containing the button. Behaviors work only with files created using ActionScript 2.0 or earlier.

Assign Button Behaviors

ADD A BEHAVIOR TO A BUTTON

1 Click ![arrow cursor].

2 Click the button symbol to which you want to add a behavior.

Note: See the section "Create a Button Symbol" to learn how to create a button.

3 Click **Window**.

4 Click **Behaviors**.

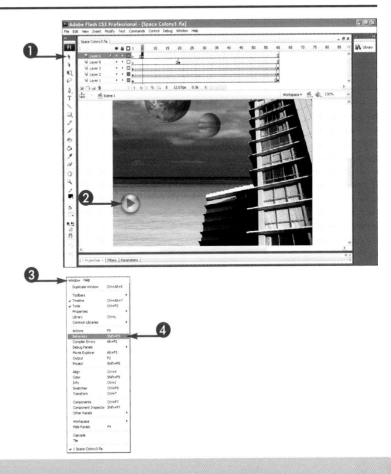

The Behaviors panel opens.

5 Click **the Add Behavior** button ().

Note: Behaviors work only with files created using ActionScript 2.0 or earlier Flash may prompt you to change the Publish settings in order to utilize behaviors.

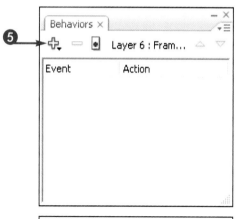

6 Click a behavior subcategory.

7 Click the behavior you want to apply.

Note: See Chapter 12 to learn more about working with Flash actions.

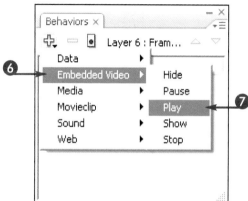

TIPS

What is an event handler?
An event handler, such as the On Mouse Event, manages the action. You can recognize the On Mouse Event in the Object Actions dialog box by the words "on," such as "on release." The words following the word "on" set the parameters for the event. See Chapter 12 to learn more about actions and using ActionScript in Flash.

I cannot select my button on the Flash Stage. Why?
If Flash activates the button when you move your 🖑 over the button, you have the Enable Simple Buttons feature turned on. Press `Ctrl`+`Alt`+`B` to disable the feature, and then click the button to select it.

continued

Behaviors are simplified programming scripts that instruct Flash how to perform a certain task, such as activating a Web page link or stopping a sound clip. Using a basic programming language, behaviors include hidden command strings to spell out exactly what behavior Flash must perform.

In addition to the behaviors you assign, Flash also automatically assigns a special event handler, called the On Mouse Event action, to the button. The On Mouse Event action acts as a manager to make sure whatever behavior you assign works properly with the button actions that are already built in to the symbol type.

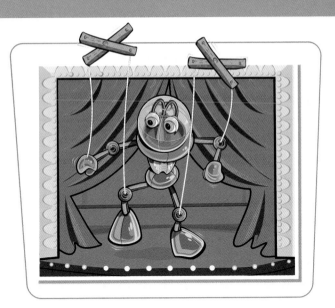

Assign Button Behaviors *(continued)*

Depending on the behavior you choose, a dialog box appears with additional parameters you can type to further define the behavior.

8 Change any parameter settings as necessary.

9 Click OK.

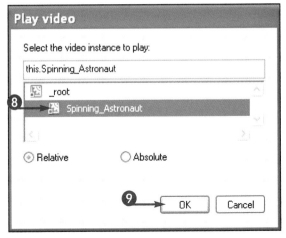

Flash adds the behavior to the list.

10 To change the event that triggers the behavior, click here.

11 Click an event.

● You can click the panel's title bar to minimize the panel, or click here to close the panel when finished.

TEST A BUTTON ACTION

⑫ Click **Control**.

⑬ Click **Test Movie**.

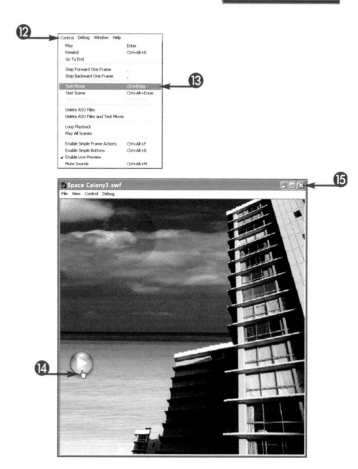

The Flash Player window opens.

⑭ Move the ↖ over the button (↖ changes to ⟨ᵐ⟩) and click to see the associated action.

⑮ When finished, click here to close the Player window.

Is it better to write my own ActionScript or use the premade behaviors?

Scripting depends entirely on how much programming you want to input. If you prefer writing your own code and plan on making lots of modifications to the script, and want others to view and edit your code, then ActionScript is a better choice to suit your needs. If you are just looking for simple coding, Flash behaviors are an easy choice to add interactivity to your project.

I activated the Enable Simple Buttons command, but I cannot test my button. Why not?

When working with behaviors, you cannot test the effects using the Enable Simple Buttons command. Instead, you must activate the Test Movie command and view the actions in the Flash Player window.

Adding Interactivity

Do you need to add some user controls to your animation? In this chapter, you learn how to add interactive Flash actions and behaviors to frames, buttons, and clips.

Introduction to Flash Actions

You can add interactivity to your Flash movies by assigning an action or behavior to a frame, a button, or movie clip instance. Actions are based on principles of cause and effect. The occurrence that triggers the action is called an *event*. An event might be a click of a button or reaching a certain frame in your movie. The result of the action is the *target*, the object that is affected by the event. For example, a target might be linking to a Web page or playing another Flash movie.

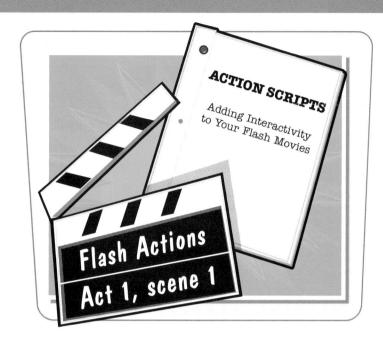

Actions and ActionScript

Flash actions are built on a programming language called ActionScript. This scripting language allows you to write instructions that control a movie. If you know how to write scripting programming code, you can certainly write your own actions in Flash. However, you do not need to know a scripting language to create actions. Flash includes hundreds of prewritten scripts, or actions, you can assign.

Using Actions in Flash

You can use the Actions panel to add actions to frames, buttons, or movie clips—mini-movies within the main movie. You can also assign any of the built-in actions found in the Behaviors panel. When you assign an action, Flash adds it to a list of actions for that particular frame or button. This list is called an *action list* or *script*. Flash then executes the actions in the list based on the order in which they appear.

Events

Anything that causes an action is called an *event*. In Flash terminology, an event triggers an action in your movie. Flash recognizes several types of events: mouse events, or button actions, keyboard events, clip events, and frame events, also called frame actions. A mouse event occurs when a user interacts with a button. Keyboard events occur when a user presses a keyboard key. Frame events are placed in keyframes in your movie. Clip events control movie clips.

Targets

A *target* is the object affected by the action. Targets are directed toward the current movie (called the *default target*), other movies (called the *Tell Target*), or a browser application (called an *external target*). For example, you might place a button in your movie that, when clicked, opens a Web page. You direct most of your frame actions toward the current movie, which is the default target.

Types of Actions

Flash groups actions into categories in the Actions panel. The most common actions include navigational actions such as Go To, Play, and Stop; browser actions, such as Get URL and Load Movie; and movie clip control actions. Although Flash offers hundreds of actions, this chapter focuses on the common navigations actions you can use in your own Flash movies.

ActionScript Versions

You can find more than one version of ActionScript in Flash. ActionScript 3.0 works best for users familiar with object-oriented programming. ActionScript 2.0 is simpler than 3.0, but is slower to execute in the Flash Player. ActionScript 1.0 is the simplest form of ActionScript. Flash Lite 2.x is a subset of ActionScript 2.0, while Flash Lite 1.x is a subset of ActionScript 1.0, and both are used to create content to run on mobile devices, such as cell phones. You can switch between versions using the Publish Settings dialog box.

Using the Actions Panel

You can use the Actions panel to add actions and write ActionScript for your Flash movies. Actions enable you to add interactivity to your movies. The Actions panel offers a scripting environment in a single panel, with a script pane for assembling scripts, an Actions Toolbox with pieces of code you can use to write scripts, and a Script Assist mode to help you write scripts accurately.

The left pane of the Actions panel, called the Actions Toolbox, lists all the categories and actions available. After you choose an action to add, it is listed in the right pane, called the script pane, along with any parameters you specify to further define the action. Above the script pane, you can find buttons you can use to help you add and work with scripts. Depending on which version of ActionScript you use, the Actions panel displays different action categories.

Using the Actions Panel

1 Click **Window**.

2 Click **Actions**.

You can also press **F9** to open the panel.

If the Property inspector is open, you can also click the **Edit Action Script** button (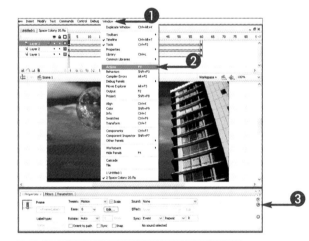).

Note: The Actions panel can be moved and resized just like the other panels you use in Flash. See Chapter 1 to learn more about panels.

- The Actions panel opens.

- The current frame or object is listed here.

- The Toolbox lists categories, subcategories, and actions you can assign.

- If you are using Flash Professional, the left pane also includes a Script navigator displaying a visual representation of your file structure.

Note: Depending on which version of ActionScript you use, the Actions panel displays different action categories. You can switch versions using the Publish Settings dialog box. Click File, Publish Settings to display the dialog box.

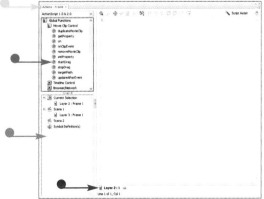

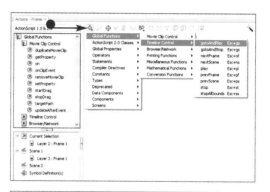

● You can also assign actions from the pop-up list that appears when you click here.

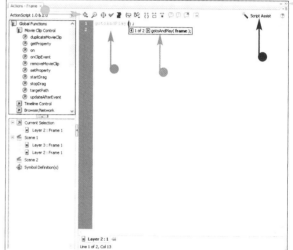

● Actions you assign are added to the actions list, also called the *script pane*. You can also type action scripts here.

● When you assign an action, a code hint tooltip appears with information about which parameters to assign.

● You can use the buttons to help you edit and construct your ActionScript statements.

● You can use the Script Assist tool to help you write script in Flash.

● To close the Actions panel, click here.

TIPS

Where can I find additional commands for working with the Actions panel?

You can click the **Panel Menu** button (▾≡) located in the upper-right corner of the Actions panel to reveal a list of related commands. A Panel Menu is available for every panel you use in Flash. To learn more about working with panels, see Chapter 1.

Can I move the panel out of the way?

You can move and resize the Actions panel just as you can with other panels available in Flash. You can also dock the panel. Click the panel's title bar to quickly hide or display the panel contents. See Chapter 1 to learn more about working with Flash panels.

Assign
Frame Actions

You can use the Actions panel to add actions to your movie. Frames can include multiple actions, but you can only assign an action one frame at a time. You add actions to the frame's *action script*, a list of actions associated with the frame. Flash performs the actions in the order they appear in the list.

When you assign an action, it appears in the actions list on the right side of the Actions panel. As soon as you assign an action to a frame, the frame is marked with a tiny icon of the letter *a*, for action. After assigning an action to a frame, you can return to the Actions panel and make changes to the action as needed.

Assign Frame Actions

1 Select the frame to which you want to add an action.

Note: You can only insert actions into keyframes, not regular frames. See Chapter 8 to learn how to add frames.

2 Open the Actions panel.

● You can press **F9** to quickly open the Actions panel or click the **Edit ActionScript** button (⟦⊚⟧) in the Property inspector.

Note: See the section "Using the Actions Panel" to learn how to display the Actions panel.

3 Click an action category.

4 Click a subcategory.

Most categories include subcategories.

5 Double-click the action you want to add or drag it from the list and drop it in the actions list.

● You can also click here to display a pop-up list of categories and actions to assign.

*Note: Depending on which version of ActionScript you use, the Actions panel displays different action categories. You can switch versions using the Publish Settings dialog box. Click **File**, **Publish Settings** to display the dialog box.*

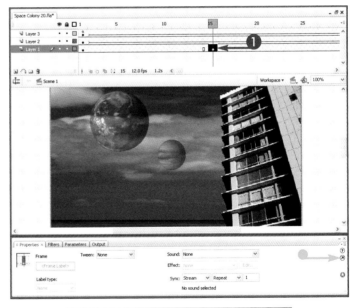

● Flash adds the action to the actions list, also called the *script pane*.

● Depending on the action you select, you may need to type parameters to further define the action.

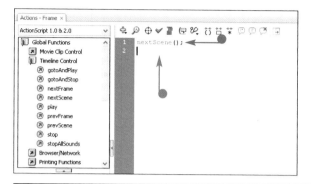

● Flash also adds a tiny letter () to indicate that an action is assigned to the frame.

When you play the movie, the frame action you assigned is carried out.

● You can click the panel's title bar to hide the panel and free up workspace on-screen.

6 When finished adding actions, click the **Close** button (⊠).

The Actions panel closes.

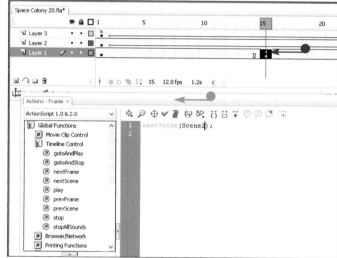

TIPS

How do I organize actions in my movie?
To help you clearly identify actions you assign to frames, consider creating a layer specifically for actions in your movie. This technique simplifies the process of finding the action you want to edit. See Chapter 6 to find out more about moving and positioning Flash layers.

How do I know what parameters to fill in for an action?
Click the **Show Code Hint** button (📖) in the Actions panel to display a code hint tooltip detailing what parameters you need to type to complete the action script. Be sure to enclose each parameter with quote marks.

Add Actions to Movie Clips

You can add actions to movie clip instances that appear in your main movie. For example, you may have an animation sequence of a moving car that includes movie clips for making each wheel rotate. To make the car seem to animate from parked status to moving, you can target the movie clips that comprise the wheels of the car and stop each wheel's rotation.

Any actions you attach to a movie clip instance apply only to that instance, not the original movie clip. Movie clip actions respond to the event much like button actions respond to on events. When assigning actions to instances, it is important to name your movie clip instances. Depending on which version of ActionScript you use, the Actions panel displays different action categories. The steps in this section show ActionScript 2.0 actions.

Add Actions to Movie Clips

① Click the movie clip instance to which you want to add an action

Note: See Chapter 8 to learn how to create movie clips.

② Display the Property inspector.

Note: See Chapter 1 to learn how to work with the Property inspector.

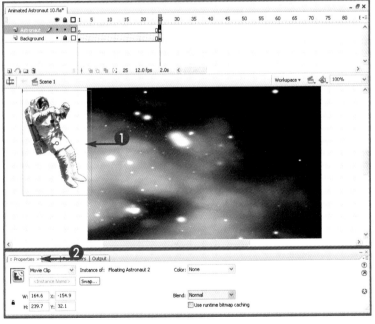

③ Click in the instance name field and type a new name for the instance.

④ Press **Enter** (**Return**).

● You can click the Property inspector's title bar to hide the panel.

5 Open the Actions panel.

You can press **F9** to quickly open the Actions panel or click the **Edit ActionScript** button (⊡) in the Property inspector.

6 Click the **Add** button (⊞).

7 Click an action category.

8 Click a subcategory.

Most categories include subcategories.

9 Click the action you want to add.

● You can also click and drag an action from the Actions Toolbox.

Note: *Depending on which version of ActionScript you use, the Actions panel displays different action categories. You can switch versions using the Publish Settings dialog box. Click File, Publish Settings to display the dialog box.*

● Flash assigns the action to the clip and you can set parameters as needed.

You can add additional actions to the clip, if needed.

● When finished adding actions, close or hide the Actions panel.

Note: *See Chapter 11 to learn how to add actions to buttons.*

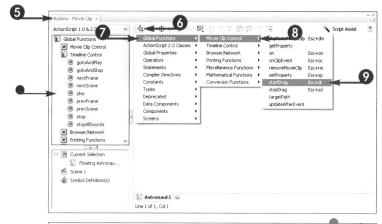

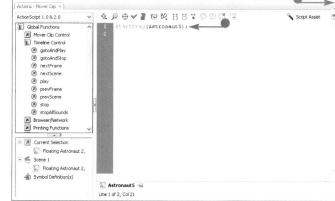

How do movie clips differ from graphic or button instances?

Movie clips are independent movies, and as such, they play all their frames when an instance of the clip is added to the Stage, whether it is one frame or 120. Movie clips also loop unless you add a Stop action to the last frame of the clip. Unlike graphic instances, movie clip instances do not play when you scrub, or drag, the Timeline's playhead. To see clips play, open the Flash Player window. See Chapter 8 to learn more about previewing movies.

Which category in the Actions panel lists movie clip actions?

If you are using ActionScript 2.0, Flash groups the majority of movie clip actions under the Movie Clip Control subcategory in the Actions panel, under the the Global Functions category. You can also apply other actions to control movie clips, not just those listed under Movie Clip Control. When you select a movie clip instance on the Stage, grayed-out actions in the panel cannot be applied to the clip. In ActionScript 3.0, you can find movie clip actions in the Index category.

Jump to a Specific Frame or Scene

You can assign a Go To action that tells Flash to start playing a particular frame in your movie. You can use the Go To action with frames, buttons, or movie clips. When Flash follows a Go To action, it jumps to, or goes to a specified target frame.

The Go To action includes parameters you can define to play a specific frame. When you assign the Go To action using the Actions panel, you can type a frame number as the target frame, or if your frames are organized with labels, you can type the label of the target frame.

ADD A GO TO ACTION TO A FRAME

① Select the keyframe to which you want to add the action.

② Open the Actions panel.

You can press **F9** to quickly open the Actions panel, or if the Property inspector is open, you can also click ⬚.

③ Click the **Global Functions** category.

④ Click **Timeline Control**.

⑤ Double-click **gotoAndPlay**.

You can also click and drag the action from the list and drop it in the script area.

Note: *Depending on which version of ActionScript you use, the Actions panel displays different action categories. This example uses ActionScript 2.0. You can switch versions using the Publish Settings dialog box. Click **File**, **Publish Settings** to display the dialog box.*

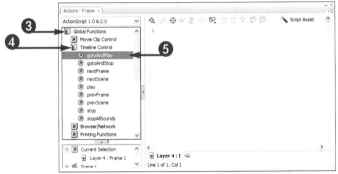

- Flash adds the action to the actions list.

- Flash also adds an to the frame to indicate that an action is assigned.

Note: *If you assign an action to a button, Flash does not display the tiny letter "a."*

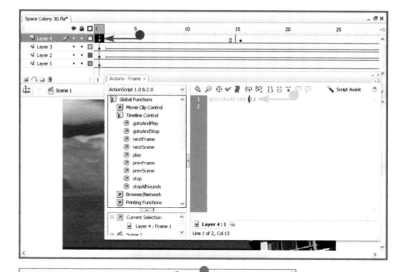

6 Type the number of the frame you want to go to in the parameter's parentheses.

You can also type a frame label or scene name to jump to a particular frame.

When you play the movie, Flash follows the frame action you assigned.

- To hide the Actions panel, click the panel's title bar.

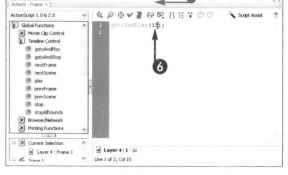

TIPS

What is a scene?

Scenes are blocks of the animation frames turned into their own independent Timelines. You can use scenes to organize a large movie into smaller segments. You can learn more about creating scenes in Chapter 8.

If my frame has a label instead of a number, how do I define the parameter?

Instead of typing a frame number for the parameter, type the frame label. Frame labels allow you to give frames distinct titles that more readily tell you about the frame's content. Labeling frames is particularly helpful with longer Flash movies. You can use labels to tell you when a key change occurs in an animation or to indicate a new element that appears in the movie. Labeling is an organizational tool and can help you with keeping your actions organized as well. To learn more about assigning labels to frames, see Chapter 8.

Assign Stop and Play Actions

You can assign a Stop action to stop a movie from playing, or you can assign a Play action to play it again. For example, perhaps one of the keyframes in your movie is text heavy and you want to allow the user to read the text. You can create a button and assign a Stop action that allows the user to stop the movie and assign a Play action to another button that allows the user to play the movie again.

Stop and Play actions are two of the basic Flash navigation and interaction buttons. The Stop and Play actions are commonly used with buttons. Depending on which version of ActionScript you use, the Actions panel displays different action categories. The steps in this section show ActionScript 2.0 actions.

Assign Stop and Play Actions

ADD A STOP ACTION

① Click the frame or button to which you want to add a Stop action.

Note: See Chapter 11 to learn how to create buttons.

② Open the Actions panel.

You can press `F9` to quickly open the Actions panel, or if the Property inspector is open, you can also click ⌷.

③ Click the **Global Functions** category.

④ Click **Movie Clip Control**.

⑤ Double-click **on**.

● The on action is added to the script along with a parameter to define.

⑥ Double-click **release**.

*Note: Depending on which version of ActionScript you use, the Actions panel displays different action categories. This example uses ActionScript 2.0. You can switch versions using the Publish Settings dialog box. Click **File**, **Publish Settings** to display the dialog box.*

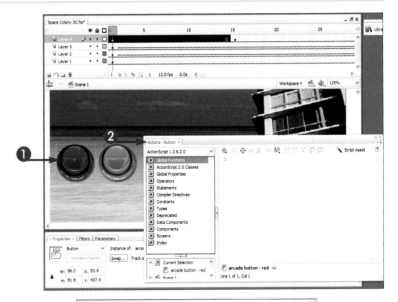

⑦ Click the end of the first script line and press **Enter** (**Return**).

⑧ Click the **Global Functions** category.

⑨ Click **Movie Clip Control**.

⑩ Double-click **stop**.

● Flash adds the stop action, which has no parameters, to the script.

Note: If you assign an action to a button, Flash does not display the ▣ *icon in the Timeline.*

ADD A PLAY ACTION

⑪ Hide the Actions panel or move it out of the way.

You can click the panel's title bar to minimize and maximize the panel at any time.

⑫ Click the frame or button to which you want to add a Play action.

Note: See Chapter 11 to learn how to create buttons.

⑬ Click the Actions panel title bar to display the panel again.

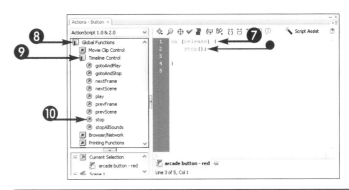

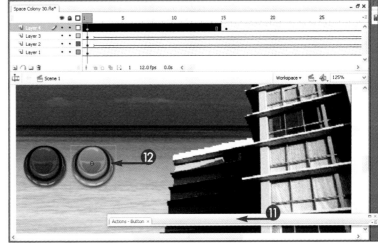

What is the difference between frame actions and object actions?

Actions can be applied to frames or buttons, which are treated as objects in Flash. Frame actions are assigned to frames and control how a movie plays. Button actions, as demonstrated in the following steps, are assigned to buttons and require input from the user. For example, a Stop action assigned to a button enables the user to stop a movie by clicking the button to which the action is assigned. You can assign Stop and Play actions to frames or buttons, but remember that button actions require user input in order to carry out the action.

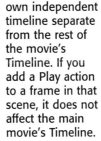

Does a Play action in a scene affect the rest of the movie's Timeline?

No. A scene has its own independent timeline separate from the rest of the movie's Timeline. If you add a Play action to a frame in that scene, it does not affect the main movie's Timeline.

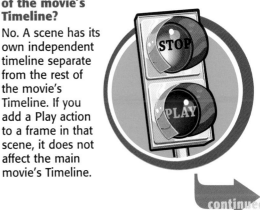

continued

Assign Stop and Play Actions *(continued)*

Assign the Stop and Play actions to give users control over the movie's playback. Stop and Play actions act much like the controls found on a DVD, VCR or CD player. In many cases, you will want to use the two commands together because the Stop action ceases the movie from playing while the Play action starts a movie previously stopped with the Stop action.

Depending on which version of ActionScript you use, the Actions panel displays different action categories. The steps in this section show ActionScript 2.0 actions.

Assign Stop and Play Actions *(continued)*

⑭ Click the **Global Functions** category.

⑮ Click **Movie Clip Control**.

⑯ Double-click **on**.

● The on action is added to the script along with a parameter to define.

⑰ Double-click **release**.

Note: *Depending on which version of ActionScript you use, the Actions panel displays different action categories. This example uses ActionScript 2.0. You can switch versions using the Publish Settings dialog box. Click **File**, **Publish Settings** to display the dialog box.*

⑱ Click the end of the first script line and press Enter (Return).

⑲ Click the **Global Functions** category.

⑳ Click **Timeline Control**.

㉑ Double-click **play**.

● The play action is added to the script.

No parameters are available for the play action.

㉒ Click the title bar to minimize the Actions panel.

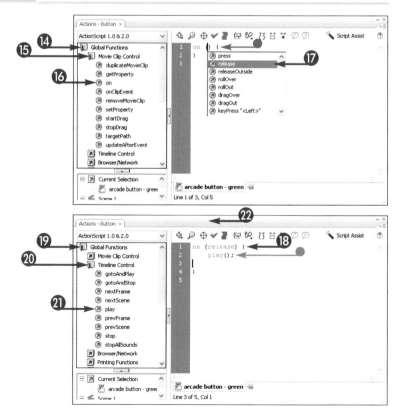

TEST THE ACTIONS

㉓ Click **Control**.

㉔ Click **Test Movie**.

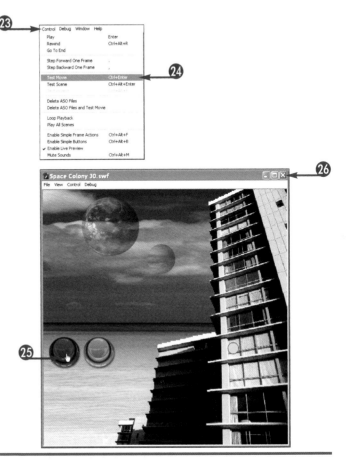

The Flash Player window opens and plays the movie.

㉕ Click the buttons to perform the Stop and Play actions.

㉖ Click the Close button (☒) to exit the Player window.

Can I resize the type in the actions list?

Click the **Panel Menu** button (▼≡) to display a pop-up menu. Click **Preferences** to open the Preferences dialog box to the ActionScript category to find options for changing the text font and size. To learn more about customizing the panel, see the section "Customize the Actions Panel" later in this chapter.

Does Flash support a Pause action?

No. However, a Stop action acts like a pause action in that your movie stops playing and rests on the frame to which the Stop action is activated. You can place a Stop action at the start of a movie to keep the movie from playing automatically when opened as a self-playing projector file. Do not forget to add a button with a Play action so users can start the movie.

Load a New Movie into the Current Movie

You can use the Load Movie action to start a movie file within your current movie. Use this action to replace the current movie with another, or play the loaded movie on top of the current movie as if it were another layer.

The Load Movie action can help you create layered animation action. For example, you might create a movie of a wooded background. In the middle of the movie, you can load a movie of a man walking. By loading the walking man in the middle of the background movie, you can combine the two movies to make it look as if the man is walking through the woods.

Depending on which version of ActionScript you use, the Actions panel displays different action categories. The steps in this section show ActionScript 2.0 actions.

Load a New Movie into the Current Movie

① Select the keyframe to which you want to add the action.

② Open the Actions panel.

You can press F9 to quickly open the Actions panel, or if the Property inspector is open, you can also click 🗷.

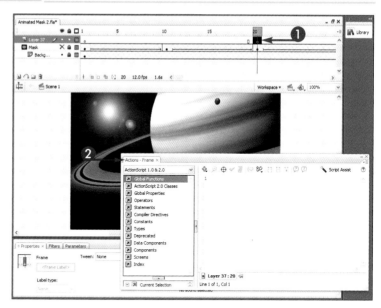

③ Click the **Global Functions** category.

④ Click **Browser/Network**.

⑤ Double-click **loadMovie**.

● Flash adds the action to the actions list and displays a code hint tooltip demonstrating what parameters to set.

Note: Depending on which version of ActionScript you use, the Actions panel displays different action categories. This example uses ActionScript 2.0. You can switch versions using the Publish Settings dialog box. Click **File, Publish Settings** to display the dialog box.

6 Click inside the parentheses and type the first parameter, which defines the name of the Flash movie file you want to load.

Be sure to include quote marks around the movie name.

● The code in this example loads the Flash movie Animated Astronaut 20.swf.

7 Type a comma, and then the second parameter, which defines the target movie clip.

● The code in this example targets a movie clip instance named *mc*.

● You can test the action by clicking **Control**, then **Test Movie** to play the movie in the Flash Player window.

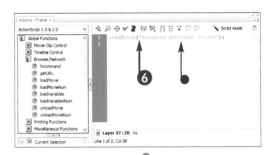

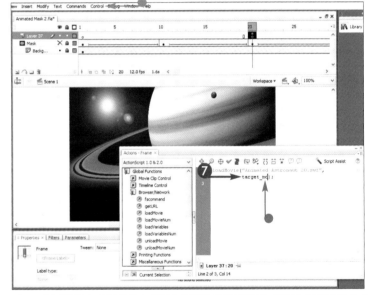

What are movie levels?

Flash handles the playing of multiple movies as *levels*. The current movie is always playing at level 0. When you play a second movie with the Load Movie action, it plays at the level you designate, starting with Level 1 or higher. Like stacking, movies play on top of the bottom level, so a movie set to play at Level 2 visually appears on top of movies at Levels 1 and 0. If you specify Level 0 for the location level with the Load Movie action, the new movie replaces the existing movie. If you assign another level, the new movie plays on top of the existing movie.

LEVEL 1 - Sky
LEVEL 2 - Flowers
LEVEL 3 - Hummingbird

How can I check my script for errors?

You can click the **Script Assist** button (Script Assist) in the Actions panel to display the parameters as fields and check over your coding. You can click Script Assist again to toggle the feature off.

ACTIONSCRIPTS

Script OK!

Control Instances with Behaviors

You can use behaviors to control instances and movie clips without writing ActionScript. Behaviors are prewritten ActionScript scripts. Behaviors are an easy way to perform basic actions such as changing the stacking order of instances, loading other movies to play within your current movie, jumping to a specific frame, and more.

To use behaviors, you can assign an identifier name to the instance or clip. You can then use the Behaviors panel to assign behaviors. Behaviors work only with ActionScript 2.0. If your file was created using ActionScript 1.0 or 3.0, you can switch to ActionScript 2.0 using the Publish Settings dialog box. See Chapter 15 to learn more about publishing Flash files.

Control Instances with Behaviors

① Open the Library panel.

You can press **Ctrl**+**L** (**⌘**+**L**) to quickly open the Library panel.

② Right-click over the instance or movie clip you want to use.

③ Click **Linkage**.

Note: *Behaviors only work with ActionScript 2.0. You can switch ActionScript versions using the Publish Settings dialog box. Click* **File**, **Publish Settings** *to display the dialog box.*

The Linkage Properties dialog box appears.

④ Select the **Export for ActionScript** check box (☐ changes to ☑).

⑤ Type an identifier for the instance or clip.

⑥ Click **OK**.

You can press **Ctrl**+**L** (**⌘**+**L**) to close the Library panel again.

⑦ Select the object to which you want to assign a behavior.

⑧ Click **Window**.

⑨ Click **Behaviors**.

You can also press Shift + F3 to open the panel.

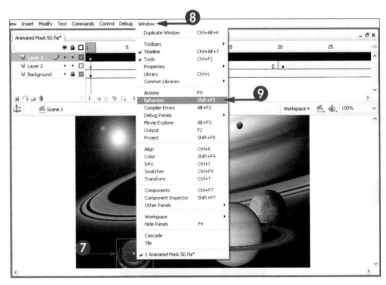

The Behaviors panel opens.

⑩ Click the **Add Behavior** button (⊕).

⑪ Click a behavior category.

⑫ Click a behavior.

In this example, the behavior duplicates a movie clip within the main movie.

How do I undock the Behaviors panel?

The Behaviors panel works just like any other panel in Flash, which means you can move, dock, undock, minimize, and maximize the panel. To undock a docked panel or move a floating panel, simply click and drag the far left side of the panel's title bar. To dock a panel, click the same area on the title bar and drag it to the far right side of the program window. To minimize the panel to hide its contents, click the title bar.

Is there an easy way to organize actions and behaviors I add to my Flash movies?

You can add a layer to your Timeline and keep all the actions organized at the top of the Timeline. This way, you can always know where to find the keyframes that contain actions. This also makes it easier for other users who work on the file to quickly find and view frame actions. To add a layer to the top of the Timeline, click the current top layer and click the **Insert Layer** button (⬚). See Chapter 6 to learn more about using layers in Flash.

continued

You can control behaviors by specifying an object to trigger the behavior and a target object that is affected by the behavior. One way to use navigational behaviors is to assign them to buttons in your movie. When assigning behaviors to buttons, the On Release event is assigned by default unless you specify another event. This means that the behavior activates when the user clicks the button and releases the mouse pointer.

Control Instances with Behaviors *(continued)*

- Depending on which behavior you select, an additional dialog box may open.

⑬ Type the appropriate information or select from the available options.

- In this example, the dialog box prompts you to select a movie clip to target.

⑭ Click **OK**.

- Flash assigns the behavior.

- To change the event handler, click here and choose another.

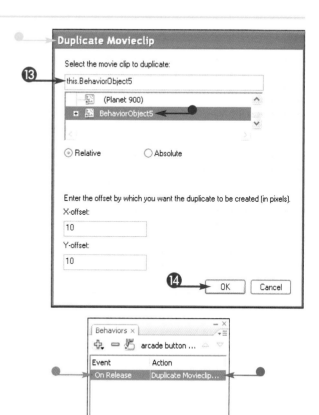

15 Click **Control**.

16 Click **Test Movie**.

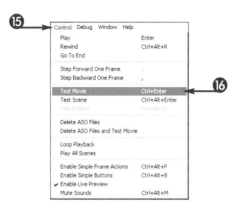

The Flash Player window opens.

18 Click the button or instance to test the behavior.

● In this example, clicking the button duplicates a movie clip that is already playing, creating two playing clips.

19 Click ⊠ when finished.

Flash returns you to the program window.

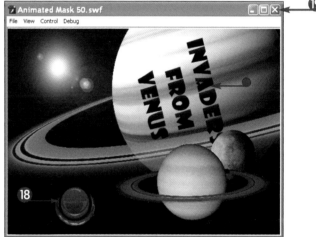

Can I delete behaviors after I assign them?

Yes. Select the object to which the behavior is assigned, and reopen the Behaviors panel. Select the behavior you want to remove, and click the **Delete Behavior** button (⊟). Flash removes the behavior from the list.

When I use the Behaviors panel to insert scripts, Flash inserts a blank line at the top. Why?

Any time you use behaviors to add script to your movie, Flash leaves the first line at the top of the script blank. You can use this line to add comments about the behavior and help you keep notes about how you want to use the script. All comments are preceded by //. For example, you might leave a comment like //MovieClip GotoandStop Behavior.

Link a Button to a Web Page

You can use the Go to Web Page behavior to take users to other files or Web pages. When you assign this behavior to a button or frame, it acts as an HTML hyperlink. For example, you might insert a Go to Web Page behavior in a stand-alone Flash Player projector movie, which, when activated, opens a browser window and downloads the specified HTML page.

Behaviors work only with ActionScript 2.0. If your file was created using ActionScript 1.0 or 3.0, you can switch to ActionScript 2.0 using the Publish Settings dialog box. See Chapter 15 to learn more about publishing Flash files.

① Select the object to which you want to assign a behavior.

Note: See Chapter 11 to learn how to create buttons.

② Click **Window**.

③ Click **Behaviors**.

You can also press Shift + F3 to open the panel.

Note: Behaviors only work with ActionScript 2.0. You can switch ActionScript versions using the Publish Settings dialog box. Click File, Publish Settings to display the dialog box.

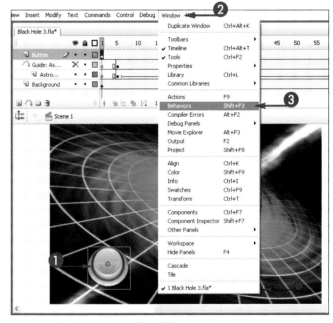

The Behaviors panel opens.

④ Click the **Add Behavior** button (⬚).

⑤ Click **Web**.

⑥ Click **Go to Web Page**.

The Go to URL dialog box appears.

⑦ Type the path to the Web page you want to open.

⑧ Click the Open in ☑ and click a target.

You can select _blank to open the Web page in a new browser window.

⑨ Click **OK**.

● The behavior is added to the list.

● To change the event that triggers the Web page, click here and choose another.

● To test the behavior, click **Control**, **Test Movie**, and click the object to activate the hyperlink.

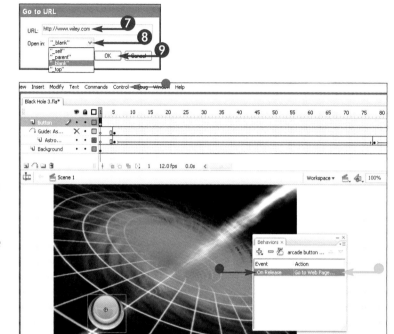

Can I also use the Get URL action?

Yes. You can use the Get URL action in the Actions panel to take users to other files or Web pages. There are four targets you can specify in the Get URL action's parameters. _self opens the designated HTML page in the current frame of the current browser window. _blank opens the designated file in a completely new browser window, _parent opens the page in the parent of the current browser, and _top opens the page in the top-level frame of the current window.

What other targets can I use for the link?

The example in this section shows the _blank target, which opens the URL in a new browser window. You can also choose three other targets. The _self target opens the URL in the same frame of the browser window as the current content, the _parent target opens the URL in the parent of the current frame, and the _top target opens the URL in the top-level frame of the current browser window.

Customize the Actions Panel

You can customize the Actions panel to change the appearance of scripts and make the panel easier to view. For example, to see more of the scripts listed in the script pane, you can resize the panel, or you can change the font and font size for the script text to make it easier to read. You can use the Preferences dialog box to make changes to how ActionScript appears in the panel.

RESIZE THE PANEL

① Open the Actions panel.

You can press **F9** to quickly display the Actions panel.

② Move ▷ over the border you want to resize (▷ changes to ↨).

③ Click and drag the border to a new size.

You can drag the corner of the panel to resize both sides at once.

● Flash resizes the panel.

● You can click and drag the panel's title bar to move the panel around the program window.

You can also click the panel's title bar to minimize or maximize the panel.

Note: *See Chapter 1 to learn more about working with panels in Flash.*

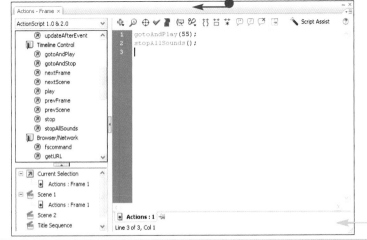

RESIZE THE PANEL

1 Open the Actions panel.

You can press **F9** to quickly display the Actions panel.

2 Click the **Panel Menu** button (▾≡).

3 Click **Preferences**.

The Preferences dialog box appears to the ActionScript category.

4 Change any preferences you want to set for the panel.

● To change the font for the script coding, click ▾ and click a new font.

● To change the font size, click ▾ and click a new size.

5 Click **OK**.

Flash applies the new preferences.

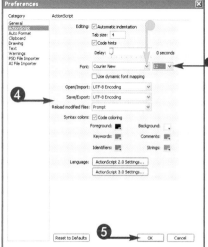

 TIPS

What other preferences can I set for the panel?

The Preferences dialog box includes several advanced options you can apply to your ActionScript endeavors. For example, if you are experienced with writing script code, you can change the syntax colors to help you identify coding in the list. You can also set the number of indents you want to see for each tab you type, or whether code hints appear as you type coding. To learn more about customizing ActionScript in Flash, see the Flash help files.

Can I pin a script in the Actions panel?

Yes. You can pin individual scripts in the panel to keep the location assessable. To pin a script, select the script in the script pane and click the **Pin Active Script** icon (⊣). Flash pins the line and the pushpin icon changes to ⊿. You can click ⊿ to unpin the script.

Add a Component

You can use components to add instant interactivity to your movie projects. Components are simply prebuilt, complex movie clips for user interface elements such as radio buttons and list boxes. You can add just one of these components to a movie, combine them, or use all of them to create a very simple user interface for a Web page form. Components only work with ActionScript 2.0.

After you add a component to the Stage, you can customize the data contained within the component. For example, if you add a combo box that offers the user a drop-down list of menu choices, you can control exactly what menu choices appear in the list.

① Click **Window**.

② Click **Components**.

The Components panel opens.

Note: Flash panels can be undocked and moved around the screen. See Chapter 1 to learn more about working with panels.

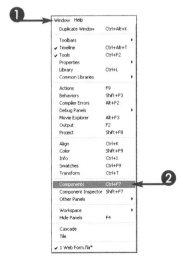

③ Click the User Interface category.

④ Click and drag a component onto the Stage.

In this example, a check box is added.

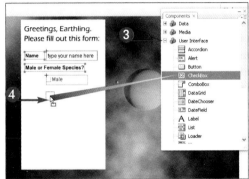

⑤ Open the Property inspector.

You can press `Ctrl`+`F3` (`⌘`+`F`) to display the Property inspector.

⑥ Click the **Parameters** tab.

⑦ Type the component parameters you want to define.

Parameters vary for each component and may involve setting dimensions, labels, and values.

● In this example, a check box label is needed.

You can add additional components to your movie to continue building an interactive form.

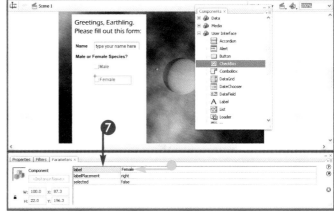

What types of components can I use in my Flash movies?

Flash components include the following common user interface elements: radio buttons, check boxes, pushbuttons, combo boxes, scroll panes, text scroll bars, and list boxes. Each of these elements is typically found in Web page forms and used for basic navigation. When you insert a component instance on the Stage, the component's graphic elements are automatically added to your movie's Library. Called *skins* in Flash terminology, you can edit the component's graphical elements to match the appearance of other elements in your movie.

Why is my Component panel empty?

Flash components only work with ActionScript version 2.0. If you create the file using ActionScript 3.0, you can switch to version 2.0 using the Publish Settings dialog box. Click **File**, **Publish Settings** to display the dialog box; click the **Flash** tab, then click the **ActionScript Version** ☑ and choose **ActionScript 2.0**. Click **OK** to save the new setting. You can now use the Components panel as described in this section.

Adding Sound

Does your animation need some sound? In this chapter, you learn how to add sound files to your animation frames and control how they play.

Import a Sound Clip

Although you cannot record sounds in Flash, you can import sounds from other sources for use with movies. For example, you might download an MP3 file from the Internet and add it to a movie, or import a saved recording to play with a Flash button. Flash supports popular sound file formats, such as WAV and AIF.

When assigning sounds in Flash, you add them to keyframes the same way you add graphics and buttons. Before you can add a sound to a frame, you must first import it into your movie's Library. Flash stores the sounds as symbols, and you can add an instance to your movie whenever you want the sound to play.

Import a Sound Clip

① Click **File**.

② Click **Import**.

③ Click **Import to Library**.

Note: You can also use the Import to Stage command to import sound files directly to the Stage as well as the Library.

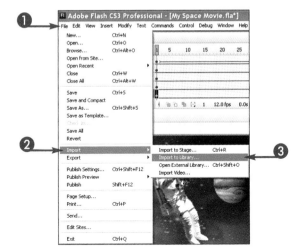

The Import to Library dialog box opens.

④ Click the sound file you want to import.

● You can click here to look for the file in another folder or drive.

● You can click here to look for a particular type of sound file.

⑤ Click **Open**.

Flash imports the sound file and places it in the Library.

6 Open the Library panel.

If the Library panel is not displayed, you can press **F11** to quickly display the panel. You can also click **Window**, **Library**.

Note: See Chapter 7 to learn more about using the Library.

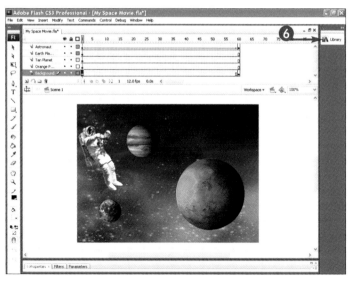

7 Click the sound file.

8 Click the **Play** button (▶).

Flash plays the file.

Note: See the sections "Assign a Sound to a Frame" or "Assign a Sound to a Button" to learn more about using sound files in Flash.

How many sounds can I use in a Flash project?

You can use as many sound files as you need for your project, and you can use different sounds. For example, you might use multiple sounds to create a layered sound effect, such as a narration over background music, or the sound of a doorbell over background ambient sounds. Sounds are placed in the layers in your movie's Timeline. Overlapping sounds play together, so the user hears both at the same time.

Do I need to worry about the size of my sound file?

Yes. When you use large sound files, such as background music, they take longer to download when users are accessing files from your Web site. It is a good idea to make sure that your sound clips are as short as you can possibly make them. Trim off excess parts of the clip or use an audio clip that loops.

Assign a Sound to a Frame

You can enliven any animation sequence with a sound clip whether you add a single sound effect or an entire soundtrack. You use sound files as instances that you can insert into frames on the Timeline and use throughout your movie. Flash represents sounds as waveforms in frames.

Depending on the length of the sound clip, the sound may play through several frames of your movie. Unlike a graphic or button symbol, however, sound clips appear as outlines on the Stage and the waveform for the sound appears in the designated layer and frame in the Timeline.

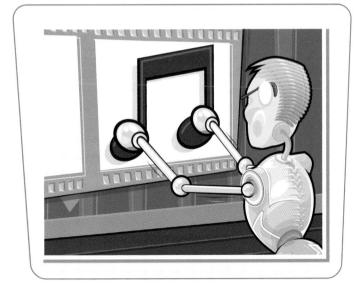

Assign a Sound to a Frame

ADD A SOUND USING THE LIBRARY PANEL

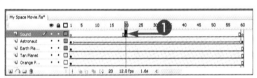

① Click the frame to which you want to add a sound.

Note: See the section "Import a Sound File" to learn how to add sound clips to the Library.

② Insert a keyframe.

You can press **F6** to quickly insert a keyframe.

③ Display the Library panel.

You can press **F11** to quickly open the Library.

④ Click and drag the sound clip from the Library and drop it onto the Stage.

The sound's waveform appears in the frame.

Note: By default, Flash assigns all sounds Event synchronization status unless you specify otherwise. See the next section to learn more.

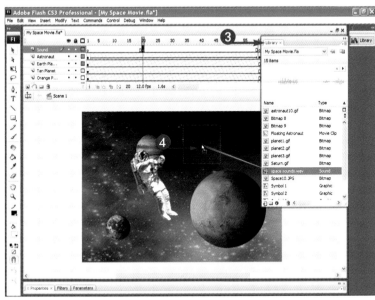

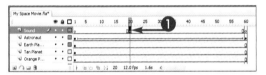

ADD A SOUND USING THE PROPERTY INSPECTOR

1 Click the frame to which you want to add a sound.

Note: See the section "Import a Sound File" to learn how to add sound clips to the Library.

2 Insert a keyframe.

You can press `F6` to quickly insert a keyframe.

3 Display the Property inspector.

You can press `Ctrl`+`F3` (`⌘`+`F3`) to open the Property inspector.

4 Click the **Sound** ☑.

5 Click the sound you want to assign.

● The sound's waveform appears in the frame.

Note: By default, Flash assigns all sounds Event synchronization status unless you specify otherwise. See the next section to learn more.

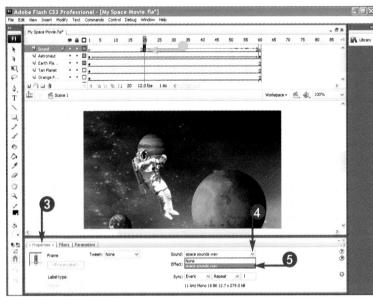

TIPS

Should I place my sounds in separate layers?

To keep your movie elements organized, it is always a good idea to place sounds on separate layers. This way you can always easily locate the sound you want to edit and quickly view how the sound relates to other movie elements. By placing sounds on separate layers, you can treat them as audio channels in your movie. Give each sound layer a unique name. To learn more about adding layers, see Chapter 6.

Why does my sound's waveform appear compressed into one frame?

If you assign a sound file to a keyframe that appears at the end of your movie, or if you have yet to add additional frames or keyframes to your movie, the sound's waveform appears only in the frame in which you assigned it, typically as a straight line. You can enlarge the frames to better view waveforms. Simply click the Timeline's Panel Menu button (≡) and click another frame size to display.

Assign a Sound to a Button

You can add sounds to buttons to help people know how to interact with the buttons or just to give the buttons added flair. For example, you might add a clicking sound that the user hears when he or she clicks a button.

If your buttons are part of a graphic or page background, adding a sound to the button's rollover state helps users find the buttons on the page.

Assign a Sound to a Button

① Open the button to which you want to add a sound in Symbol Edit mode.

Note: *See Chapter 11 to learn more about creating buttons.*

② Click the **Insert Layer** button (![icon]).

③ Assign a name to the layer.

Note: *See Chapter 6 to learn how to add and name a layer.*

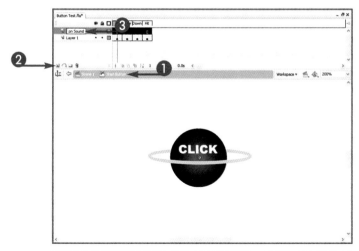

④ Click the frame to which you want to add a sound.

⑤ Insert a keyframe if the frame does not already have one.

You can press **F6** to quickly insert a keyframe.

⑥ Display the Library panel.

You can press **Ctrl**+**L** or **⌘**+**L** to open the Library.

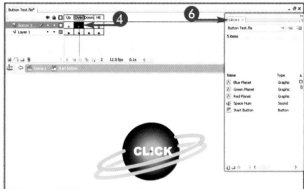

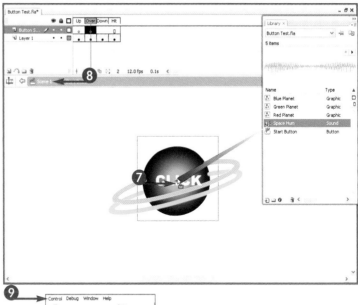

⑦ Click and drag the sound clip from the Library and drop it onto the Stage.

The sound's waveform appears in the frame.

Note: *See the section "Import a Sound File" to learn how to add sounds to the Library.*

⑧ Switch to Movie Edit mode by clicking the scene name.

Note: *See Chapter 11 to learn how to enable buttons in Movie Edit mode.*

⑨ Click **Control**.

⑩ Click **Enable Simple Buttons**.

You can now move ▷ over the button or click the button and Flash plays the assigned sound.

 TIPS

To which button frame should I assign a sound?

The most practical frames to use when assigning sounds are the Over and Down frames, but you can assign sounds to any button frame. For example, you might want the button to beep when the user rolls over the button with the mouse pointer. To do this, assign a sound to the Over frame.

Flash does not let me add a sound to a frame. Why not?

You can add sounds to only keyframes, not to regular frames in the Timeline. Be sure you insert a keyframe before attempting to add the sound. See Chapter 8 to learn more about using frames and keyframes in Flash.

Set Synchronization Properties

You can tell Flash how you want a sound to synchronize with your movie by setting sound properties. Sounds fall into two categories: *event driven* and *streamed*. You assign an event sound to a specific keyframe and it continues to play independently of your movie's Timeline. Use event sounds when you do not want to synchronize the sound with your movie.

Streamed sounds download as they are needed and start playing even if the rest of the clip has not yet loaded. Flash synchronizes streamed sounds with your movie's frames and attempts to keep any animation in sync with the streamed sound.

Set Synchronization Properties

① Click the keyframe containing the sound you want to edit.

Note: See the section "Add a Sound to a Frame" to learn how to assign sound clips.

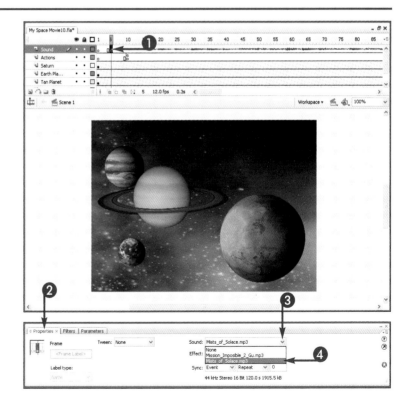

② Open the Property inspector.

You can press **Ctrl** + **F3** to quickly display the Property inspector.

③ Click the **Sound** ⊡.

④ Click the sound you want to edit.

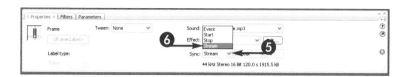

⑤ Click the **Sync** ☑.

⑥ Click **Event** or **Stream**.

Choose **Event** to trigger a sound at a particular frame or action. Event sounds play independently of the movie timeline.

Choose **Stream** to synchronize the sound clip to your movie frames.

Note: By default, Flash sets all sound to Event sounds unless you specify otherwise.

⑦ Click the Sound Loop ☑.

⑧ Click **Repeat** or **Loop**.

If you choose **Repeat**, specify how many times the clip should play.

If you choose **Loop**, the clip plays continuously.

You can now test your sound.

Note: Click Control, Test Movie to open the Player window and test the sound.

TIPS

How do I remove a sound clip I no longer want in the movie?

First, click the frame containing the sound and open the Property inspector. Next, click the **Sound** ☑ and click **None**. The sound is no longer associated with the keyframe, but the clip is still stored in your movie's Library. You can reuse it again, if needed.

If I repeat or loop a sound, does it affect my file size?

Yes. For example, if you repeat a streamed sound more than once, or loop it to play continually, your overall file size will increase. For that reason, be careful in choosing streaming sounds for your movie if your goal is to keep the overall file size down, and use caution when playing the sounds more than once.

Add Sound Effects

You can use the Effect properties to adjust the way in which a sound clip plays in your movie. For example, you can make a sound appear to fade in or out, or you can simulate a stereo audio channel effect. You can find sound effect controls in the Property inspector panel.

Add Sound Effects

① Click the frame containing the sound you want to edit.

Note: See the section "Add a Sound to a Frame" to learn how to assign sound clips.

② Open the Property inspector.

You can press **Ctrl** + **F3** to quickly display the Property inspector.

③ Click the **Sound** ☑.

④ Click the sound you want to edit.

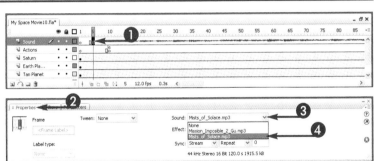

5 Click the **Effect** ☑.

6 Click a sound effect.

Flash assigns the new sound effect to the clip.

7 Press **Enter** (**Return**) to play the sound.

● Flash plays the sound effect, and the playhead moves across the Timeline.

Note: *You can also click* **Control**, **Test Movie** *to open the Player window and test the sound.*

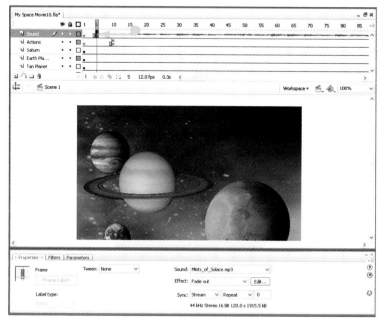

What are the sound effects I can apply?

Flash offers six sound effects you can apply. The Left Channel and Right Channel effects play sounds only in the left or right speaker. The Fade Left to Right and Fade Right to Left effects make the sound move from one speaker to another. The Fade In and Fade Out effects make the sound gradually increase or decrease in volume.

How do I create a Custom effect?

You can apply some rudimentary editing to your Flash sounds using the Custom sound effect control. For example, you can adjust the sound volume or length. See the section "Edit Sounds" later in this chapter to learn more about this control.

Load a Sound Using a Behavior

You can use the Load Sound from Library behavior to control the playback of a sound clip in your movie. Behaviors are prewritten ActionScript you can assign to an object in your movie to control another object, such as a sound clip. You can assign the behavior to a button that plays the sound clip when clicked.

To set up the Load Sound from Library behavior, you must first import a sound clip into your movie's Library and assign an identifier name to the clip.

Load a Sound Using a Behavior

① Open the Library panel.

You can press **F11** to open the Library.

② Right-click over the sound clip you want to use.

③ Click **Linkage**.

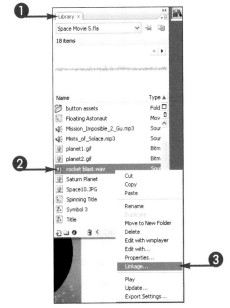

The Linkage Properties dialog box appears.

④ Select the **Export for ActionScript** check box (☐ changes to ☑).

⑤ Type an identifier for the clip.

Note: *If you created the Flash file for ActionScript 3.0, you cannot use behaviors. To change the Publish setting, click File, Publish Settings and then click the Flash tab to change the ActionScript version to ActionScript 2.0 or earlier.*

⑥ Click **OK**.

You can press **F11** to close the Library panel.

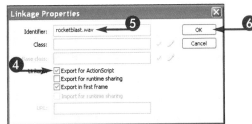

⑦ Select the object to which you want to assign a sound behavior.

In this example, a button will trigger the sound.

⑧ Click **Window**.

⑨ Click **Behaviors**.

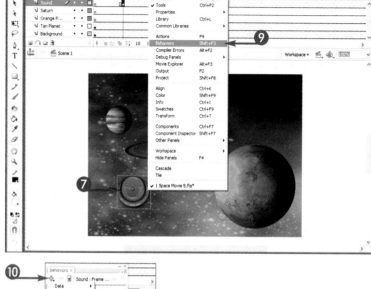

The Behaviors panel opens.

⑩ Click the **Add** button (🖭).

⑪ Click **Sound**.

⑫ Click **Load Sound from Library**.

TIPS

What other behaviors can I assign to sounds?

Flash includes five sound behaviors. You can use the Play Sound, Stop Sound, and Stop All Sounds behaviors to control how sounds play in the movie. You can use the Load Streaming MP3 File behavior to load an external MP3 file into your movie without increasing the overall file size. You can use the Behaviors panel to assign the sound behaviors to frames and buttons. In order to use several of the behaviors, you must first set the sound to Export for ActionScript, Export in First Frame, and assign a linkage identifier string.

Can I also write ActionScript to control sounds?

Yes. If you are familiar with writing script coding, you can use ActionScript to write all kinds of instructions for controlling sounds. You can use ActionScript to control everything from basic playback actions to controlling volume panning and more. Before you can work with sounds, you must first set the sound to Export for ActionScript, Export in First Frame, and assign a linkage indentifier, as shown in the steps in this section. To learn more about Flash actions, see Chapter 12.

continued

You can control sound behaviors by specifying an event or action. By default, the On Release event is assigned to the behavior unless you specify another event. This means that the sound clip plays when the user clicks the button and releases the mouse button. You can also set up other events, such as On Press or On Rollover.

Load a Sound Using a Behavior *(continued)*

The Load Sound from Library dialog box appears.

⓭ Type the identifier name you typed in Step **5**.

⓮ Type an instance name.

⓯ Deselect the **Play this sound when loaded** check box (☑ changes to ☐).

⓰ Click **OK**.

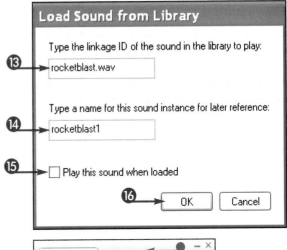

● Flash assigns the sound behavior.

● To change the event handler, click here and choose another.

● You can click the panel's title bar to minimize the Behaviors panel.

⑰ Click **Control**.

⑱ Click **Test Movie**.

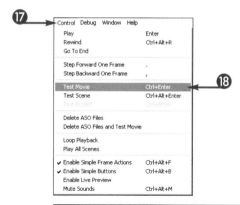

The Flash Player window opens.

⑲ Click the button to test the sound.

⑳ Click the **Close** button (☒) when finished.

Flash returns you to the program window.

TIPS

How do I remove a sound behavior I no longer want?

Select the object to which the sound behavior is assigned, and then reopen the Behaviors panel. Select the behavior you want to remove and click the **Delete Behavior** button (⊟). Flash removes the behavior from the list.

How do I move the Behaviors panel?

You can move, dock, undock, minimize, and maximize the Behaviors panel. To undock a docked panel or move a floating panel, simply click and drag the far-left side of the panel's title bar. To dock a panel, click the same area on the title bar and drag it to the far-right side of the program window. You can dock a panel on any side of the program window.

Assign Start and Stop Sounds

You can use the Flash Start and Stop sound controls to start and stop sounds in your movie. Use the Start control to start a new instance of a sound. The Start sound command is handy when you want to synchronize a sound with your animation.

Use the Stop control to stop a sound from playing. For example, if your animation ends on a particular frame, but your sound clip goes on much longer, you can put a Stop command in the frame to end the sound.

Assign Start and Stop Sounds

SET A START SOUND

1 Insert a keyframe where you want to start the sound again.

You can press **F6** to insert a keyframe.

2 Open the Property inspector.

You can press **Ctrl** + **F3** to quickly display the Property inspector.

3 Click the **Sound** ☑.

4 Click the sound you want to start.

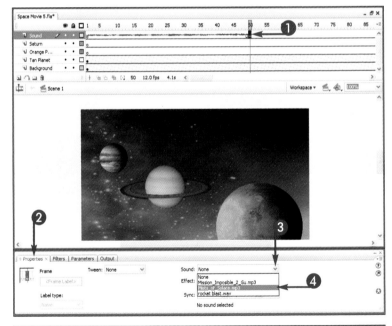

5 Click the **Sync** ☑.

6 Click **Start**.

When the movie reaches the keyframe with the Start control assigned, Flash plays the sound clip.

SET A STOP SOUND

① Insert a keyframe where you want to stop the sound.

You can press F6 to insert a keyframe.

② Open the Property inspector.

You can press Ctrl + F3 to quickly display the Property inspector.

③ Click the **Sound** ⌄.

④ Click the sound you want to stop.

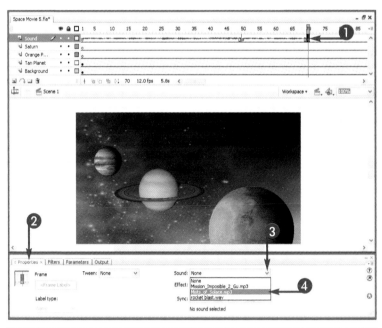

⑤ Set the Sync field to **Stop**.

The next time you play the movie, Flash stops the clip from playing when the movie reaches the keyframe with the Stop control assigned.

TIPS

Does the Stop command have to be in the same layer?

No. You can place a Stop command on any layer to stop the sound. The command immediately stops any playback of the sound regardless of where the sound is assigned. Although keeping sounds separate from other movie elements in their own layers is always a good way to organize your movie, the placement of Stop Sound and Play Sound behaviors can appear where needed in the movie. To learn more about layers, see Chapter 6.

Can I use sound behaviors to start and stop sounds?

Yes. You can apply the Play Sound, Stop Sound, and Stop All Sounds behaviors to control sounds in your movies. To use behaviors with sounds, your sound clips require an identifier, a name to identify the sound object for ActionScript actions. To learn more about behaviors, see the section "Load a Sound Using a Behavior" earlier in this chapter.

Edit Sounds

When you import a sound into Flash, its file includes information about the sound's length, volume, and stereo settings. You can fine-tune these settings using the Edit Envelope dialog box. Flash's sound-editing controls enable you to define start and endpoints for sounds, or to adjust the volume at different points in the sound.

For example, you can make your sound files smaller in size if you define the exact point at which a sound starts to play, or define the point where the sound ends.

Edit Sounds

① Click the frame containing the sound you want to edit.

② Open the Property inspector panel.

You can press **Ctrl** + **F3** to quickly display the Property inspector.

③ Click the **Sound** ☑.

④ Click the sound you want to edit.

⑤ Click **Edit**.

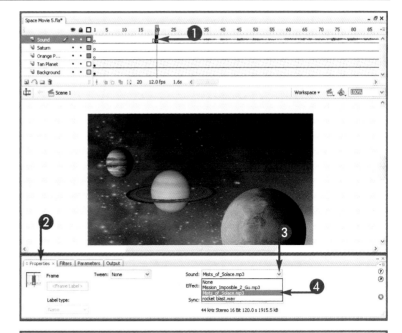

The Edit Envelope dialog box appears.

6 Click the waveform channel that you want to edit.

Flash places an envelope handle (▭) on the waveform.

Note: You can add up to eight envelope handles to either channel.

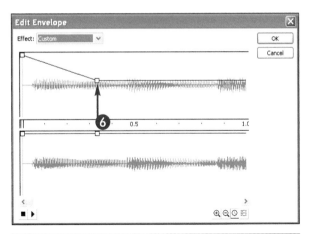

7 Click and drag the handle up or down to adjust the sound's volume.

8 To hear the sound, click the **Play** button (▶).

Continue adjusting the sound as needed.

Note: For greater sound-editing controls, you might need a full-featured sound-editing program.

9 Click **OK**.

Flash applies your edits to the sound.

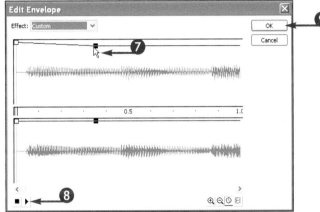

 TIPS

How do I create start point and endpoint for my sound?

Click and drag the Time In control marker, which is located at the far-left side of the Sound Timeline bar separating the two channels in the Edit Envelope dialog box, to create a new start point for your sound. To create a new endpoint, click and drag the Time Out control marker, located at the far-right side of the Sound Timeline bar.

Can I change the panning for a sound channel?

Yes. *Panning* refers to the stereo effects of a sound, adjusting the left and right audio channels. You can adjust the volume by clicking and dragging envelope handles in either audio channel in the Edit Envelope dialog box to create panning effects for your movie.

Set Audio Output for Export

You can control how sounds are exported in your Flash files. You can find options for optimizing your sound files for export in the Publish Settings dialog box. Options include settings for compressing your sounds in ADPCM, MP3, or RAW format. By default, Flash exports sounds in MP3 format using a bit rate of 16 Kbps. MP3 is the emerging standard for distributing audio on the Internet.

Set Audio Output for Export

① Click **File.**

② Click **Publish Settings.**

The Publish Settings dialog box appears.

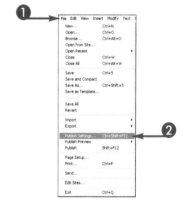

③ Click the **Flash** tab.

④ Click the **Set** button corresponding to the audio type you want to control.

You can control the export quality of both streaming and event sounds.

Clicking either Set button opens the Sound Settings dialog box.

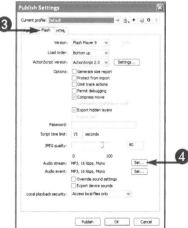

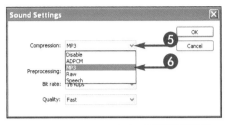

⑤ Click ▾ to view available compression formats.

⑥ Select a compression format to apply.

Depending on the format you select, the remaining options in the Sound Settings dialog box reflect settings associated with your selection.

You can make changes to the remaining settings.

⑦ Click **OK** to close the Sound Settings dialog box.

⑧ Click **OK**.

The Publish Settings dialog box closes and Flash saves your settings.

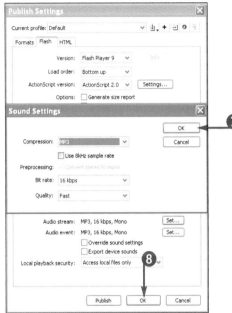

TIPS

What is a good bit rate for MP3?

MP3 efficiently compresses audio files, resulting in high bit rates — therefore better quality — and small file sizes. This is why MP3 is emerging as the standard for distributing sounds on the Internet, especially on Web pages. For large music files, try a setting of 64 Kbps. For speech or voice files, try 24 or 32 Kbps. To set near CD quality, use a setting of 113 or 138 Kbps. Use 16 Kbps settings for simple button sounds, or larger audio sounds where quality is not crucial.

How can I minimize my file size when it comes to sounds?

You can apply several methods regarding movie sounds to help cut down on overall file size. If you plan on looping Event sounds in your movie, be sure to use short sound clips. Avoid looping streaming sounds because they take longer to download. You can apply a few editing techniques, such as fading and panning, to make the same sounds work more efficiently in your movie.

Working with Video

You can add video clips to your Flash projects and manage how they play using playback controls. You can add QuickTime videos, Windows Media, MPEG clips, and more. This chapter shows you several basic techniques for playing video clips in your Flash movies.

Using Progressive Download to Play a Video

You can play external videos within your Flash project using the progressive download feature. Ordinarily, when you publish a Flash file, it is saved as a SWF file type. If you embed a video, it increases the size of the SWF file. If you want to play a particularly long video without increasing the Flash file's size, use the progressive download feature.

Using the Import Video Wizard, you can set up the progressive download feature to convert the video file to a Flash Video file (FLV). You can then upload the video to your Web server so it is ready to go. Anytime the video is activated, it begins playing, using HTTP streaming, as soon as the first segment is downloaded.

Using Progressive Download to Play a Video

① Click **File**.

② Click **Import**.

③ Click **Import Video**.

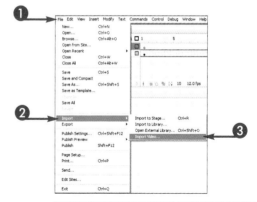

The Select Video page appears in the Import Video Wizard.

④ Click **Browse**.

The Open dialog box appears.

5 Click the video file you want to use.

● You can click here to navigate to the folder or drive containing the file.

● You can click here to list a particular file type.

6 Click **Open**.

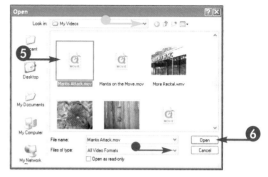

● The path to the file appears here.

● If your video clip is already uploaded to a server, you can select this option (○ changes to ◉) and type the URL.

Note: URL stands for Uniform Resource Locator and identifies the exact location of a site or page on the Web.

7 Click **Next**.

TIPS

What is streaming video?

Streaming video is a delivery method for multimedia content that is continuously sent by a provider and received by and displayed to the end user. With streaming video, the users do not have to wait for the entire file to download before they can start viewing the content. Instead, the media is sent in a steady stream and plays as soon as it arrives to a player, such as the Flash Player. You can use the progressive download feature to stream an external video to your Flash project.

What are the advantages and disadvantages of using progressive download for my videos?

The biggest advantage is file size — by storing the video clip as an external file, you can save on overall file size consumed by the Flash file. As an external file, the video loads onto the user's hard drive into the SWF file, so you do not need to worry as much about the size or duration of the clip. Because the video streams, you also do not need to worry about synchronizing the audio with the video or making sure the frame rate is the same as the Flash file. On the downside, the external file must be uploaded separately to the Web server.

continued

You can assign a skin for your video that determines how the video control bar appears. The control bar includes buttons for playing, stopping, pausing, rewinding, and forwarding the video. Flash includes several preset skins you can choose from. You can also create your own custom skins.

At the end of the Import Video Wizard, the Finish Video Import page explains the final steps for completing the encoding. Flash saves the video as an FLV file, adds a video component to the Stage, and adds the skin information to your SWF file. You need to remember to manually upload the video to your Web server when you are ready to post your Flash project on the Internet.

Using Progressive Download to Play a Video *(continued)*

The Deployment page appears.

⑧ Select **Progressive download from a web server** (○ changes to ◉).

⑨ Click **Next**.

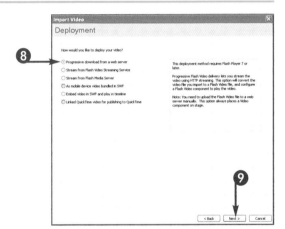

The Encoding page appears.

⑩ Click here and choose a quality level.

● You can click tabs to customize the video clip settings.

● You can edit the video clip's start point and endpoint using these icons.

⑪ Click **Next**.

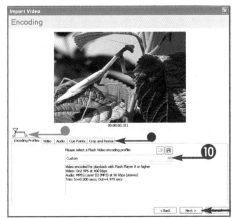

The Skinning page appears.

⑫ Click here and then select a skin.

● You can change the color of the playback controls by clicking here.

⑬ Click **Next**.

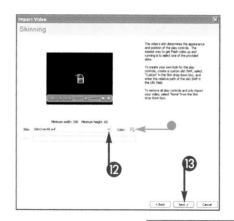

The Finish Video Import page appears.

⑭ Click **Finish**.

The Save As dialog box appears.

⑮ Type a name for the external video file.

⑯ Click **Save**.

Flash encodes the video file and displays the Flash Video Encoding Progress dialog box during the process. When Flash has finished encoding the video file, you can upload it to the server when you are ready to publish your Flash project to the Web.

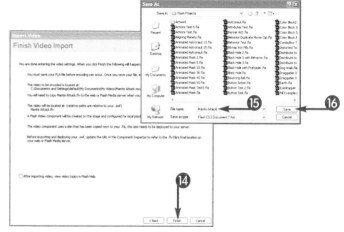

What quality setting should I pick for the encoding process?

When you reach the Encoding page of the Import Video Wizard, you can choose from low-, medium-, or high-quality encoding options, each tailored for a specific version of the Flash Player. The higher the quality setting, the larger the video file. The wizard dialog box displays details about each quality setting you select.

What can I do with the other tabs on the wizard's Encoding page?

The Import Video Wizard displays the Encoding Profiles tab by default. You can use the other tabs to customize the video settings. For example, you can click the **Video** tab to find options for setting a video codec and frame rate. You can click the **Audio** tab to set a data rate. You can click the **Cue Points** tab to set cue points for navigating the video with the Forward and Rewind buttons. You can click the **Crop and Resize** tab to crop the video window.

Embed a Video Clip

You can embed video clips from other sources into your Flash projects. Keep in mind that embedding a video clip can increase the overall file size of the Flash movie file, which in turn creates slower download times for users. For best results, use small clips that last 10 seconds or less. As soon as you embed a clip, Flash adds it to the Stage and to the Library. You can use the Import Video Wizard to guide you through the embedding process.

Unlike streaming video clips, when you embed a video clip, the user must download the entire file before the clip starts playing.

Embed a Video Clip

① Click **File**.

② Click **Import**.

③ Click **Import Video**.

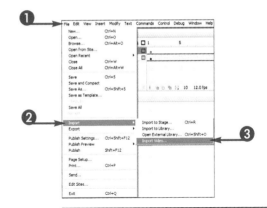

The Select Video page appears in the Import Video Wizard.

④ Click **Browse**.

The Open dialog box appears.

⑤ Click the video file you want to embed.

● You can click here to navigate to the folder or drive containing the file you want to use.

● You can click here to list a particular file type.

⑥ Click **Open**.

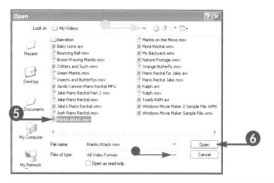

● The path to the file appears here.

⑦ Click **Next**.

TIPS

What is the difference between the video symbol types?

If you choose to import the clip as an embedded video, Flash displays each frame of the clip as separate frames in the main Timeline. If you change the symbol type to movie clip, Flash displays the video frames as a separate timeline from the file's main Timeline. If you import the video as a graphic, it appears as a static image on the Stage and you cannot use ActionScript, including actions or behaviors, on the clip.

What types of video files can I use in Flash?

If QuickTime 6.5 (Windows), DirectX 9 or later (Windows), or QuickTime 7 (Mac) is installed, Flash supports Audio Video Interleaved (AVI), Digital Video (DV), Motion Picture Experts Group (MPG, MPEG), and QuickTime Video (MOV). If DirectX 9 or later (Windows) is installed, Flash also supports Windows Media (WMV, ASF).

continued

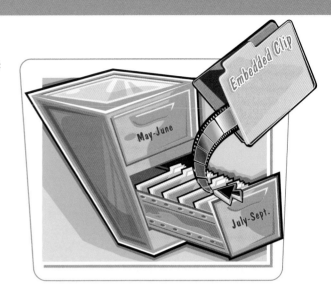

When embedding a video clip, the frame rate for the clip must match the frame rate of your Flash movie. If it does not match, the video playback may not be smooth. The Embedding page of the Import Video Wizard has several options you can control, including whether the Timeline expands to fit all the necessary frames.

After you import an embedded video clip, Flash places an instance of the clip on the Stage and stores the clip in the file's Library.

The Deployment page appears in the Import Video Wizard.

⑧ Select **Embed video in SWF and play in timeline** (◯ changes to ◉).

⑨ Click **Next**.

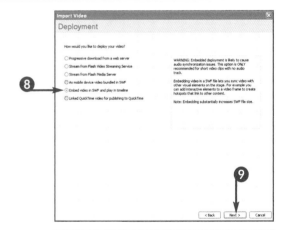

The Embedding page appears.

⑩ Click here and then select **Embedded video**.

● Leave these two check boxes checked.

⑪ Click **Next**.

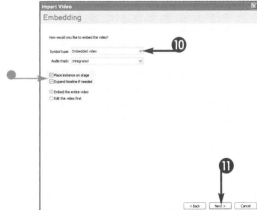

The Encoding page appears.

⑫ Click here and select a quality level.

● You can click the tabs to customize the video clip settings.

● You can edit the video clip's start and endpoints by clicking and dragging these two triangular markers.

⑬ Click **Next**.

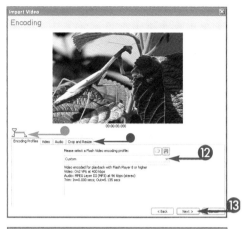

The Finish Video Import page appears.

⑭ Click **Finish**.

Flash embeds the video file and places an instance of the clip on the Stage.

![TIPS]

How do I play an embedded video clip?

You can use the Control menu's commands to play the Flash file and view the clip. Click **Control**, and then **Play** to see the entire Flash Timeline, including the video clip. You can also view the clip in the Flash Player window. To do so, click **Control**, **Test Movie**.

Can I edit the video clip's size on the Stage?

Yes. To change the clip-viewing window size, click the **Free Transform** tool (⊞) and click the **Scale** modifier (⊡). You can then resize the clip object's handles to resize the clip's appearance. You can also move the clip around on the Stage just like any other object you place on the Stage.

Assign an Embedded Video Stop Behavior

When you embed a video file, it continues to loop unless you give it an instruction to stop. You can use Flash behaviors to control an embedded video. Behaviors are preset ActionScript scripts you can use to add interactivity to your Flash projects. You can choose a particular frame in which to assign an Embedded Video Stop behavior. You can also assign the behavior to a button or a movie clip. For example, if you want the user to be able to stop a video, you can assign the behavior to a button.

When assigning an Embedded Video Behavior, you must first make sure the instance is named. You can use the Property inspector to assign instance names. To learn more about instances, see Chapter 7. Embedded video behaviors work only with files created using ActionScript 2.0 or earlier.

Assign an Embedded Video Stop Behavior

① Embed a video clip.

Note: See the section "Embed a Video Clip" to learn how to import a video clip into Flash.

② Using the Property inspector, assign a name to the video clip instance.

Note: See Chapter 12 to learn more about using Flash actions. See Chapter 1 to learn more about the Property inspector.

③ Click the frame, button, or movie clip to which you want to insert a **Stop** behavior.

④ Press **Shift** + **F3** to display the Behaviors panel.

You can also click the **Window** menu and click **Behaviors**.

Flash opens the Behaviors panel.

⑤ Click the **Add Behavior** button (⊞).

⑥ Click **Embedded Video**.

⑦ Click **Stop**.

Note: Embedded video behaviors work only with files created using ActionScript 2.0 or earlier.

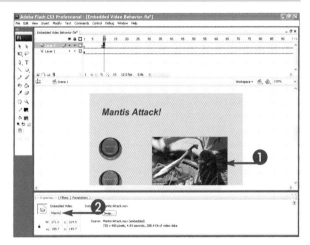

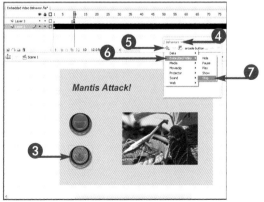

The Stop video dialog box appears.

⑧ Click the name of the video clip.

⑨ Click **OK**.

Flash assigns the Stop behavior.

Note: If you assign the behavior to a button or movie clip, Flash adds the On Release event to the action. You can change the event, if needed.

● You can test the behavior by clicking the **Control** menu and then **Test Movie**.

● You can click here to close the panel at any time.

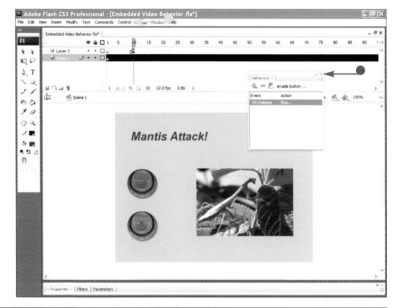

 TIPS

What other video behaviors can I assign?
Flash includes seven embedded video behaviors you can use to control a video clip in a Flash file. You can use the same steps shown in this section to assign other embedded video behaviors. Simply target the instance you want to use in each case. The following table outlines popular behaviors.

Behavior	Action
Play	Plays a video
Stop	Stops a video
Pause	Pauses the video
Hide	Hides the video
Show	Shows the video

How do I remove a behavior?
Click the frame, button, or movie clip with the assigned behavior and display the Behaviors panel. Click the behavior you want to remove in the Action column, then click the **Delete Behavior** button (⊟). Flash removes the behavior from the list.

Distributing Flash Movies

Are you ready to distribute your Flash creations to others? Learn how to export Flash files to the Web, to CD disks, or as self-playing files.

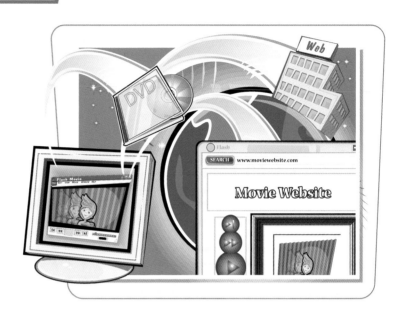

You can distribute your Flash projects to an audience in several ways. You might publish a Flash movie to a Web page, save it as a QuickTime movie to send to another user via e-mail, or deliver the movie as a self-playing file. You can assign a distribution method using the Publish Settings dialog box, or you can export your movie as another file type using the Export Movie dialog box.

Start with an Authoring File

When you create content in Flash, you start by creating an *authoring file*. The authoring file is where you draw and animate your movie's content. This file contains all the elements that make up your movie, such as bitmap objects, sounds, symbols, buttons, text, and so on. The authoring file can be quite large in file size. Authoring files use the .fla extension.

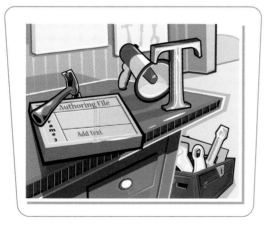

Create an Export File

After you create the authoring file and get it working just the way you want, you can turn it into an *export file.* When you create an export file, you create a file that is separate from the authoring file. Flash offers two exporting features, Export Movie and Publish. The feature you select depends on what you want to do with your Flash content.

Export or Publish

When you export a movie using the Export Movie feature, you export your file as a specific file type to be used in another program, such as QuickTime. When you publish a movie, you turn your content into a file type viewable from the Web. The process of publishing compresses the file contents, making it easier for others to view the file. The resulting file is uneditable, so you cannot change its contents. Published Flash movie files use the .swf extension.

Publish in Flash Player Format

Your Flash creations really shine when you publish them in the original program format — Flash Player format. When you distribute a movie as a movie file, Flash saves it in the SWF file format, and the format requires the Flash Player application or plug-in for a user to view. The Flash Player is the most widely used player on the Web and comes preinstalled with most computers and Web browsers today.

Publish as a Projector

Another way to distribute your movie is to turn it into a *projector*. A projector is a stand-alone player that runs the movie without the need of another application. Use the Projector feature to distribute your Flash creations to users who do not have access to the Flash Player or plug-in.

Using the Bandwidth Profiler

When preparing a movie for publishing, Flash offers a handy tool to help you check for quality and optimal playback. The Bandwidth Profiler is a valuable tool that can help you fix problem areas that hold up your movie while downloading into the browser window. Use the Profiler to help you fix problems before you post the Flash file on a Web page.

Publish a Movie as a Flash Movie File

When you complete a Flash movie, you can publish the movie as a Flash movie file you can share with others. You use two phases to publish your movie. First, you prepare the files for publishing using the Publish Settings dialog box, then you publish the movie using the Publish command.

By default, Flash is set up to publish your movie as an SWF file, but you can choose to publish in other formats. For example, you might publish your movie as a GIF, JPEG, or PNG image, or as a self-playing Windows or Mac file, or as a QuickTime movie.

Publish a Movie as a Flash Movie File

PREPARE FILES FOR PUBLISHING

1 Click **File**.

2 Click **Publish Settings**.

The Publish Settings dialog box appears.

Note: If you have already published your file, tabs from your last changes appear in the dialog box.

3 Click the **Formats** tab.

4 Select the Format type you want to use (☐ changes to ☑).

Depending on which formats you select, additional tabs appear with options related to that format.

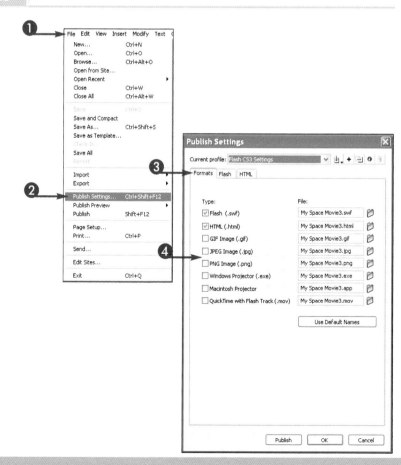

- To assign a different file name other than the default supplied by Flash, you can click inside the **File** field and type a new name in the format's text box.

Flash publishes your files to the My Documents folder unless you specify another folder and file name path in the File box.

- To change the folder location, you can click here and choose a destination folder.

⑤ When you are ready to publish the movie using the settings you selected, click **Publish**.

Flash generates the necessary files for the movie.

⑥ Click **OK** to save the settings and close the Publish Settings dialog box.

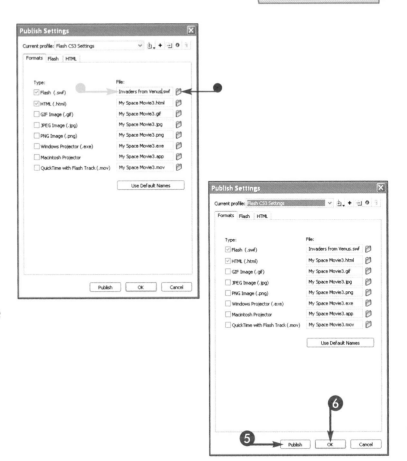

TIPS

How does the Publish feature differ from the Export Movie feature?

You use the Publish feature specifically for publishing your work for use on the Web. The Export Movie feature enables you to save your Flash project as another file type, so you can use it in another program. To learn more about these features, see the section "Introduction to Distribution Methods."

Do I always have to publish a movie through the Publish Settings dialog box?

No. If you want to publish the movie using the previous settings you set up in the Publish Settings dialog box, you can click the **File** menu and then click **Publish**. Flash does not give you a chance to name the file if you choose to publish directly and bypass the Publish Settings dialog box.

You can save a movie as a Web page and Flash generates all the necessary HTML code for you, including the tags you need to view your page in both Microsoft Internet Explorer and Netscape Navigator. You can then upload the document to your Web server.

Flash bases the HTML document you create on a template that contains basic HTML coding. By default, Flash assigns the Flash Only template, which is the simplest template to use to create an HTML document. You can choose from other templates.

① Click **File**.

② Click **Publish Settings**.

The Publish Settings dialog box appears.

Note: If you have already published your file, tabs from your last changes appear in the dialog box.

③ Click the **Formats** tab.

④ Leave the **HTML** type checked.

● The Flash format (.swf) is also selected by default.

Note: The Flash and HTML formats are selected by default the first time you use the Publish Settings dialog box.

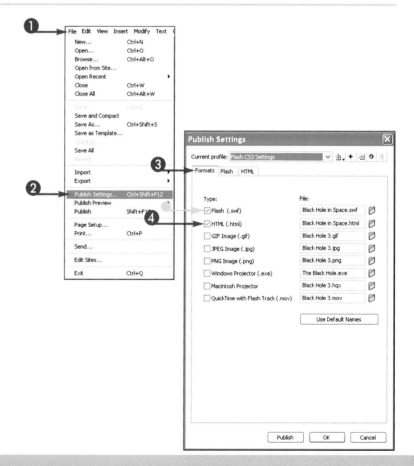

⑤ Click the **HTML** tab.

Flash displays options associated with generating a Web page, such as playback options and movie dimensions.

⑥ Select any options you want to apply.

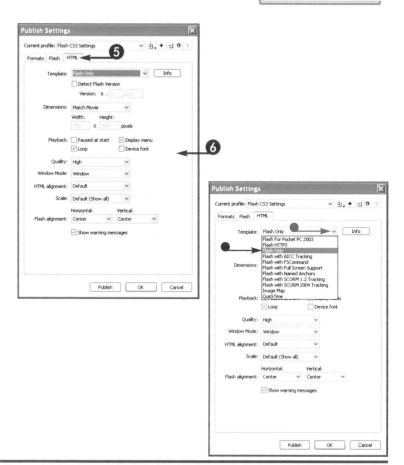

● The default Flash Only template allows other Flash users to view your movie. Users without the Flash plug-in cannot view the movie.

● You can click the **Template** ⌄ and select another template from the list.

What HTML tags does Flash insert into the HTML document?

The Publish feature inserts the tags necessary for playing a Flash movie file in the browser window, including the OBJECT tag for Microsoft's Internet Explorer browser and the EMBED tag for Netscape's Navigator browser. Flash also inserts the IMG tag for displaying the movie file in another format, such as animated GIF or JPEG. The OBJECT, EMBED, and IMG tags create the movie display window used to play the Flash movie.

Can I make my own HTML templates for Flash?

Yes. You can set up your own HTML templates or customize existing templates. Be sure to save any HTML templates in the HTML subfolder within the Flash application folder on your computer system. Flash looks for all HTML templates in the HTML folder. The template must also include a title that starts with the recognized HTML title code $TT, such as $TTMy Template.

continued

The HTML tab in the Publish Settings dialog box has a variety of options for controlling how your movie plays in the browser window. You can set alignment, dimensions, and even playback options. Any changes you make to the settings override any previous settings for the file.

You can control exactly how a movie starts, indicating whether the user starts the movie manually or if the movie loops continuously or not. You can also specify new movie dimensions that differ from the movie's original screen size dimensions.

- You can click the **Dimensions** ☑ to set width and height attribute values for the movie display window – the area where the Flash plug-in plays the movie.

- You can select a Playback option to control how the movie plays on the Web page (☐ changes to ☑).

- You can click the **Quality** ☑ and select options for controlling the image quality during playback.

- You can click the **Window Mode** ☑ and select options for playing your movie on a regular, opaque, or transparent background (Windows browsers only).

- You can click the **HTML alignment** ☑ and change the alignment of your movie as it relates to other Web page elements.

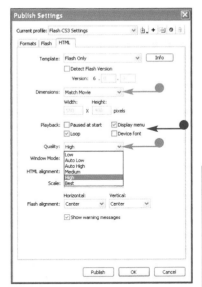

● If you choose to set new dimensions for the movie, you can click the **Scale** ☑ to rescale movie elements to fit the new size.

● You can click the **Horizontal** and **Vertical** ☑ settings and designate how the movie aligns in the movie window area.

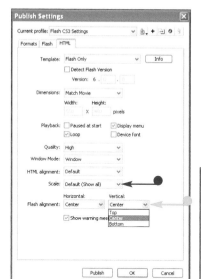

7 When you are ready to publish the movie using your settings, click **Publish**.

Flash generates the necessary files for the HTML document.

8 Click **OK** to save the settings.

The Publish Settings dialog box closes.

Note: By default, all files are saved to the last location to which you saved a file, unless you specify another folder and file name path in the Formats tab.

How do I make my movie full size in the browser window?

To make your Flash movie appear at full screen size in the browser window, you can change the dimension settings of your movie. To do so, click the **Dimensions** ☑ in the Publish Settings dialog box, and select **Percent**. Finally, type **100** as the percent values in both the Width and Height text boxes.

How can I tell which HTML template does what?

The HTML tab in the Publish Settings dialog box offers a variety of templates. To learn what each template does, select the template you want to know more about by clicking the **Template** ☑. Next, click **Info** in the Publish Settings dialog box to see a description of the selected template.

Publish a Movie as a Projector File

You can publish a movie that plays in its own Flash Player window without the benefit of another application, which means that anyone receiving the file does not need to install the Flash Player application. Flash projectors are simply self-extracting, self-sufficient mini-applications designed to play movies in real time.

Because the projector files are self-sufficient, you can easily place the files on discs or send them as e-mail file attachments. The only catch is that you must publish the projector file to a format appropriate to the computer platform the end user needs.

Publish a Movie as a Projector File

PUBLISH THE MOVIE AS A PROJECTOR

① Click **File**.

② Click **Publish Settings**.

The Publish Settings dialog box appears.

Note: If you have previously published your file, tabs from your last changes appear in the dialog box.

③ Click the **Formats** tab.

④ Select either **Windows Projector** or **Macintosh Projector** as the format (☐ changes to ☑).

● If you do not want to publish your movie for the Web, you can deselect the **Flash** and **HTML** format check boxes (☑ changes to ☐).

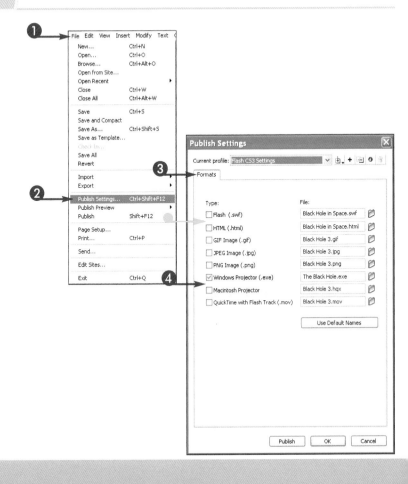

● You can assign a different file name by typing directly in the File field.

5 Click **Publish**.

Flash generates the necessary files for the movie with an .exe (Windows) or .hqx (Mac) file extension.

6 Click **OK**.

The Publish Settings dialog box closes and Flash publishes the movie.

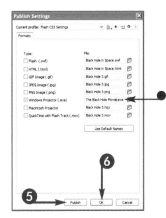

PLAY THE MOVIE

1 Test the movie by double-clicking its name.

● In this example, the file opens through the Windows XP My Documents window.

● The Flash Player window opens and plays the movie.

2 Click ☒ to close the window when the movie stops.

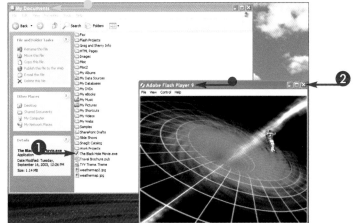

 TIPS

Do I need to worry about licensing my projector file?

Adobe allows free distribution of its Flash Player and Projector product. If you distribute your movie for commercial purposes, however, check the Adobe Web site for information about crediting Adobe. Visit www.adobe.com/support/ programs/mwm. You need to include the Made with Adobe logo on your packaging and give proper credits on your credit screen.

What is the difference between a stand-alone player and a projector?

When you save a file as a Projector file, you are making an executable copy of your Flash movie. This file does not require a player or plug-in. It comes with everything necessary to run the movie. A regular SWF file packs only the movie data, not the player. Regular SWF files require the Flash Player in order to view the movie.

Export to Another File Format

You can easily export a Flash movie into another file format for use with other applications. For example, you might save your movie as a Windows AVI file or as a QuickTime file, or perhaps you want to save each frame as a bitmap sequence. Flash allows for more than a dozen file formats for export in both Windows and Mac platforms.

The Export feature differs from the Publish feature in that it creates editable Flash content. You use the Publish feature when you want to generate Web-based content. Unlike the Publish feature, export savings are not saved with the movie file.

① Click **File**.

② Click **Export**.

③ Click **Export Movie**.

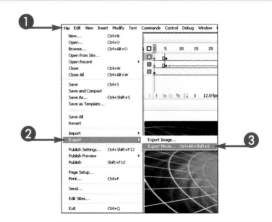

The Export Movie dialog box appears.

④ Type a name for the file.

⑤ Click the **Save as Type** ☑ and select a file format from the list.

⑥ Click **Save**.

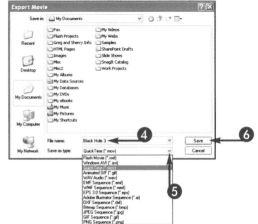

● Depending on the file type you select, an additional Export dialog box appears with options for size, sound, and video format. You can make any selections necessary.

⑦ Click **Export**.

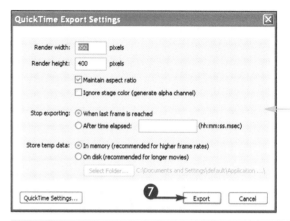

● Flash exports the movie to the designated file type.

Note: *Depending on the file type, another dialog box may open first. Make any selections necessary, and click **OK** to continue exporting.*

Note: *Interactive elements you include in your Flash movies might not export to other file formats properly.*

 TIPS

What is the difference between exporting a movie and publishing a movie?

When you publish a movie, you can publish to Flash (SWF), HTML, GIF, JPEG, PNG, Windows Projector, Macintosh Projector, and QuickTime, formats. When you export a movie, you can save the file in more than a dozen file formats, such as Windows AVI or Animated GIF. The two features share some of the formats and options, but when you publish a movie as opposed to exporting it, Flash saves information about the movie's Publish settings along with the movie file. When you export a movie, you are saving it to a single format.

Can I export a single frame rather than an entire movie?

Yes. First, select the frame you want to save as an export file. Click the **File** menu and then **Export**, **Export Image**. This opens the Export Image dialog box. Give the file a distinct name and format type, then click **Save**. Depending on the format you select, additional parameters may appear for you to set.

You can use the Flash Player to play your published movie files. You can play movies from within Flash or outside the confines of the program window by using the Flash Player window. The Flash Player, version 9, is installed when you install Flash onto your computer.

The Flash Player is a separate application for viewing Flash multimedia files. As such, when you download a Flash file, it opens into its own window along with several menu commands for controlling how a movie plays.

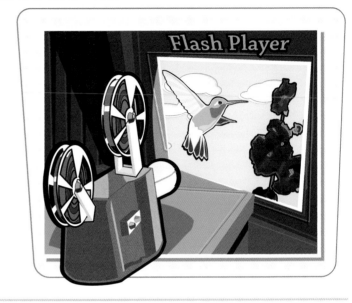

Play a Flash Movie in Flash

① Click **File.**

② Click **Open.**

Note: The Flash Player window and test movie window are one and the same. You can also open the Flash Player by clicking Control, Test Movie.

Note: Published movie files use the .swf file extension and are identified by a different icon than the Flash authoring files.

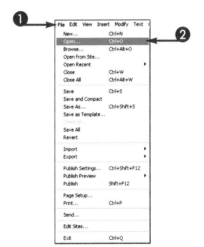

The Open dialog box appears.

● You can click here to navigate to the folder containing the Flash movie file you want to play.

③ Click the Flash movie file you want to play.

④ Click **Open**.

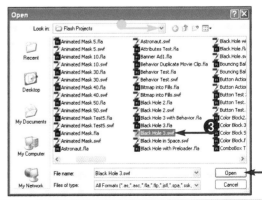

● The Flash Player window opens and plays the movie.

Note: When opening the Flash Player from within the Flash program, the Player fits inside the Flash program window and has a separate set of window controls and menu commands.

To stop the movie, press Esc ; to resume play, press **Enter** or **Return**.

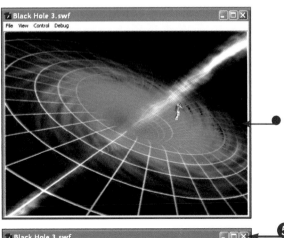

5 Click ⊠.

The Flash Player application closes and you are returned to the Flash program window.

Note: To open a movie for editing, you must open the movie's FLA file.

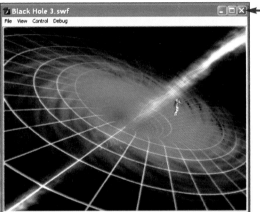

How do I stop the movie from looping?

The Flash Player window has a few tools you can use to control how the movie plays. Click the **Control** menu to see the available commands. The Loop command is turned on by default. To deactivate the command, click **Loop**. To stop the movie from playing, click **Stop** or just press **Esc**.

How do I open another movie to play in the Flash Player window?

As long as the Flash Player window is open, you can view other Flash movies. To view another movie, click the **File** menu, then click **Open**. Click **Browse** and navigate to the next movie file you want to play. Double-click the movie file name. When you click **OK**, the movie starts playing.

Play a Flash Movie in a Browser

You can play a Flash movie using the browser's Flash plug-in. Most browsers, such as Microsoft Internet Explorer and Netscape Navigator, include the Flash Player plug-in program for playing SWF files.

Most Internet users can access Flash Web content without needing to download the Flash Player application separately, which makes the Flash Player the most widely used player on the Internet. Most of today's browsers and computer systems come with the Flash Player preinstalled.

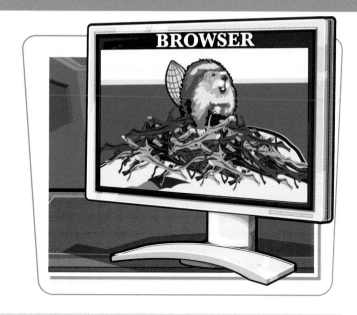

Play a Flash Movie in a Browser

① Open the browser you want to use.

This example uses Microsoft Internet Explorer.

② Click **File**.

③ Click **Open**.

The Open dialog box appears.

④ Click **Browse**.

⑤ In the dialog box that appears, click the Flash movie file you want to play.

● Click here to navigate to the folder containing the file you want to open.

● If you cannot find your file, click ⊡ and select **All Files** for a complete list of files.

⑥ Click **Open**.

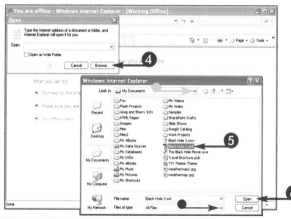

7 Click **OK**.

The browser window begins playing the movie.

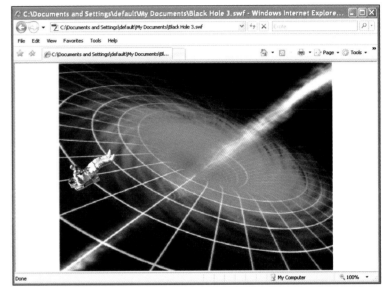

 TIPS

Can older browser versions view Flash movies?

It depends on how old the version of the browser program is. The latest version of the Flash Player plug-in is version 9, which is supported in Netscape Navigator, or Microsoft Internet Explorer. Earlier versions of these browsers may not include the Flash Player plug-in.

How do I control the movie's screen size?

The movie's screen size is set when you define the Stage area measurements. To learn how to set the Stage size, see Chapter 1. You can also control the size of the movie display window that appears inside the browser window when a Flash movie plays. You can find movie-display controls in the Publish Settings dialog box. Learn more about these controls in the section "Publish a Movie in HTML Format."

Test Movie Bandwidth

You can use the Flash Bandwidth Profiler to help you determine which movie frames might cause problems during playback on the Web. File size and the user's data-transfer rate affect how smoothly and quickly your movie downloads and plays.

With the Bandwidth Profiler you can test six different modem speeds and gauge which frames in your movie use the most bytes. This information helps you to see exactly where your movie might slow down during playback.

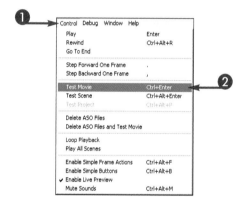

OPEN THE BANDWIDTH PROFILER

① Click **Control**.

② Click **Test Movie**.

The Flash Player window opens and starts playing the movie.

You can press **Esc** to stop the movie from playing.

③ Click **View**.

④ Click **Download Settings**.

⑤ Select a download speed to test.

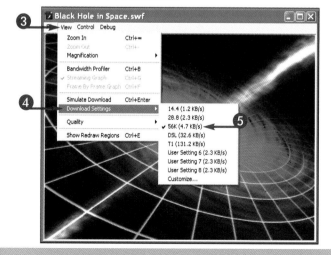

6 Click **View**.

7 Click **Bandwidth Profiler**.

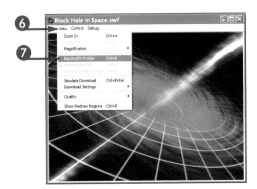

The Bandwidth Profiler appears at the top of the window.

● The left side of the Profiler shows information about the movie, such as file size and dimensions.

● The bars on the right represent individual frames and the total size, in bytes, of data in the frame.

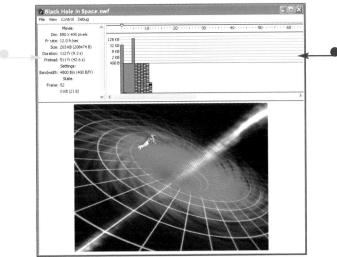

TIPS

Can I customize the download speed I want to test?

Yes. To customize the modem speed, click the **View** menu in the Flash Player window. Click **Download Settings**, **Customize** to open the Custom Download Settings dialog box. You can then set a speed to simulate in the test. For example, you can change an existing speed settings' bit rate by typing another bit rate. Or you can type a custom speed in a **User Setting** box and a bit rate to test for that speed. Click **OK** to save your changes.

Can I save the test settings for use with another movie?

Yes. Leave the Bandwidth Profiler open in the Flash Player window. You can open another movie from the player window, or you can return to the player window at a later time and use the same Profiler settings. To open another movie without leaving the player window, click **File**, then click **Open**. Double-click the movie you want to view and it begins playing in the player window.

continued

You can use two different views in the Flash Bandwidth Profiler to see how the frames play in your movie: Streaming Graph mode or Frame by Frame Graph mode. The default view is Streaming Graph mode. Depending on the view you select, the right section of the Profiler displays data differently.

A vertical bar on the graph represents a single frame in the movie. The bars correspond with the frame number shown in the Timeline.

Test Movie Bandwidth *(continued)*

RESIZE THE GRAPH

To make sure you are viewing all the movie's information on the left side of the Profiler, resize the Profiler graph.

⑧ Click and drag the border to resize the Profiler graph (⬚ becomes ⬄).

The Bandwidth Profiler resizes.

● You can also drag the border between the panels to resize panels.

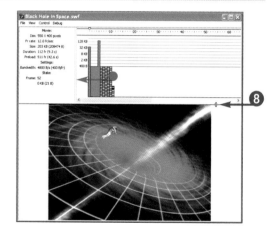

CHANGE THE GRAPH VIEW

To check which frames might be causing a slowdown, switch to Frame by Frame Graph mode.

⑨ Click **View**.

⑩ Click **Frame By Frame Graph**.

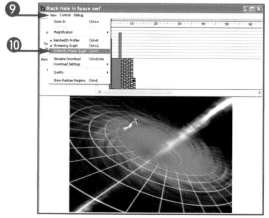

- The Profiler graph displays Frame by Frame Graph mode.

- You can use the scroll bar to scroll through the movie's Timeline and view other frames.

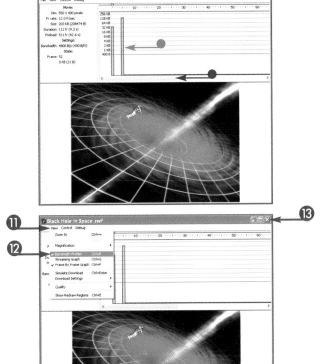

CLOSE THE PROFILER

⑪ To close the Bandwidth Profiler, click **View**.

⑫ Click **Bandwidth Profiler**.

⑬ To close the Flash Player window, click ☒.

Flash closes the Bandwidth Profiler and the Player window.

TIPS

How do I view a specific frame in the Profiler?

Use the scroll bar arrows (◁ and ▷) to move left or right in the Profiler Timeline at the top of the Profiler graph. To view a specific frame, drag the playhead to the frame, or click the playhead where you want it to go.

Does the Bandwidth Profiler test the exact modem speed?

No. The Profiler estimates typical Internet connection speeds to estimate downloading time. DSL, cable modem, and especially dial-up modem speeds are typically never full strength. For example, a 28.8 Kbps modem can download 3.5 kilobytes of data per second under perfect conditions, but in real life, there are no perfect conditions when connecting to the Internet. In real-life conditions, a 28.8 Kbps modem is lucky to download 2.3 kilobytes of data per second. The same is true of broadband connections which may experience heavy traffic usage at peak periods and slow the downloading process. Flash gears each modem test speed setting in the Profiler toward real-life connection speeds.

28.8 Kbps!!

(your actual speed may vary)

Print Movie Frames

Some Flash projects may require you to print out a frame or series of frames. You might print out frame content to show a storyboard of the movie. You can use the Page Setup dialog box (Windows) or Print Margins dialog box (Mac) to specify a layout, then use the Print dialog box to specify which pages to print.

You can specify a variety of printing options for frames. You can print a single frame and designate margins, alignment, page orientation and paper size for the printout. You can print thumbnails — miniatures of your movie's frames.

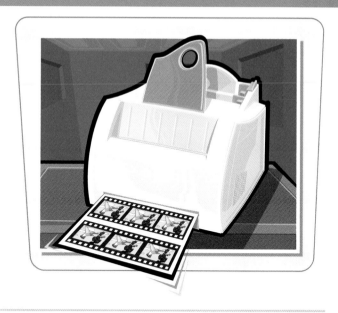

Print Movie Frames

① Click **File**.

② Click **Page Setup**.

The Page Setup dialog box appears.

③ Click the **Frames** ▼.

④ Click **All frames**.

You can use the **First Frame Only** option if you want to print just the first frame of the movie.

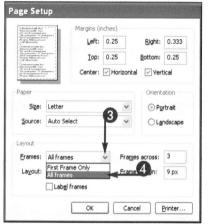

⑤ Click the **Layout** ☑ to view layout options.

⑥ Click an option.

Select **Storyboard-Boxes** to print in storyboard boxes.

Select **Storyboard-Grid** to print in a grid pattern.

Select **Storyboard-Blank** to print only the graphic items of each frame.

⑦ Click **OK**.

The Page Setup dialog box closes.

⑧ Click **File**.

⑨ Click **Print**.

The Print dialog box appears.

⑩ Click **OK**.

● From within the Print dialog box you can specify print options such as number of copies.

Flash prints the specified pages and layout.

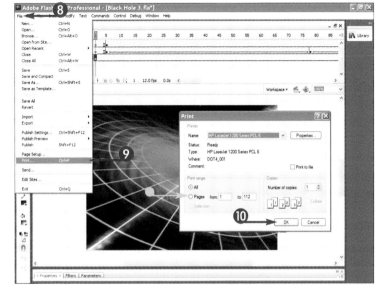

Can I add labels to each printed frame?

Yes. If you select one of the storyboard layout options in the Print dialog box, a Label frames check box appears. Click this check box (☐ changes to ☑) to print the scene and frame number for each frame you print out in the storyboard.

Will Flash print any symbols I place in the work area off of the Stage?

No. Flash prints only the symbols and objects found on the Stage area of any given frame. If you move a symbol off the Stage to place in a later frame or insert later, the symbol does not display in your printout.

Index

Index

Index

Index

Index

Index

Index

Index

V

vector graphics, converting bitmaps into, 80–81
Version setting, 206
vertical lines, 33
video. *See also* movies
    progressive download feature
        advantages/disadvantages of, 289
        encoding process, 291
        Import Video Wizard, 291
        streaming video, 289
video clips
    embedded, 292–295
    Embedded Video Stop behavior, 296–297
Video tab, 291
View menu, 21, 65, 155, 317
View tools, 31

W

waveforms, 269
Web pages
    linking buttons to, 258–259
    publishing movies as
        HTML tags, 305
        HTML templates, 305, 307
        resizing, 307
Web Safe color palette, 67
Welcome screen, 8, 9
Wide Library View button, 122
Window menu, 9, 16, 17, 296
Workspace button, 17
workspaces, 17

Z

zooming in/out, 18–19

Read Less–Learn More®

Visual™

There's a Visual book for every learning level...

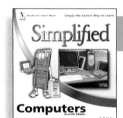

Simplified®

The place to start if you're new to computers. Full color.

- Computers
- Creating Web Pages
- Mac OS
- Office
- Windows

Teach Yourself VISUALLY™

Get beginning to intermediate-level training in a variety of topics. Full color.

- Access
- Bridge
- Chess
- Computers
- Crocheting
- Digital Photography
- Dog training
- Dreamweaver
- Excel
- Flash
- Golf
- Guitar
- Handspinning
- HTML
- Jewelry Making & Beading
- Knitting
- Mac OS
- Office
- Photoshop
- Photoshop Elements
- Piano
- Poker
- PowerPoint
- Quilting
- Scrapbooking
- Sewing
- Windows
- Wireless Networking
- Word

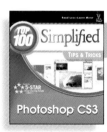

Top 100 Simplified® Tips & Tricks

Tips and techniques to take your skills beyond the basics. Full color.

- Digital Photography
- eBay
- Excel
- Google
- Internet
- Mac OS
- Office
- Photoshop
- Photoshop Elements
- PowerPoint
- Windows